# DON'T LAUGH, IT'LL ONLY ENCOURAGE HER

# Exclusively Signed

# First Edition

DAISY MAY COOPER

*October 2021*

MICHAEL  JOSEPH

# DAISY MAY COOPER

# DON'T LAUGH, IT'LL ONLY ENCOURAGE HER

MICHAEL  JOSEPH

MICHAEL JOSEPH

UK | USA | Canada | Ireland | Australia
India | New Zealand | South Africa

Michael Joseph is part of the Penguin Random House group of companies
whose addresses can be found at global.penguinrandomhouse.com.

First published 2021

001

Copyright © Daisy May Cooper, 2021

Lyrics for 'Fly Me to the Moon' on page 49:
TRO Essex Music Limited of Suite 2.07, Plaza 535 Kings Road, London sw10 0sz.
International Copyright Secured. All Rights Reserved. Used by Permission

The moral right of the author has been asserted

Every effort has been made to trace copyright holders and to obtain their
permission for the use of copyright material. The publisher apologizes for any
errors or omissions and would be grateful to be notified of any corrections
that should be incorporated in future editions of this book

Set in 13.5/17.5 pt Garamond

Typeset by Couper Street Type Co.

Printed and bound in Great Britain by Clays Ltd, Elcograf S.p.A.

The authorized representative in the EEA is Penguin Random House Ireland,
Morrison Chambers, 32 Nassau Street, Dublin D02 YH68

A CIP catalogue record for this book is available from the British Library

HARDBACK ISBN: 978–0–241–50358–4
TRADE PAPERBACK ISBN: 978–0–241–50359–1

www.greenpenguin.co.uk

Penguin Random House is committed to a
sustainable future for our business, our readers
and our planet. This book is made from Forest
Stewardship Council® certified paper.

For Ben Shephard,
because he's fucking fit

# Contents

Introduction                                                    1

1. The Borrowers                                                3

2. Spawn of Satan                                              19

3. High Spirits                                                37

4. A Cooper Christmas Special                                 63

5. The Hedge Trimmer                                          81

6. The Coopers Go Continental                                91

7. Matchmakers                                               111

8. Souped-up Renault Clio                                    133

9. Working Nine to Five                                      151

10. Shepherd's Bush                                          171

11. Brian, Bo' Selecta! and
        the Missing Monologue                               191

12. Thaddeus-Mothafucking-Toogood                           227

13. RADA                                                     259

14. The Wilderness                                          289

15. The Job Centre                                          311

16. *Doc Martin*                                            323

17. *Kerry's Camera*                                        355

18. *This Country*                                          383

Scripts                                                     403

# Introduction

When things were really bad, Mum would always say to me:

'Don't worry, it will be a good read for your memoir one day.'

I suppose that's a weird way of coping, isn't it? Trying to turn the bleakest, most dire situations into positives?

'Mum, I auditioned to be a stripper by snogging a pole and was laughed off the stage by a bunch of topless dancers.'

'Well, that can go in the memoir.'

'Mum, I accidentally spent all my student loan on a penthouse suite in a fancy hotel in Marble Arch, and now it looks like I'm going to be kicked out of drama school.'

'That's a good one for the memoir.'

'Mum, sorry I'm late for dinner. I had to work late at my cleaning job as someone balanced a Quaver packet full of piss on the radiator in the boys' toilets, and I didn't realize until I picked it up, so I had to wash the piss off while trying to learn my lines for that *Call the Midwife* audition I have in London tomorrow.'

'That will definitely be good to put in the memoir . . . it'll make people think you're down to earth.'

For fuck's sake . . .

If I didn't write this memoir, this would all just be really fucking sad.

But faced with the boredom of the national lockdown, going on the same walks and baking banana bread day after day, I decided to write some of it down. The more I wrote, the more I felt like I was writing sketches for the Chuckle Brothers. At the age of thirty-four, I have lived the most humiliating, ridiculous screw-up of a shitstorm life, and it has been an utter joy digging up all that shit and putting it down on paper. Therapeutic, even.

I'm writing this memoir because I owe it to myself to tell this story. I also really need the money as I've got an ant infestation that needs sorting.

Thank you so much for buying it. But if you haven't bought it and you are just flicking through it in Waterstones, then at least do me the favour of positioning it in front of Joe Wicks's book, because I'm pretty sure the curly-haired fitness fuck will outsell me . . .

# CHAPTER 1
# THE
# BORROWERS

know how boring the early stuff can be in auto-biographies so, for your benefit, I'm going to skip through all that crap about how I was a cute baby. (I wasn't.)

I've been writing scripts and playing out a whole cast of characters in my head for as long as I can remember. To me, it's as normal as breathing. To psychiatrists, it's a pathological disorder that needs to be addressed. I blame my parents – especially my mum. She allowed it. At no point did she step in and say, 'Oh, Daisy. Stop making it up!'

Thankfully, I've finally managed to build a career out of talking utter bollocks, but back then it wasn't as if my life's trajectory was mapped out for me.

I was born on 1 August 1986. That very same year the nuclear reactor at Chernobyl exploded, the space shuttle *Challenger* disintegrated mid-launch and, closer to home, Mad Cow Disease scared the shit out of everyone. When I entered into the world, Chris de Burgh was riding high in the charts with his erection-section classic 'Lady in Red'. The omens didn't look good . . .

**GM** 241376

1 & 2 ELIZ. 2 CH. 20

# CERTIFICATE OF BIRTH

Name and Surname *Daisy May COOPER*

Sex *Female*

Date of Birth *First August 1986*

Place of Birth
{ Registration District *Basingstoke*
Sub-district *Basingstoke*

**I,** *P Cofield* Registrar of Births and Deaths for the sub-district of Basingstoke in the Registration District of Basingstoke do hereby certify that the above particulars have been compiled from an entry in a register in my custody.

Date *18 September 1986*

*P Cofield*
Registrar of Births and Deaths.

N SAXT 188

Besides, life isn't easy when you live with a constant chatter of voices. It was so full on that I never wanted to play with other children – the characters in my head were company enough. This did worry my parents, but I didn't give much of a toss about having any friends. Who needs them? By the time I finished nursery I had a largely telepathic relationship with the pet rabbit who lived in the hutch in the playground. We could communicate non-verbally for hours, mostly about Care Bears and about how Mrs Canes was a tight bitch when it came to handing out biscuits at breaktime. It was enough.

At home, living in the Cooper household was like growing up in Aladdin's cave. Mum and Dad were permanently broke and Mum raided charity shops and car-boot sales. She was an obsessive collector of threads and yarns, materials and toys, garden furniture, books, electrical equipment and objects with absolutely no name whatsoever.

As well as all the stuff she bought from car-boot sales and charity shops, Mum also collected animals. She rescued everything, like the blind magpie that she nursed until it flew into the neighbour's spaniel's mouth. Even Mum couldn't rescue it then. Next, there was a cat with one eye that shat all over our shoes in the hallway and a pheasant with a mangled beak that had been hit by a car. Mum never wanted to pay vet's bills, but she did make

the princess
a nd The Goblin
on The hills a
Casslit Lived.
The king won did
With his men
To The trure
woods
her up
she eyes
Feel could
Some thing
Wispring to
her

An early work of genius. Just ignore the spelling . . .

us have a house mouse with a brain tumour put down once. She'd bury them all in our back garden – it was transformed into a pet cemetery. Even now, she has a dead parrot called Claude wrapped in gold tissue paper in her freezer. He's been dead for five years, but she says she's just not ready to bury him yet.

Mum was always trying to feed my young and fertile imagination. She read to me all the time. There were stories about fairies at the bottom of the garden, about goblins, ghouls, ghosts and vampires.

When she brought home the book *The Borrowers* from a charity shop, I was hooked. No one could have predicted it would be the start of my life spiralling out of control.

This family of tiny people seemed innocent enough. They lived secretly in the walls and under the floorboards of an old English house. To survive, they borrowed items from the house, which was inhabited by the 'human beans'.

I longed to make friends with them.

As long as this make-believe world I was playing out in my head was contained within the four walls of our house in Cirencester, it really wasn't a problem. It was when I was unleashed on the outside world that it seemed to upset people. Apparently, it was hard to know where my reality ended and my imagination started.

One time at nursery, we were given a thick dollop of

What ting to be a mermaid

Ariel Was sitting by the sea.

A tear droped in the sea

The prince came and said What Was the

matter. "I Want to see my Dad
and sisters" "Well I no" "how"
"in your Dremes" She Looked puzzeld"

"WW What do you mean"
"never mind" "oh but plse
please" "never mind now
thats it" then the Wold
Changed into the sea.
but the funny thing is
a minet a go she
Was on Land

and then not far a Way was a
bit of Land. then a man in
of 90 years old came
up to her and Said
"You are in the half
Land"

She Was very puzzeld
indeed. the Stupid puzzeld
face Was coming back a
gain.

I I feel home sick
tears were Wondr
ing round her
pretty Littel face
She was now
Chaging into half mermaid
and half human

I always had characters in my head. They were as real to me as my
mum or my brother sat next to me.

her self now she was
worried. "hello" "Oh
Oh Oh its you Eric"
"Yes its me Dalingn"
they Gave each Other
and masif hug and
a very Long Wonderful
Kiss "Oh" said Eric "you
have Chaneged in to haff"
"Yes" said The Littel memaid
With her tears "We have
got to solv this
Secret" said Eric
the Littel memaid
gave Eric One Last
hug With trembling
hands

cocret
The crechers of
black Water sea
Came and Eric had
to fight them The Littel
memaid had a very
Nastey scrach on
The Arm. they did
Win Then. they have
got to ride a shack
find the King of harf
Land and thats going
Liketo be finding a needle
pin in a hay stack

"and thats going to be
Mrs D Mrs i Mrs ffi
Mrs c Mrs u Mrs L t y"
it now was night
time the sun was going
down they slepted in
a frezzing barn
Z Z Z Z

cocret
The crown was macking
his call at
they Got up "Wonce
Look" there is the
skark "Now were
do you whane to go"
snaped the shark.
"to the harf city"
"Yes" snaped the
shark a gain.

"Weeeeeeeeeeee" they spuled.

"Look Look" the hats & city" it was Wondeful. every singlet Light sone brighly

Rock A Doel

Hi Ma

They soon got os the shark
What will you give me.
Well I will give you my ring the shark went a way with out saying thankyou and Grumpley went a way

They slowel walked to the city "fise said Eric We have got to book a hotel" said Eric. "I will give my ne cles for the hotel" said the Litel me maid Look said Eric theres a good hotel to book come on Lets go! said Eric"

the Littel mermaid took of her
necles and trow iron the tabel.
"here" she said        the man
at the till his eyes shon
as she thow on the tabel
"how many nights do you
    want to book 4p" said the
man at the till. "a week"
said the Littel mermaid
"yes yes madem" said
    the man at the
        till

The harf King was
saty ing in the hotel
thar they were satying
then they met in the
hotel then Aril woke
up she was just saying
that it was a bream
them she saw a scrah on
the arm and gave
a cheeky smiel

he

End

sticky clay to play with. I'm told I showed all the promise of an early Michelangelo and fashioned the most amazing clay elephant.

'I was just about to go over and tell Daisy how brilliant her work was when she took her fist to it and smashed it,' the teacher said to Mum when she collected me at the end of the day. She was clearly concerned.

'Why did you do that, Daisy?' Mum asked. I had to think on my feet. 'The Borrowers told me to. They made me start again,' I said, with some indignation. Clearly, the little people were keen on me suffering for my art.

Mum looked at the teacher as if this was a fair enough excuse.

In fact, Mum fuelled my obsession with the little people. She was always leaving notes around the house, written by the Borrowers. Post-its would be attached to the members of my burgeoning Sylvanian Family.

*Dear Daisy,*
*Hope you don't mind. We had nothing to eat off, so we just borrowed your miniature table so we could have our dinner.*

See? If proof was needed that the Borrowers existed, this was it! I'd never actually seen one, though, so much of my spare time was spent rummaging around in the backs of clocks or on the floor, looking under the beds.

My insatiable curiosity led me to an attempt to lift the floorboards in the kitchen. Mum and Dad stopped me that time. Yet, through all of this, I don't remember Mum ever breaking it to me that the Borrowers *weren't real*.

Understandably, this was causing havoc at nursery. One major bugbear for my teachers was my refusal to wear any knickers. To be fair on Mum, she had tried her best. But no sooner was she out of my sight than I whipped them off.

Normally, this didn't matter, because no one noticed. It only fully came to light when one teacher made us sit cross-legged in a large circle.

'Why did you do this, Daisy?' Oh God . . . *that* question again.

'Errr . . . the Borrowers made me?'

'What do they do?'

'They tell me to do things . . .'

Mum was called into the school and told in no uncertain terms that the whole Borrowers fantasy had to end.

'Mrs Cooper, it's horrendous. She's moving into a completely new realm . . .' the teacher warned. Not only was I getting away with murder in class, but I was starting to upset the other children, too. Especially with the knickers thing.

Fucking hell. Without the Borrowers, I might actually have to make a friend. This filled me with utter dread because there was something secretly comforting about my rejection by the other kids because of them. If I was weird, then kids wouldn't want to hang out with me. And if kids didn't want to hang out with me, then I could be weird. I was happily stuck in a vicious circle of weirdness.

Clearly terrified at the thought of proper human friendships, I pulled out all the stops and staged a dramatic reveal.

'I have voices in my head,' I announced to Mum and Dad. This scared the shit out of them. Mum took me to be assessed by experts, convinced there was something 'unusual' about me. The word 'Asperger's' got bandied around.

I was prodded and poked and had lights shone in my eyes, and doctors made me play with toys and answer ridiculous questions.

'There's absolutely nothing the matter with her,' they assured Mum in the end.

This seemed to give Mum licence to carry on with her mad-as-fuck parenting technique, which I'm sure is the primary cause of much of my insanity. But Mum didn't think it was eccentric – to her, it was all about creativity. Daisy May Cooper was on the artistic spectrum.

And I can't help feeling that had it not been for my parents, my brother Charlie and I would never have picked up a second-hand camcorder and started making up stories and filming each other. We would never have

## I magine you are a toy

I Wos bought in a Scruffy Shop

and a big Fat boy Said

I Vhot this ted and they

bought me and He Kicked me He

Chewed me and He ripped me I dotn'

like this boy and One day I got put

in The bin and that is The endoF me I thot

and I nearly got did in The bin machine
but a babby squirrel Saved me and He bought Me
To a hut and it Vos a Little Squirrels
birthday and I Whnt To The Squirrel and Vhn She
SaVl me She dancing all The Vy round The
Toon like a Flging Pig and I live Happey Vich her

what a lovely story

dreamed our big dream to make a TV sitcom called *This Country*. And we would never have ridden the peaks and troughs of hope and heartbreak for a whole *seven years* to make it a success.

# CHAPTER 2
# SPAWN OF SATAN

One of my earliest memories is meeting my brother, Charlie, for the first time. I was three years old and Dad was taking me into the hospital to see Mum and my new baby brother.

When we got there, Mum was lying on a bed in the ward and next to her in a Perspex box lay this little bundle of blankets. I remember Dad picking me up so I could see, and as I leaned over to take a look the bundle wriggled.

'Daisy, do you want to meet Charlie?' cooed Mum.

Dad lifted me up on to Mum's bed and she reached into the box and lifted Charlie out like she was handling a Fabergé egg. Mum lay him on her chest and pulled a corner of blanket to reveal his face.

*Fuck me!*

I jumped back in horror.

He was bright red and hideous. His head was cone-shaped and he was all crusty. It was as if someone had spilt Tipp-Ex all over his face and done a shit job of cleaning it up with a bit of wet kitchen roll.

For the past nine months, my parents had banged

on about the 'new baby brother' I was going to have —
you would have thought Mum was carrying Jesus Christ
Our Lord and Saviour, not this monstrosity. He was the
sort of thing you'd pay to see in some travelling carnival somewhere at the turn of the twentieth century, not
something you were related to in a maternity ward at the
end of it.

'Do you want to give him a kiss?' Mum smiled.

Absolutely not. I'd rather stick my tongue in a Polly
Pocket and clamp it shut.

Dad was winding up his disposable camera. He held
it to his eye.

'Give him a kiss.'

'No, thanks.'

'Daddy's going to take a picture. Do it for the picture.'

'No.'

'Just give him a quick kiss.'

I shook my head.

'Charlie wants to give *you* a kiss, don't you, Charlie?'

Mum pushed him towards my face and Charlie
squirmed in her arms like a pink new-born rat.

'*No!*' I screamed.

'Let's not push it, Paul,' Mum said to Dad.

'It must be hard, adjusting.'

It's not hard for me, adjusting. I just don't want to kiss
something that clearly looks like it carries the Bubonic
Plague.

After that first meet, Charlie and I were like ships in the night. It was like an unspoken agreement:

'I don't like you, you don't like me, but unfortunately we share the same parents so let's just get through this until we both fly the nest.'

And things got even worse when he was about one and a half and he was old enough to share baths with me. This really pissed me off as I had enjoyed four undisturbed years of luxury bathing at the comfortable, curved end of the bath. Now, I was being cast towards The Tap End.

'Why do I have to be at the tap end?!'

'He's younger than you,' Mum would say as she poured an old gravy jug of tepid bathwater over my head, taps jabbing into my back.

I looked at him living it up at the other end of the bath like a Roman emperor, holding a bottle of Mr Matey bubble bath and smugly sipping bathwater from the plastic sailor's hat like it was a Martini glass.

I tried not to stoop to his level and threw myself whole-heartedly into playing God with my Sylvanian Families. The population of my Sylvanian town had grown dramatically after a rather abundant Christmas. So much so, I even had duplicates of the rabbit family (thanks to a couple of crusty old aunties who can't have discussed with one another what they were getting me that year).

The rabbits were simple folk who ran the local swimming pool, which was a cereal bowl full of cold water and a slide I'd made out of an old toilet-roll tube. The badgers ran the post office. They had an illegitimate child that was actually a panda. I had lost the original badger son on a holiday in France and Dad ended up having to drive to a foreign supermarket to look for a substitute. The panda son, who was affectionately known as Christophe, was the same size as his non-biological father badger, because he was a cheap European rip-off of the Sylvanian Family brand.

It worked quite well, though. Christophe added lots of drama to the town. His oafish size was mirrored by an oafish personality. He was constantly being arrested for jumping off the church, but he always got away with it by pretending that he didn't understand the rules as he could only speak French.

However, the family that I loved the most had absolutely no drama whatsoever: the squirrels. Perfect, law-abiding citizens who ran the village shop. Squirrel father Eric was also mayor of the town, and he was firm but fair. He once made Christophe walk the plank of a Playmobil ship after he had been caught dive-bombing recklessly into the pool run by the rabbits. I was really pleased with this: it seemed like the perfect punishment. (Christophe was never seen again.)

But one afternoon, after coming back from ballet

class, I skipped upstairs into my room to find what I can only describe as the Jonestown Massacre.

All the rabbit family had had their clothes taken off and been stuffed head first into my cereal-bowl pool. If I had known anything about forensics, I would have said this homicide had happened several hours ago, as the fur had now come off in chunks in the water, revealing the translucent plastic beneath. The village post office had been ransacked: all the tiny envelopes had been torn and the post office till had been broken because someone had tried to stuff a large amount of Play-Doh into the drawer. The badger father was lying naked in the centre of the carnage, missing an arm, staring up at the ceiling with a thousand-inch stare.

But that was not the worst of it. Eric the squirrel was just a torso. I was only able to identify him by the mayor badge on his little plaid shirt. He'd been decapitated, all of his limbs had been ripped from their sockets and his tail had been pulled off and shoved into the slot of my Peter Rabbit money box.

I had never known such boiling rage. And I knew who had brought extinction to my beloved Sylvanian universe.

'Mum! Charlie's ruined my Sylvanian town!'

I stormed downstairs.

'Oh, Daisy, he doesn't know how. He's only two.'

But he knew all right.

I would have my revenge, and it would be premeditated. I thought about giving him one of Mum's favourite lipsticks to chow down on and barf up later. But no, that would have been too easy. I needed to fuck with him psychologically.

At two, he was young enough to understand what birthdays were but not old enough to know exactly when his was. This was the perfect opportunity to show him who was boss and prove how stupid he was. Mum kept birthday balloons in a drawer in the kitchen, so one morning I blew some up and placed them strategically on the stairs. I ran into his room to wake him.

'Happy birthday!'

'It's my birfday?'

Charlie spoke with a speech impediment for most of his early years after learning to talk around a dummy that was permanently in his mouth. He ended up having to see a speech therapist. It took the stupid bastard three years to pronounce his own name properly.

'Yes! There's lots of presents waiting for you in the living room!'

'Pwresents?!'

'Yup, come with me . . .'

He jumped out of bed and rushed down the stairs.

'Bawoons!' His eyes lit up, as if to say, 'It must be my birthday!'

He flung open the doors of the living room . . . to find

nothing. Just Mum sat on the sofa watching *The Clothes Show*.

His eyes became glassy. He didn't cry, he just sort of stood and stared.

I would see that exact expression again in years to come. Fast-forward to 2013, and I'm lying on the broken mattress Charlie and I shared at Mum and Dad's house. He's on the landline phone to our producer. For the last three years, we've been working on a pilot called 'Kerry', which would later become *This Country*. We've put our blood, sweat and tears into this, all the while working as night cleaners and battling poverty. I'm trying to read his face.

'Hmmm, yeah . . . yeah . . . OK, well, thank you for letting us know. Bye.'

He hung up.

'ITV are dropping the pilot.'

Silence.

'Well, fuck it, we'll just take it to another channel. What about the BBC?' I reassured him, even though I felt like someone had dropped a bowling ball into the pit of my stomach.

His eyes became glassy.

'The production company are dropping us too.'

'Well . . . we'll start again. We'll go to another production company.'

'I've already spoken to Laura.'

Laura was our agent at the time.

'She says we can't take it anywhere as the production company own all the rights. The only way we could would be to buy the rights back from them, for over £300,000.'

He didn't cry, but he looked like he was on the verge of it. We didn't have a pot to piss in, and if we were to get back the ideas and the characters we'd created, we'd have to pay the cost of a house. *Our own ideas* would cost us money?! We couldn't sell our house to cover it – we didn't even own a house; we were barely affording the £600 a month in rent.

'That's that. We had our chance, and now it's gone,' he said, staring at a stain of dog piss on the carpet.

I felt like I was bleeding out on to the broken mattress. Three years of creating, three years of hopes and dreams just bled out, and I was empty.

Charlie stormed out of the room.

'Where are you going?!' I called out after him.

'I have to get out!' he shouted back at me. I heard the front door slam. He was going somewhere to cry, or possibly kill himself.

After a rocky start, Charlie and I did end up bonding, probably when I was around eight, fuelled largely by our mutual hatred of an evil force in our midst. Mum had a friend with a son called Louis. He made Lord Voldemort look like the Andrex puppy. He was the biggest, nastiest, most horrible spoilt shit we'd ever had the pleasure of

LION BRAND

a Family Bird Book

WORK BOOK
RULED WHITE PAPER

Bird Book

Meet the Coopers . . .

ME AGED 3

MY AGE NOW - 9
faveroit food -
feast's - A Kind of ice cream
birth day - Aug 1st
star sign - Leo

parent's NAMEs -
Paul + Gillan
freind's -
Tiffany, Emily,
Mehanie.
hobby's - swimming
, icescateing, Danceing
+ faverouit vido's
Little shop of
horror's, MEET the
applegate's, A
spider film, .

My brother's name - Charlie

My Brother
Age 2
Age Now - 8
favourious food
- chips
Birthday - 16th June
star sign - cancer
parents name -
Gillian, Paul.
freinds - Scot,
Thomas + Dallis
etc.
HOBBYS - FootBall
video
fave vidios -
little shop of
Horrors, ZULU -

knowing. I found myself looking at Charlie with new-found fondness. Love, even. Two's company, three's a crowd.

Inviting Louis to our house was like welcoming in a deadly tornado and letting it sweep through every room. This was particularly annoying if we'd been made to tidy our bedrooms beforehand. He marched in, flung the cupboard doors open and yanked out our toys then spilled them on to the floor with wild abandon.

Once, he took a hammer to Mum's piano and smashed up the keys while we looked on, dumbstruck. I'm sure, subconsciously, Christophe – the oafish French addition to my Sylvanian Family – was based on the over-sized Louis.

Telling his mum on him was hopeless. He got what-ever he wanted.

'Oh, Louis. Never mind. You're such a darling,' she'd laugh adoringly, while he tried to stab our pet cat's eyes out with an Action Man harpoon.

This was so unfair, and flew in the face of all the children's stories I'd ever read where the baddie gets his comeuppance in the end.

And he could turn on the waterworks like a busted fire hydrant:

'Charlie and Daisy won't let me play Jenga with them!'

Mum would step in. 'Oh, Daisy, what have I told you about sharing?' There was no point explaining that we'd stopped him from playing because he'd pulled down his trousers and tried to topple the Jenga with raspberry fart. It would have fallen on deaf ears.

If Louis came to our house after school, he was very fucking quick to point out that he was our guest. Because of this, we were duty bound to give him first dibs on the Sega Mega Drive. But it was never limited to a first go.

Charlie and I didn't get a look in. In our own home! We spent hours sitting on the bed watching Louis's clown-like hands commandeer the console, fury boiling up inside us.

'Come on, Louis, get your stuff. It's time to go!'

We longed for this moment when his mum would call up the stairs – but that would only be after she'd polished off three bottles of Pinot with our mum. Charlie and I would shoot each other a hopeful glance. We'd been held captive for hours by the Antichrist. If we'd checked, he would've had a birthmark somewhere on his body that spelled out 666 – the number of the beast.

If Charlie and I ever got dumped at Louis's house, somehow, a different set of rules applied. Louis got first dibs on the Sega Mega Drive there, too, even though we were now *his* guests. How did that happen?

'My house, my rules,' he'd announce. We were being gaslit by an eight-year-old, and we knew it. We dug deep and drew on each other for support.

Louis didn't even want to play *Sonic the Hedgehog* with

either of us, despite it being a two-player game. He would rather battle it out with the computer than give Charlie or me the satisfaction.

This was even more gutting when it came to the game *Earthworm Jim*. Jim was a battle-hungry earthworm dressed in a bonkers cyber suit with a head like a wispy turd. He was the most unlikely superhero. He bungee-jumped and launched cows and rode hamsters as he battled through an unforgiving landscape to save Princess What's-Her-Name. Clearly, this game had been dreamed up by people who mainlined hallucinogens, but Charlie and I longed to enter Jim's surreal world.

'Can me and Charlie have a go now?' Sometimes, we checked in to see if Louis had had a personality transplant.

'No. I told you. My house, my rules,' he hissed. Charlie and I would just sit there, quietly yearning to wrench the handset from Louis and duct-tape him to the bed so we could at least get to the second level undisturbed.

I don't pretend to be in any way proud of this, but Louis was the person I had my first sexual experience with. Up until I met him, I'd never had even a sneak peek at a strange boy's bits. Then, out of the blue, he flashed his willy at me.

*Holy shit!*

It was a bright pink mushroom. At first, it was shocking, but very quickly it just got boring.

'Oh God, put the phallic fungi away!'

Louis looked undeterred by my gag-reflex action.

He was stroppy and selfish and clearly had some kind of Mummy issues. My guess is he's now a guy who sexts a dick pic as an introduction on Tinder. Either that, or he's in prison.

His parents were the proud owners of a VHS video recorder and he discovered that they owned *The Lover's Guide* on tape – billed as 'a no-holds barred exploration of the pleasures of lovemaking'. Through watching this video, I learned that it's part of the rules of relationships to run hand in hand with your partner through a field of wheat and to frolic in swimming pools on inflatable whales. Also, communication and understanding are the key to a committed union, and self-acceptance is the key to a fulfilling sex life – all incredibly handy tips when you're still at primary school.

When there were no adults in the house, Louis made Charlie and me watch it, and he often attempted to rub his naked mushroom up against my tights. This usually happened when the on-screen couple caressed each other in faux-silk underwear and soft focus.

I have absolutely no doubt whatsoever that this weird juxtaposition of *The Lover's Guide* and a boy with a face like an angry wasp with his small, pink willy out deeply affected my psyche and my future relationships with men. And it put me off mushrooms for years.

Looking back, Louis was sex-obsessed. He even tried to use Charlie as a procurer of porn. Poor Charlie. At the age of six, he had the smallest hands, and Louis persuaded him to go to the dump-bin near our house. Charlie's fingers were the perfect size to slip under the lid of the paper recycling bin and retrieve someone's stash of disposed-of jizz mags. Louis would take them back to his bedroom and salivate over them like a rabid animal.

Having met someone like Louis at such a young age, I had an idea that maybe life wasn't always going to be a bed of roses.

# CHAPTER 3
# HIGH SPIRITS

**T**his is a text sent to me recently by Debs, my cleaner:

Hi Daisy,
Just to let you know your bedroom and the green room above has a spirit that hasn't crossed over, possibly a few. There was a hanging tree there. People hanged themselves in that tree, and that's why you have so many spirits in the area. Also, you have a Roman that walks through your front door, through the wardrobe and the wall, through the kitchen door and the kitchen and on to the grass by the tree. He's a lovely man, though. Just had to share with you as soon as I found out.
xx
PS: Your spirit box was doing what sounded like Morse code. I'm seeing if I can decipher it. Also, I've managed to get that stain out of the coffee table.

I can't ever sack Debs. She's in her late fifties, she's a bit dumpy with a brown hat which she refuses to take off, even when she is cleaning. She used to clean for my mum, which is how I know her. And she's lent me money in the past, even when she's been broke herself. She says she's a medium and gets possessed all the time. When she's reaching for the Mr Muscle, she says things like:

'Daisy, I don't mean to alarm you, but there's a high-wayman next to your door. He's right behind you. He's in my peripheral, and he's doffing his cap to you.'

Right you are, Debs.

But I think if you tell people you're a medium, they're unlikely to fuck with you, right?

'What do you mean, you used Domestos to clean my apples?'

'So sorry, Dais, but I wasn't thinking. The Roman stopped for a chat. He was telling me about all his near-death experiences before he was fatally stabbed while urinating on the side of a newly built road. Apparently, the culmination of a long-running feud with an emperor who wanted it named after him.'

'It's OK, Debs, just don't do it again.'

'Maggots ate his genitalia, Dais. It's why he walks funny.'

For legal reasons, I would like to point out that the above conversation is *not real* and Debs has never bleached my fruit. She comes highly recommended and is always available for work – no job too small – in the Cirencester area.

But her 'special talent' has given her licence to say exactly what's in her head.

'Daisy. You really shouldn't wear that orange top. You look like a sun-dried Donald Trump. Now it's not me who's saying this, you understand. It's your gran coming through. She says blue is definitely more your colour.'

I have bought a shitload of spirit-detection paraphernalia just in case, though.

- 1 x rechargeable headlamp
- 1 x movement sensor
- 1 x heat sensor
- 1 x voice recorder
- 1 x electromagnetic field detector

The DPD delivery driver wouldn't have known whether he'd be greeted by a coal miner or Psychic Sally.

Also, Debs reads Tarot. But I hate her offering to read mine because she's never yet given me a positive reading. If you ask me, it's very fucking passive aggressive. Especially as she refuses to reveal what she's seen.

'I don't want to say, Daisy. Nope. I said to myself, "Don't say it, Debs . . . don't say it."'

'Just tell me!'

'Nope. "Don't say it, Debs."'

'Fucking hell – what is it? Am I going to die? I need to know.'

'Daisy . . . Don't go in the car tomorrow.'

Debs always clasps my hand and squeezes it.

'Why?'

'I can't say. Just . . . just don't ask me any more.'

This is another classic:

'I know your career's going really well at the moment . . . but do you have a Plan B, Daisy?'

'No! Of course I fucking haven't. Acting is *all I've ever wanted to do*. Where have you been living these past few years? A fucking cupboard?'

'Nope. "Don't say it, Debs. Keep your big trap shut."'

'What is it? I've suffered every war, famine and pestilence the Four Horsemen of the Apocalypse could chuck at me. For the love of Jesus, just tell me!'

'You need to start looking for another line of work, that's all. In three or four months' time, it's all going to come out in the press. Your career will be ruined, but it's no biggie. You'll pick yourself up and move on.'

'What will come out?'

'I can't say. Just . . . just don't ask me any more.'

I also can't sack her because even if a Roman has never walked through my wardrobe, I want to believe that he does. I really, really want to believe that he does. I definitely get this from my mum. I don't know whether it's a curse or a blessing.

It all goes back to when I was around four and Charlie was one, when Mum's younger sister, Auntie Alison, died in a car accident. One night she crashed her car on her drive home. She was pronounced brain dead not long after and her life-support machine got switched off. It was so shocking how someone could be there one minute and not the next. The only experience of loss I'd ever had was a Russian hamster called Sniffles who ended up dying of whiplash on his own hamster wheel.

Unsurprisingly, this was a very weird time in our house. Looking back, I think Mum was trying to process all this dark stuff that had happened. And my grandmother was devastated.

At home, Mum tried to look after Alison's kids, who were toddlers at the time. I loved that they visited most weekends, but there were always tears and sad music playing in the house. Sometimes, I'd walk into the living room and Mum and Gran would be sat in silence, rocking drunkenly to 'Take My Breath Away' by Berlin, playing it over and over again.

Now, Mum says that I remind her of Alison. If she'd lived, she might have gone on to be a performer. She had the sharpest sense of humour and she could really hold a room – it was as if she had her own personal spotlight that lit her in stardust. Now that I have kids I understand how hard Mum must have found it to cope and to bring us up in that atmosphere of grief.

And I was really quite naughty . . .

One time I was such a little shit that Mum shut me in my bedroom cupboard. I'd been inspired by the TV series *Changing Rooms* and started painting the front door in Mum's coral nail varnish. What she failed to understand was that, had there been enough nail varnish (10,000 bottles), it would have gone really well with the curtains. All that she could see was a dripping circle above the letterbox.

When she shut me in the bedroom cupboard I thought she had locked it, but she says now she only pretended to. Instead, she waited outside and held the door while Charlie sat in his baby bouncer giggling – a bit too much, for my liking.

I held off being angry with him. Strategically, he could come in useful. I waited until I couldn't hear voices any more before I attempted to enrol him in my masterplan.

'Charlie,' I whispered. 'Charlie, listen to me . . . I need you to go and get a shovel and dig underneath the door because I'm planning my escape.'

To be fair, Charlie was at an age when he couldn't even wipe his own bum. He was hardly Morgan Freeman in *The Shawshank Redemption*. And I wasn't exactly Andy Dufresne. Besides, I was guilty. I was never going to painstakingly carve a chess set from the rocks in the prison yard or build a library up from scratch to prove my innocence.

Mum's threats of punishment always had a touch of the macabre about them.

'If you keep misbehaving, I'm going to poke your eyes out and chop your nose off and chop your head off.'

Apparently, I couldn't give a flying fuck. I spun round and stomped off, head turning in a final flourish to deliver my killer line.

'What was that last one again?'

I don't know when Mum's hoarding started, but I reckon it must have been around this time. They say the root of hoarding is loss or trauma and, for Mum, losing Auntie Alison hit that spot. Before then, she designed greetings cards, but all her cardboard and glitter and craft stuff now sat in bags gathering dust. The one certainty in our lives then was that we could pretty much always find her in bed.

Weirdly, Mum took me to loads of séances and to see psychics and mediums when I was really quite small. They were always in the back rooms of the shittiest pubs, with rows of rickety wooden chairs and a carpet that was so swirly it was as if someone had vomited rainbow-flecked pilau rice over it.

Naturally, I didn't have a clue what was going on, but I was very interested to find out. Mum would tell me beforehand that we were going to see if we could talk to Auntie Alison. She spent lots of money trying to get a hotline to the spirit world. Grief makes people splash what little cash they have in so many weird ways.

'Maybe this time we'll get a message from the other side,' she'd say. I could hear the hope in her voice. It was heartbreaking.

I often felt annoyed on her behalf, especially when we sat there all night and Auntie Alison couldn't even be arsed to put in an appearance. I can't imagine there's much to do in heaven, other than watch reruns of *Neighbours*, so it's not like she didn't have the time.

Mum said the connection must be weak, like the medium needed to call a BT engineer to sort it or something.

One place we were regulars at was really bad.

Every week in the back room of the Wheatsheaf Pub there was a guy who looked like a seedier Roy Orbison – if that's even possible. He'd set up his PA system and when we arrived he'd be shouting into the mic and tapping it with his fingers, which were covered in gold rings: 'One, two. One, two.'

His wife was on the door, slumped into her mobility scooter. She looked much older than him and her belly hung over the top of the elasticated waist of her polyester trousers.

When they weren't being mediums, we used to see them in Tesco together, arguing in the cereal aisle. You could pick up Roy Orbison's gold glinting like a talisman before you ever clocked him.

'That'll be £10 each, but we've got a family offer on at the moment: two for the price of one,' she'd say. We'd pay our money, hoping to get a chance to speak to Alison from the other side, but Roy's wife never thought to include Auntie Alison in the offer, so we assumed it was a sign that she might be lost in transition.

The room was always packed. And people often turned up in black. Maybe if you showed respect, your dead relative would be more willing to talk?

Mum always held my hand as the lights faded and the room went dark. A spotlight would illuminate Roy, who'd always be wearing fake Ray-Bans and be pacing up and down the stage.

'Someone's coming to me,' he'd say with a hint of a northern accent while he closed his eyes and opened up his chest, spreading his arms out wide. Mum's hand would grip me tighter.

One time, it was: 'I'm getting . . . I'm getting a caravan . . .'

A ripple of excitement ran through the crowd. Mum's hand eased off.

'Hold on . . . yes . . . it's clearer now. A caravan. It's got floral upholstery.'

For fuck's sake . . . don't all caravans have floral upholstery?

A hand shot up from the crowd.

'Yes . . . it's possibly a second-hand Swift Danette five-berth . . . can't quite make out the name . . .'

Roy really was full of shit.

'That's me!' A woman with a poodle perm in the second row looked close to exploding. Like me and Mum, it was difficult to know whether she actually believed or whether she just wanted to believe.

'What's your name, my lovely?'

'Pam,' she said, wide-eyed.

'All right, Pam. It's your husband, isn't it?'

Pam nodded quietly, her face crumpled like a crisp bag, and she leaned down to get a tissue from her handbag.

'OK, let's just give Pam a minute . . .'

Pam was now dabbing the tears from around her eyes.

'Oh . . . the signal's really strong now, Pam . . .'

Pam looked up adoringly into Roy's sunglasses.

'He wants you to know he's safe and at peace. And he forgives you for the chemical-toilet disaster . . . Oh, no . . . hang on . . . he's gone a bit fuzzy . . . yes, he has forgiven you, but he wants to remind you that you never listen. He says it was a bugbear throughout his whole forty-year marriage. And that he'd given clear instructions that the toilet only needed two pumps on the flush, otherwise it could explode in someone's face.'

The room shuffled uncomfortably. That was very specific. The side of Pam's mouth turned up with a knowing smile, but she looked relieved.

'OK, ladies and gentlemen. I think we all need a bit of light relief after that, don't we, Pam? Drinks and snacks are available at the bar. If you want to stretch your legs or phone a friend, feel free.' He waited for a titter from the audience. No one laughed.

48

*Beep . . . beep . . . beep . . . beep.* Roy's wife's mobility scooter was already reversing.

She'd been here before.

Roy leaned over, pressed play on the CD drive of his PA system. He smoothed back his toupé gently so it didn't slide off and patted the chains on his hairy chest, his shirt half unbuttoned.

His foot started tapping jauntily as he took the mic in his hand, and his eyes glinted. It was obvious that him being a medium was just a smokescreen to crowbar in his love of the Rat Pack.

'Ah-one, two, three, four . . . Fly me to the moon. Let me play among the stars . . .'

Roy seemed to be in a world of his own as he crooned out Frank Sinatra. He'd created a bottleneck at the bar but persisted for a good few tracks until everyone was back in their seats.

'Maybe Auntie Alison will visit in the second half,' Mum said, downheartedly.

To be clear, Auntie Alison did not visit. Ever.

Roy always finished with a raffle. At the back of the room there was a trestle table covered in a black cloth with all the prizes laid out: Roses chocolates, Martini Rosso, Malibu, Lambrini, scented tea-lights, a Frisbee, hoodie and baseball cap ensemble, an LA Gear hold-all and a mug.

This was on a good night.

We never won any of that either. I've yet to work out what a raffle ever had to do with the spirit world.

Mum also took me to spiritualist churches. Mainly, these were held at the Old Memorial Hospital, which has since been demolished. It was an eerie Tudor cottage on the edge of town which accommodated the History Society, the Cyber Café and anyone wanting to contact a loved one, sadly deceased. Next door was a Second World War air-raid shelter that was a favourite for school trips. Later, I had a couple of snogs outside it too.

The hospital smelled damp, and the mediums appeared weekly, on some sort of rotation. They never seemed quite as successful as Roy. If any medium had a terrible night, they always blamed it on too much spiritual traffic from the air-raid shelter, which was weird, because shelters were designed to save lives . . .

This other world seemed to spill over into my school life. Lots of the stories I wrote in English had twisted endings. Even the happy ones. And I loved those horror-book covers with the overly dramatic tag-lines: *The Boyfriend – he will love you to death.*

I'll never forget the time one teacher called Mum into the school. She was worried that I was writing dark shit. On one story she marked, she wrote in the margin for Mum to come and see her, so I would get a literary ticking-off (which Mum never did). I felt mortified that a piece of my writing could be judged – that you could be told off simply for *having an idea*. Instead of it holding me back, though, it made me determined to write more.

So I dreamed up the ghost of Rebecca Powell.

Rebecca Powell was the founder of my Catholic primary in Victorian times. A painting of her hung in the school library and her piercing eyes stared down. She had 'miserable bitch' written all over her. One day, I got sent to the library to pick up a textbook. There was a deathly silence as I creaked open the door. My mind started working overtime.

'You'll never guess what happened,' I told my mates when I arrived back to the classroom all panicky and breathless. (I liked acting even then.)

'What?'

'It was awful,' I gasped.

'What?' I had the back of the class in the palm of my hand. Even Robert Pope, the class sceptic, was hanging off my every word.

'Rebecca Powell's eyes followed me around the room.'

'No way!'

'Then, one by one, the books started flying off the shelves!'

If any one of them had had a brain cell between them, they would have realized that this bit was taken straight from the film *Poltergeist*.

Surprisingly, they swallowed the whole tale. Then the

rumour got out of control. But there was an upside. I noticed that I had a growing audience gravitating towards me. So I made up more stories . . .

'Not long after she founded the school, she had her heart broken by a lover and jumped off the roof.'

Mouths were agape.

'And she's been spotted late at night running between the two old buildings laughing and wearing a long white petticoat, her long brown hair flying out behind her.'

They lapped it up. So much so that kids were walking into the library and fainting at the sight of Rebecca Powell. It was crazy. I caused total chaos, and I was loving every bloody second of it.

Rebecca Powell made the time pass far quicker in lessons. Especially maths, which I hated. I'd always skulked around at the back of the classroom making people laugh, but now I burst into fake tears and started jerking my body around in weird, seemingly involuntary movements, like I was having a stroke.

'It's Rebecca Powell. She's possessed me! She's entering my very soul.'

I said all of this in a plummy English accent, which, if I do say so myself, was rather impressive.

Soon, other kids were reporting even more fantastical sightings of Rebecca Powell. This pissed me right off. I felt like Danger Mouse when Count Duckula got his own successful spin-off series.

I wasn't going to let my hardcore followers be distracted by rivals, so I upped my game and brought in Mum's Ouija board.

I invented another ghost called Gary, partly because if the name was any longer my classmates would have realized it was my hand pushing the glass across the board. Also, I had a major crush on Gary Barlow at the time. Gary the ghost was definitely more street. I pictured him with a beanie hat and baggy trousers that made him look desperate for a crap whenever he walked. He made Rebecca Powell look like a fucking nun. He made pictures clatter off walls and one girl's mum turned up on my mum's doorstep to complain about how much I had terrified her.

The headmistress caught wind of the growing supernatural crisis sweeping the school and called an emergency lunchtime assembly. Apparently, other parents had been complaining that their kids were also too scared to turn up for lessons.

'There is no ghost of Rebecca Powell,' she announced with a scowl. It felt like me telling Charlie that Santa didn't exist out of spite. Rude.

This sudden curtailment of my ghostly fantasies gnawed away at me for years. Actually, right up until 2014, when I formed the Cirencester Ghost Society and wrote a guide to the haunted landmarks of Cirencester town.

LINCOLN

1997 - 2001!

To Daisy,
All the best
for next year

Miss. McCormick
—

(Looking forward
to seeing your
name up in
lights!)

Some teachers recognized how utterly crap I
was at everything but Drama.

Whereas in the 1990s I'd had to rely on word of mouth – which, let me tell you, was as slow as a snail on ketamine – by now social media had been invented. It comes in handy when you are trying to disseminate fake news.

It was as if all the hard work I'd put in at primary school had led up to this one moment. I was Sigourney Weaver in *Ghostbusters*, and the words started spewing out of my keyboard like pure ectoplasm.

I will list my tales, readers, because they will give you a fascinating window into my crazy mind. It will also assist Gloucestershire Tourist Board, because, let's face it, tourism needs all the help it can get at the moment . . .

## The Black Horse pub haunting

There have been several ghostly apparitions in this popular pub. In one incident an evil-looking lady appeared in a bedroom and scratched a signature in a black window before disappearing. Others have smelled lavender by the pub's fireplace. It is thought that it comes from the ghost of a previous cleaner who always sprayed lavender polish near the fireplace.

## *The WHSmith poltergeist*

As well as being home to many books, magazines and stationery, WHSmith is said to be home to a terrifying poltergeist. In an incident during a refit in 1995, staff reported stock vanishing, books flying around a room and doors slamming.

The bookstore was a garage at the beginning of the twentieth century and many believe that the garage owner still haunts the building.

## *Ghosts of little girls at House of Fraser*

Many staff have seen the ghosts of two little girls and a little boy in the stock rooms at the top of the building. The children often like to play hide and seek when staff are doing stock counts late into the evening and can be heard singing.

## *Faceless monk and ghosts at the King's Head Hotel*

This hotel has the reputation of being one of the most haunted places in Cirencester. A ghostly monk with no face reportedly scared one member of staff into quitting her job. Guests have also reported strange paranormal activity, such as their room doors opening and a figure in armour walking through the ballroom.

## The White Girl, Cirencester Memorial Hospital

There have been many chilling reports of a little girl dressed in white being seen at the top window of the hospital. Many who have seen the pale and very frail girl say she forces them to smile and puts up her bony arm to wave at them before disappearing within the blink of an eye. It is said that those who have seen the girl are overcome with sadness and are reduced to tears.

## Grey Lady, Cirencester Parish Church

One myth states that this church is haunted by a grey lady who is often seen carrying freshly cut flowers. Legend has it that she is taking them to the grave of her child, who died after catching smallpox.

### US airforce pilot at Queen Anne's Column in Cirencester Park

A young American pilot has been spotted talking to members of the public then vanishing after speaking a single sentence.

### Old man at the abbey grounds

An old gentleman with a humped back and a stick dressed in Victorian clothing is said to walk past the bandstand towards the river.

He is usually seen between 10 p.m. and 2 a.m. on clear nights, often shaking his head and grumbling to himself.

### Headless dog, Coxwell Street, Cirencester

There are reports of people seeing a whippet or grey-hound bound towards them when walking down Coxwell Street late at night. Some have chased the dog in an effort to return it to its owner. It responds by running in the other direction. Its head disappears, and then it vanishes entirely.

\*

My page went up on Facebook in August 2014 with a spooky picture of a haunted house I ripped from Google. By October, I had my first victim – a hungry reporter from the *Wilts and Glos Standard*.

It must have been a slow news day and I suspect he was desperate to find something scary yet heart-warming from the local community for the Halloween special. I couldn't believe my luck when he left a message. When he asked if he could feature all my ghoulish stories, I almost wet myself with excitement. The story appeared under the following headline:

### MOST HAUNTED PLACES IN
### CIRENCESTER REVEALED

Yes! Yes! Yes! My powers were back. And, unlike at school, my supremacy went unchallenged. The next year, near enough the same article appeared in the same newspaper, albeit with a slightly less dramatic headline:

### CIRENCESTER'S MOST SPOOKY LOCATIONS

Then, a lady from the tiny, shit museum in town called me (I know that sounds mean, but it really is shit). She wanted to create a ghost tour around Cirencester based on all the sightings on my Facebook page; suitable footwear and a rain jacket strongly advised.

**Student: Daisy Cooper**
**Assignment Title: Beauty and the Beast**
**Deadline: 19.12.02**
**Grades:**
Theatre for Children: Pass
Voice 1: Distinction
Movement 1: Distinction
Devising: Pass

---

**Lecturers feedback**:

Daisy, you handed in your log book and evaluation very late (after the xmas break) and your grades for Theatre for Children and Devising have been reduced to a pass because of this. This is such a shame, because you demonstrated through your practical work that you have an excellent understanding of the concerns when performing for children and produced an excellent characterization that was highly engaging for the target audience. Your movement skills were highly effective within the characterisation of Gabrielle. You used larger than life gestures and general physicality to communicate the relationships on stage and really transformed into this beastly sister. Your physical contact with Suzanne (eg the fight) was really well executed and you were never afraid of experimenting in rehearsal to find the right pace for this.

Your vocal skills were also excellent. Your projection and diction were unsurpassed and you used an extremely large range of dynamics, rhythms and intonations to communicate the text. You achieved effective audience responses at specific moments in the play and really worked hard to bring out the humour in the family scenes. The other actors in your cast all benefited from your tremendous energy on the stage and the whole piece picked up in pace the moment you walked on stage. Well done.

You joined the group late and missed some of the early adaptation work but still contributed to the devising of movement and song later in the process. You have not documented the changes to the original script in your log, although your character profile and evaluation work is very strong. Don't forget to check through the required contents for the log before you submit – and get it in on time next project!

---

Signed (lecturer) ...................... Date ......Jan 03..........

STUDENT: DAISY MAY COOPER    TUTOR: [REDACTED]

SCHOOL: PERFORMING ART    COURSE: NATIONAL DIPLOMA

YEAR: (1) 2 3    TERM: 1 (2) 3    DATE: 13/3/03

TUTORIAL NUMBER: 1    TIME: 2.30

**Purpose of Tutorial/Issues Discussed:**

Serious concerns over attendance, brought up by several teachers.

**Report on progress (Tutor to record):**

Daisy shows excellent potential on the course. And promises to become an outstanding member of the group if her attendance 100%

**Comments recorded by Student/Candidate:**

I definetly need to ~~approve~~ improve my attendance. overall, I am really enjoying ~~was~~ The Course.

**Agreed Action (Recorded by Student/Candidate)** improves.    **By When:**    **Date Completed:**

100% improved attendance, Try and aim for no absences for the next term.

Tutor's Signature: [REDACTED]    Student's Signature: Daisy may Cooper    Date of next meeting:

Student's Destination: ...........

White copy - Student    Pink copy - Tutor's file    Photocopy to: ..........................................(if agreed)

For years, I'd been dreaming of this moment: this moment when all of my fucked-up childhood could finally be given meaning. Suddenly, everything made sense.

All those nights when I'd watch slightly creepy Roy channel the spirit world. All those nights when I'd heard the *beep . . . beep . . . beep . . . beep* of his wife's mobility scooter making a quick getaway before 'Fly Me to the fucking Moon' kicked in. All those times I'd been forced to watch a dozen Pams with poodle perms look adoringly into Roy's eyes as he spun them a line of pure bollocks. All those times I had to listen to 'Take My Breath Away' by Berlin.

All those times I'd seen the heartbreak on Mum's face, and know she was so desperate to believe that she'd see Auntie Alison again . . .

# CHAPTER 4
# A COOPER CHRISTMAS SPECIAL

'How do I look?' I proudly twirled around in the living room, beaming from ear to ear.

The day had almost arrived when I could show off my costume, lovingly constructed with Mum's help, at the school nativity play.

Dad and Charlie grunted and tried to look pleased for me, but they only succeeded in looking pissed off because I was blocking their view of the telly.

'You'll steal the show,' Mum cooed, stepping in quickly to the fill the silence.

I will, I thought. *This* is my moment to shine. *This* is the moment when all the kids who thought I was weird realized that I'd actually been hiding a show-stopping talent. I'd be like the Beast woken by Beauty's kiss, or Olivia Newton-John at the end of *Grease*. Transformed from zero to hero. My natural magnetism would sprinkle itself over my audience.

The run-up to the school nativity had been epic. Mum was in her element. She *loves* Christmas. And of course I did too. When you are little, everything glitters and

A friend made this card. They clearly knew how mad-as-fuck Christmas was in our house.

shimmers and there's the slightest possibility you might get given the toy you dreamed of all year round.

I remember poring over the Argos catalogue for days on end, making lists of every toy that was crying out to be owned by me. We cut out the pictures and posted them in a never-ending stream of letters to the North Pole.

Mum was brilliant at make-believe and also encouraged us to make Christmas decorations. And she really loved it when it came to making costumes for the nativity play. Out came the sewing machine and she'd work her magic, using remnants of material.

Charlie and I always looked amazing. We had sparkles and diamante sewn into all of our costumes. However, I occasionally caught a glimpse of Mrs Oldershaw's face backstage, her jaw dropping ever so slightly at the sight of us. I'm not sure Mum always got it right. I mean, exactly how many shepherds keeping watch over their flock by night sport fairy-lights as a headdress?

My star turn came in Year Five, when Mrs Lewis picked me to play the Angel Gabriel. I was over the moon. I told absolutely everyone. I swooped and dived all around the playground with imaginary wings, behaving more like a demented bat than a would-be angel.

And, of course, as soon as she heard about my lead part, Mum got involved.

We turned out to be a dream team. For weeks, Mum

wasn't shouting at me, like she usually did. I was the model daughter she had always wanted. I clung on to her as we traipsed through town picking up scraps of material from bargain buckets.

Dad and Charlie retreated and became almost invisible as Mum and I locked ourselves in our secret world. We bent coat-hanger wire, pulled gauze, sewed on sparkles and stuck on feathers, all the while checking and double-checking the sewing patterns in our quest for the perfect set of wings.

I dreamed about my debut. I reckoned that whatever assignments the Angel Gabriel had undertaken in the past for the Lord, delivering the message to Mary that she would be pushing out the Messiah would have been a real career highlight. I wanted to do the part justice.

How a virgin could conceive was less clear. And she didn't seem to ask many questions about it either. None of it made sense. Nevertheless, I practised my lines in front of the mirror until I was pitch perfect: 'You will give birth to a son, and call him Jesus.'

Before long, it was time for the dress rehearsal. My wings and dress were carefully packed away and Dad drove to school with my costume. But as he popped the lid of the boot it became clear that one of the wings had got hideously bent in transit. I was beside myself and threw the most massive tantrum. Mrs Lewis had to calm everyone down.

'Daisy. It's a dress rehearsal. Wear your dress today and say your lines without the wings this time. You can repair them for the big night.'

It worked, although my wings had given me a certain confidence that I wasn't sure how to fake. I didn't feel half as cocky on stage – a little naked, if I'm honest. Thankfully, I managed to get through it, albeit a little sulkily.

Mrs Lewis said I was perfect, but she may have been being kind. I did look as if I was about to cry at any moment.

Finally, the big night arrived. Dad dropped me off again, this time with the wings intact. 'Break a leg, Dais,' he said, and smiled and winked as I disappeared from view.

'Thanks, Dad. Love you.'

I remember thinking the wings required a bit of man-handling to get through the double swing doors and into the classroom that served as our dressing room, but it was a fleeting thought as I rushed to get ready.

In the dressing room, the atmosphere was electric. Robert Pope was jumping from one foot to the other, saying he needed the toilet. Mary and Joseph were having a fight over who got to hold the plastic Jesus. The shepherds in their tea towels were trying to give each other dead legs, and there was a donkey swapping Pokémon cards with a Wise Man.

I was a heady mix of nerves and excitement, so much so that I was yakking ten to the dozen and Mrs Lewis shouted at me. I was also busy bobbing out and along the corridor and peeking round to enjoy the frisson of parents and siblings arriving in the hall. I looked expectantly around to see if I could spot Mum and Dad and Charlie. *Yes!* They were in the front row.

With my dress on, I felt like a million dollars. Now, it was time for my wings. God, I loved them. I ran my child fingers across the sequins and gauze and the experimental tufts of gold taffeta and feathers, like I was Jean Paul Gaultier about to unleash his latest collection.

Because I was playing the Angel Gabriel, I had a separate entrance at the back of the stage. Just as we'd practised, I would glide in, spotlight shining on me, as bright as the North Star.

The play began.

'A long, long time ago, a woman called Mary lived in a city called Nazareth. She was married to Joseph, a simple carpenter. One day the Angel Gabriel appeared to her . . .' I heard the narrator say.

This was my cue. I stepped out into the silence of the stage. I took a deep breath and, in a suitably angelic voice, I delivered my lines:

'You will give birth to a son, and his name will be Jesus.' I smiled a self-satisfied grin and turned to exit stage left. At no point had anyone told me that, in typical Cooper fashion, Mum had made the wings *fucking huge*.

As I turned gracefully, one of the tips batted Joe Ferris in the eye. He was waiting patiently at the back as Joseph, ready to lead Mary out on the journey to Bethlehem with the donkey.

He swerved violently and knocked into Mary, played by Jemima Platt. She had been looking wistfully into the distance and had not expected that at all. She squealed and started crying.

When I turned to see what all the fuss was about, I sent one of the shepherds – Joel Atkins – hurtling into one of the Three Wise Men. Everyone was falling like dominoes.

The more I turned from side to side to see what was happening, the more chaos descended on stage, but I couldn't see properly over my enormous golden wings. When I turned to face the audience, Mum's hands were covering her face. Meanwhile, Dad and Charlie couldn't contain themselves and looked as though they were choking with laughter, tears streaming down their faces.

Parents, on the brink of hysteria, started leaping up on stage to rescue their fallen children. It was mayhem.

'For God's sake, stand still, Daisy!' I could hear Mrs Lewis shouting from one side of the stage.

'Daisy!' Someone else was calling my name. It was Mr Bates, who was standing at the other side of the stage.

'*Daisy!*' Mrs Lewis called again. I didn't know who to turn to, so I just kept turning from side to side, frozen on the spot, wondering whether to tiptoe out backwards or run towards the safety of one of them.

Arrgghhhh! The whole thing was so confusing.

As I continued to swivel left then right, more carnage was being done to the cast.

Finally, I was on my own. My enormous golden wings, bent and skewed, hung around me, making me look like a pissed-up butterfly. I could feel the tears welling up inside as I stared out into the hall. I was numb. Then I felt someone's hands grabbing me. It was Mum. She scooped me up and we both ran for the exit.

After that, the incident was never mentioned. Not at school, nor at home. It was as if it had never taken place. In the playground, I was back to playing by myself. I didn't get invited to parties for a long time either. I still remember those wings with fondness, though. They may have been utterly ridiculous, but they were mine and Mum's and we'd spent weeks making them together, just me and her.

Mum's unabated enthusiasm for glitz and bling and making something out of nothing was very contagious. But as I got older, I did become disenchanted when I found out that Father Christmas was just Dad in a dodgy cotton-wool beard and a red Santa suit.

At the time, Dad was an electronics salesman. It was a soulless job, travelling to industrial estates in the middle of nowhere trying to persuade buyers they needed LED screens. He was like a sadder David Brent. Often, I'd hear him making endless phone calls to would-be clients who showed no interest whatsoever, so a lot of the day he'd play Solitaire on his computer.

The twenty-fifth of December started to become a date I didn't wholeheartedly look forward to. We never had a great deal of money and that made everything look that bit more desperate.

Gone were the days of innocence, when I loved the dressing-up, the anticipation of presents and chocolate and stockings. Sometimes, though, even with so little money, we managed to pull off a Christmas we would remember.

We nicknamed it Crimbo – I think it was a Liver-pudlian thing Dad picked up from John Lennon when he was talking about Christmas on a chat show back in the 1960s. Strange, the things you remember.

Anyway, there was one year that was *awful*. There was even talk about cancelling Christmas. All of us wanted to bury our heads in the sand and pretend the whole shebang wasn't happening.

All of us except Mum.

She wasn't having any of it. In fact, the grinding pov-erty of that particular year seemed to give her renewed determination to make Christmas *amazing*. And she did an *amazing* job, but somehow it all felt a bit sad.

The best bit was the Secret Santa. We were under strict instructions to only spend £5 on each other. The raids on the charity shops became a race between us, hunting high and low to get the best or the worst gift. Our finds included *The Full Monty* on VHS, Ian Botham's auto-biography and a framed collection of beer mats.

Mum had a board game ready for the big day that she'd no doubt picked up at a car-boot – of course some of the pieces were missing. That year we played Monopoly by candlelight. The electric had run out and there wasn't any money to put in the meter. Charlie and I felt like the impoverished Cratchit family in Dickens's *Christmas Carol* – up shit creek without a paddle but grateful to be surrounded by family.

Admittedly, other Christmases were a bit less terrible. Sometimes, Mum's Aunt Joan and Uncle John came – more so after her parents, my Grannie and Grandad Eddie, passed away. Grannie first, followed by Grandad three months later. Mum's family had been close, espe-cially after Auntie Alison's death, so it was a very difficult time for Mum.

John and Joan travelled to ours for the big day. I dreaded them coming, as I'd have to give up my bed-room and sleep on the sofa downstairs. Joan had a perm so solid it looked like it had been chiselled out of rock.

She'd also had a mastectomy and was always leaving her fake silicone boob around the house. John looked like Victor Meldrew and I was mesmerized by one eyebrow hair that protruded inches out from his forehead. Once, when he fell asleep on the sofa, I tried to pluck it.

They took pleasure in the simplest of things and they loved visiting Cirencester and lapping up its olde-worlde charm.

'Golden Egg Tea Room this afternoon?' They'd be itching to get there. We went to the Golden Egg without fail every time they visited. They were people who liked routine. They liked what they liked in the way that they liked it. Given that they were in their seventies, we forgave them.

Charlie and I could recite the conversation there'd be between them and Mum as soon as we got seated. We may as well have had a checklist.

'Will the waitress remember to bring the hot water with the tea?'

'Oh, I don't know, John. I hope so. She did last time . . .'

It was a real cliffhanger.

'Have they still got crumpets on the menu?'

To be fair, what self-respecting tea shop wouldn't have crumpets?

'Is it butter or margarine?' Woe betide the Golden Egg if it was margarine. Or, worse, one of those spreads that 'looks like butter, tastes like butter, but isn't actually butter'. The devil's work, according to John.

In the evening, Uncle John would pop out and treat us all to a fish-and-chip supper and we'd all sit around enduring *The Generation Game* or *Kids Say the Funniest Things*. I hated the children on it, as I always thought I was much funnier.

But Joan and John's outward cheerfulness hid a darker side. The slightest upset could send John into a deep sulk that lasted for hours. Joan, on the other hand, was fonder of a side swipe, often muttered under her breath. She'd say things like:

'Daisy, I couldn't tell if you were a girl or a boy with that new haircut.'

We had many an interesting Christmas with them, but the Coke Can Incident was probably the most talked about for years. Of course, yours truly was right at the centre of it.

Our fridge never held anything particularly exciting. Occasionally, there would be a tasty treat in there, but the Tesco Value range featured heavily. If there were brand names, they came via Poundland.

I distinctly remember arriving home one Christmas Eve. I skipped into the kitchen and opened the fridge, hoping to find something tasty to eat and drink that wasn't reserved for the Big Day.

Normally, any munchie mission would have left me

disappointed, but fuck me, not this time. There, glowing on the middle shelf like a tart under a tanning lamp, was a proper can of Coke. Honestly, it was begging for it. I didn't even stop to question why this impostor was in our fridge.

Without giving it a second thought, I grabbed it and, like a greedy goblin, popped the tab. In one swig, I downed the sweet, delicious fizz. I flipped the empty can into the rubbish bin and bounded up the stairs to lie down, head spinning from the caffeine kick.

My glee was broken a few moments later.

'Joan! Joan! Where's my can of Coca-Cola?' squealed Uncle John, followed by an almighty slamming of the fridge door.

'Come on. Who's had it?'

I sank into the duvet and tried to tell myself it would all die down, still trying to savour the unmistakable taste in my mouth. Own brand was never quite the same as the real thing.

Suddenly, I heard Uncle John pounding up the stairs like the Terminator. Holy shit. He had the ability to go from zero to a hundred on the rage scale over the most trivial of things, like not being able to find the remote control or losing a Werther's Original down the side of the sofa.

I figured it was hardly the crime of the century, so I made an executive decision to keep quiet.

But Uncle John's fury was like an atomic bomb exploding. He was so cross he kung-fu kicked a door wedge like he was Eric Cantona kicking the Crystal Palace fan in that premiership game in 1995.

'You leave one thing in the fridge in this house, and that's it. It's gone. Like living with a bunch of bloody magpies,' he raged.

The shit truly hit the fan. Even Mum got exasperated.

'It's only a can of Coke, John. Next time I go shopping, I'll buy another one for you.'

'No. You can't. It's Christmas Eve and the shops are shut for two bloody days. And I need that can now!'

Auntie Joan was trying to calm him down by rubbing his back.

Uncle John sounded more like a petulant toddler than a pensioner. I felt bad that he was giving Mum a hard time, but I still couldn't bring myself to own up. I'd kept quiet far too long to crack now. Besides, Mum was right, it was only a can of Coke, for fuck's sake.

'Why? What's so special about the Coke!' I could hear Mum getting very irritated.

'A cold can helps to ease the swelling of my haemorrhoids.'

A stony silence descended over the kitchen. I shot up from bed. I barely had enough time to process the full horror of Uncle John squatting, butt cheeks parted, with a can of the ice-cold classic pressed against his purple piles.

I ran to the bathroom and barfed the entire can, heaving with every grim vision that entered my mind. Even now, I cannot look at one of those iconic red cans without being reminded of Uncle John and his fat arse.

# CHAPTER 5
# THE HEDGE TRIMMER

'm standing behind a trestle table, not much shorter than me. A man saunters up and starts to survey our offerings. His eyes meticulously undress every item we've laid out on the cloth. He's mid-fifties with greying stubble and he looks like a 1970s porn director. He looks down at me like I really shouldn't be manning this stall alone.

He picks up a back scratcher.

'What's this for?' he asks.

'I dunno.'

'How do you not know? It's your stall.'

I'm seven years old, for fuck's sake. I'm not Philip Green. My only experience of trading is swapping Pogs in the playground. I'm out of my depth here.

Fuck, where's Dad?

Dad has nipped off to use the Portaloo at the back of the car-boot site, leaving me alone to shift the bric-a-brac from our garage. We've been here since 6.30 a.m. and sold absolutely fuck all. But Dad says this month we need the money. The entrance fee to the car boot is £2, so at the very least we have to break even. Ideally, Dad wants profit.

I look up. The man is running his hands across some cotton bed sheets that are neatly folded on the table. 'Please, please don't open them up,' I beg silently. When we brought them out from the garage they had a thin line of green mould in the creases from the damp. They've been folded strategically so it's not visible.

He loses interest in them and casts his eyes over a Whitney Houston CD.

Thank fuck.

On the next-door stall there's a guy in a baseball cap whose table is overflowing with goodies: a lava lamp, a plastic crate full of CDs, a video collection top heavy with the works of Jean-Claude Van Damme, a huge Staffordshire bull terrier figurine, several lamp stands and a collection of still-boxed Yardley toiletries.

This guy knows exactly how to cajole pennies and pounds out of wallets and pockets:

'Special offer. Two for a pound. Come on, love, you know you want it. Soft, velvety . . . just imagine waking up every morning with that all over your face.'

This guy knows exactly how to work the crowd too. A few people have gathered, like he's doing a cookery demonstration in House of Fraser. A woman walks away with two brushed-cotton pillowcases she probably never knew she needed.

'How much for the Scrabble set?' The porn director looks at me. Fuck. Not the Scrabble set. I start to panic. Dad says we shouldn't really sell it. It's got a T and a B missing, which could spell trouble.

'Errr . . .' I look around, desperate to catch a glimpse of Dad striding back from the bog. He's absolutely nowhere to be seen.

'Err . . . 20p?' I pluck a number from the air. I can see him doing a 'value for money' calculation in his head. It's 20p, for fuck's sake. We're not talking about a massive financial investment here. He points out some water damage on the side of the box.

Two old ladies walk by, rubbernecking two of our crocheted tea cosies. I have high hopes for the home-made stuff. Gives our pitch the edge. These are made by Mum's fair hand, but also found abandoned in the garage because, of course, she can't bring herself to throw anything out.

The ladies look like Miss Marple and Jessica Fletcher scouring the site for crimes against society.

'Didn't you need a tea cosy, Jean?' One nudges the other and points.

'I did, Sue, but not one like that . . .' she whispers, loud enough for me to hear.

'No, Jean, not really your cup of tea, those ones . . .'

I sink back towards the safety of the open car boot, sending them daggers with my eyes. I'm wounded.

Sue may have a point, though.

One tea cosy has been fashioned to resemble Elvis Presley – arguably, at the height of his addiction to prescription opioids, tranquillizers and barbiturates. The other has been inspired by the natural beauty of the Cotswolds and is a blue tit. Mum didn't get the eyes quite right or the facial markings, so it looks more like Hitler at the Nuremberg Rallies.

After sifting through its contents, the man decides against the Scrabble set. He gives me a pained expression as he continues on his treasure hunt.

Everyone else's pitch looks like they have a plan. It looks as though they've handpicked items knowing exactly the mark-up they can get on them. Ours looks as if we've raided a skip. There are dolls with dirt on them and their plastic hands chewed off.

The man looks more animated now. He's clearly seen something that catches his eye. Ah, yes . . . it's the *pièce de résistance* of our collection: the hedge trimmer. It's a Flymo. 'Top of the range,' Dad said when he loaded it into the car. It's still in its box.

'Does it work?'

For fuck's sake. All these questions. I shrug politely.

'Yeah, absolutely,' I say.

I'm a hundred per cent sure it doesn't work, but by the time he's taken it home and plugged it in I'll be long gone, like a guff in the wind. Serves him right for being sniffy about the Scrabble set.

I've never seen anyone actually use the hedge trimmer, though. It'll be one of those items Mum's picked up in a charity shop and filed it under 'That'll come in handy one day.' We know it won't and that it will sit there, like lots of Mum's items, until we're in need of cash, on days like this.

The guy next door is really going for it now. He's the sort who's got there early after studying the pitch map like it's horseracing form. He's even got a flask of coffee. Clearly in it for the long haul.

'You look like a gent in need of a trim,' he says, bringing out an electric beard trimmer and moving up and down in the air while simulating a buzzing sound. An old man who looks like Merlin seems half tempted.

'Looks brand new!' My guy is now peering inside the Flymo box.

*Yes!* Is this a sale? I dare to hope. Fucking brilliant. I play out a scene in my head. Dad returns from the Portaloo. I run towards him, arms open wide. In one hand, I'm waving a fiver. 'Look!' I'm shouting. 'I sold the hedge trimmer!' He twirls me round in a heart-warming father–daughter embrace and lifts me high above his head, smiling lovingly.

Mr 1970s Porno is pulling the Flymo out of its box now. All my hopes and dreams are tied up in its bright orange handle.

'Mmmmm . . .' He inspects it, eyes glistening.

The retractable wire and plug are incorporated into the handle. I can see he is quietly very impressed by this.

'It's a new model,' I say, capitalizing on his obvious enthusiasm. I've been taking notes from Theo Paphitis next door.

He pulls on the plug and starts to draw the wire out. It stops. He tugs on it some more. It stops again. Full length, the wire looks approximately thirty centimetres long.

'Has it got stuck?'

'Don't think so.'

He runs his finger across the wire. Suddenly, the reason someone wanted to part with it in the first place becomes patently clear. The blade has sliced through the wire in some extreme hedge-trimming incident and someone has tried to mend it with a piece of cable shorter than my school ruler.

My heart sinks.

He keeps pulling on it. He can't quite believe that anyone would try and repair it like that.

He tuts. He purses his lips and looks at me like I'm a rip-off merchant. I sink further back into the car boot and pray that Dad turns up soon.

'Sorry,' I say, embarrassed.

He bundles the Flymo back into the box. I take it from him and place it in the back of the car so he knows I didn't deliberately try to con him. It was an honest oversight, and I curse Mum under my breath.

Next door, Merlin has bought the electric beard trimmer. He wanders off, clearly thinking about his new look. Maybe he'll go for some minimalist man-strap? Or a rap-industry-standard goatee? Or maybe he's bought it for an anniversary present for his wife's beard?

Mr 1970s Porno is, surprisingly, still here. Now, he's got sidetracked by the metal fire grate. He's determined to find something on our table. Perhaps he feels sorry for me.

He turns it over in his hands. It's the real deal. Mum and Dad had it in the living room in our first house, but they don't use it any more because Mum replaced it with a superior charity-shop find with a drawer underneath to collect the ashes.

'How much?'

I feel guilty about the cordless hedge trimmer. More than that, I have no idea what the fire grate is worth. I turn around one last time, desperate to see Dad striding across the field. He is nowhere to be seen.

I reckon Dad would sell it for £1, so I drop the price to be sure of a sale.

'30p,' I say.

The guy smiles and reaches into his pocket, pulling out a handful of change and counting out three 10p pieces. When he places the coins on the table, a warm glow spreads through me. Dad is going to be so proud of me.

I sit on the car bumper, swinging my legs. I don't even care if we don't see another customer all day.

'OK, Dais? Hold the fort all right?' Dad's back from his waz. Says there was a queue and that's why he took so long.

'Any interest?'

'Sold the fire grate, Dad,' I say, looking like I've just scored a goal.

'That's my girl! How much for?'

I proudly point to the 30p sitting in a white mug with a crap cartoon of Jarvis Cocker on it and the phrase 'Sorted for Teas and Whizz'.

Silence.

'Daisy! That was our most expensive item! Thirty fucking pence? For fuck's sake!'

My head drops. I feel a prickle of shame and a clenching of my stomach.

'Sorry, Dad . . .'

'We could've got a fucking fiver for that . . .' Dad is very angry. He is sucking his teeth and pacing back and forth.

'. . . and why the fuck is the hedge trimmer in the boot?'

# CHAPTER 6
# THE COOPERS GO CONTINENTAL

As an adult, I have a far better relationship with my parents than I could ever have predicted. I consider this a major achievement because, quite frankly, some of the shit they put me through as a teenager is unforgivable. Well, I say unforgivable . . . On a one-to-ten scale of child cruelty, it feels like an eight. In reality, it's probably a four. But when you're a teenager, any whiff of your parents looking like twats to the outside world and drawing attention to your family dysfunction feels totally shaming.

And, on occasion, my parents have looked like utter twats.

Despite their constant financial worries, they always managed to take us on holiday – paid for on a credit card, of course. Back then, loan companies didn't run credit checks so it was far easier to spunk money on one card and then, when the interest got too high, abandon it and take out another. Or move house before any debt-collection agency could track you down.

Mostly, our holidays began and ended in Weymouth. Mum loved the seaside and, money-wise, it was all they could stretch to. Don't get me wrong, for a ten-year-old, the esplanade there was like being in beach heaven: Punch and Judy shows, beach rides on a donkey, ice cream, fish and chips.

But, historically, Weymouth was also the port through which the Black Death entered – and when I became a teenager, it felt more like this. There were only so many times you could hear the words 'How about the Sea Life Centre today?' or skulk around the penny arcades on the promenade without losing the will to live.

Then, one year, something strange happened. Mum and Dad booked a Eurocamp holiday in the south of France. Dad was beside himself. You'd have thought it was the first time he'd ever been camping, even though that's all his parents did – albeit only ever in the West Country, where, I might add, they also happened to live.

Maybe Mum had forced it. Even though Weymouth appeared to be her spiritual homeland, she'd been brought up on far more exotic trips. Her dad, Eddie, was a racing jockey and always went to amazing places like India and Hong Kong. Her and Grannie and her two sisters would get on a plane to visit him, and sometimes they would even live with him for a while, wherever he was.

As we'd never known a holiday like that, the south of France had all the promise of an adventure – it was like *Around the World in Eighty Days.*

A welcome pack arrived at home, handed to us by the postman. This was also a novelty because we were always instructed to avoid the postman at all costs in case he handed us an envelope which we then couldn't deny we had received – like a county court judgement or a utility bill with angry red writing on it.

'This is going to be the best holiday we've ever had!' Dad really built it up. He tantalizingly undid the envelope and spilled its contents on to the living-room floor to his own mock fanfare. Inside was a large map of the site, which he spread out.

'This is where we'll pitch out tent,' he said, matching up the coordinates detailed on the welcome letter, like he was about to conquer Mount Everest. There was a brochure with photos of ecstatic holidaymakers scream-ing their way down long and twisty multicoloured water chutes under clear blue skies. Nuclear families laughed and smiled adoringly at each other over escargots and coq au vin at the terrace restaurant.

Inside, there were also kids' packs of crayons and colouring books. Dad talked us through every item, even though we could see what they were ourselves. In the end, Charlie got bored and wandered off and Mum made an excuse to do something in the kitchen. The welcome pack had arrived eight months before the holiday. Charlie and Mum must have sensed that many more evenings like this one were to follow.

However, Dad's enthusiasm was so infectious that I got drawn in. I can picture it now. Me sitting by him, hanging on his every word. Him running down the list of on-site activities, from crazy-golf to aqua aerobics, from tree-top adventures to throwing shapes on the dance floor at the kids' disco.

'It's going to be amazing, Daisy,' he said, his eyes gazing dreamily off to a faraway land. For once, it was just me and him. We weren't angry or shouting at each other. There was no one kicking off about money. No one was blaming anyone for anything. Just a few precious moments where we laughed and smiled and dreamed of French sunshine and French food and shouting *Bonjour!* at everybody as we skipped to the on-site bakery to buy croissants – these were the only two French words we knew.

This soon wore off. Instead of putting the pack away until holiday time, Dad got it out at every opportunity. There wasn't a single visitor who didn't know we were going: the time, the date, the place. Oh . . . my . . . god . . . Dad became a holiday bore. The pack was kept in a corner of the living room and if anyone sensed him heading towards it they evaporated like a fucking will-o'-the-wisp. Best vanishing trick ever.

Eventually, the day was upon us when we had to leave. The excitement of packing up soon descended into the usual Cooper chaos. Once I'd picked out my skimpy crop tops and shorts and placed them in my suitcase, it was time to turn my attention to the in-car entertainment.

'Charlie. It's my turn to have the Walkman!'

'No, it isn't! You had it for the journey to Weymouth last year! And you pretended to be a fucking Spice Girl for the whole holiday.'

It will come as no surprise that I didn't opt for Posh.

Outside, Mum and Dad argued about how to pack the car.

As usual, Mum wanted to take the entire contents of the kitchen, just in case we couldn't get anything on site. One suitcase was filled with sliced bread, because she was so worried that the French only ate baguettes.

And no one ever bothered to mention that the journey to the south of France would last *for ever*. There was quite a lot of England to get through before we even got to the ferry, and even more road once we'd hit the continent. *In the August heat*. It wasn't long before Charlie and I were licking the windows like demented hounds in a hot car. I was fucking livid from Swindon onwards.

By the time we arrived at the campsite we were all cross and desperate to get to our tent, which turned out to be more challenging than the Crystal Maze.

'Speak English!' Dad kept saying to the site staff, which was a bit fucking rude, considering they were French. He was behaving like a language lout, so much so that Mum stepped in and, surprisingly, held it together with some schoolgirl phrases.

'*Excusez-moi, où est la tente?*' We were secretly very impressed. After a while, Mum was able to direct Dad there, with a smug sense of satisfaction.

In my mind's eye, we were going to be in campsite heaven. The site would be just like Dad had described endlessly from the brochure. There would be tall pines swaying in the breeze, clear blue skies and a golden sandy beach with azure sea lapping gently on the shore.

As we weaved our way through to reach our tent it became clear that reality never quite matches the imagination. There were pine trees – around three. And the sky was blue – all the fucking time. I never knew how much I could miss the cooling English drizzle. And the balmy wind didn't help – it just wafted hot air round the campsite like a hairdryer on full blast.

The next morning, we discovered that the beach was gold and sandy, but the brochure had failed to mention it was fucking miles away. Carrying our towels and sun cream and inflatable flamingo and windbreak down there was like a full-on assault course. In the end, we opted to stay by the pool.

Ha! I use the word 'pool' liberally. It was a concrete outpost with no shade. The multicoloured spaghetti junction of slides and chutes I had been dreaming about turned out to be an aquatic area containing a slightly dodgy metal contraption that fried your arse.

Dad loved it. He spent his days on the sun lounger sipping French beer and leering at the twenty-something women bathing topless just centimetres from his sock-and-sandal ensemble. But even then he looked like he was on the back end of a twenty-mile queue on the M1. Miserable fucker.

Mum, on the other hand, had managed to corner an English family and was busy suggesting a plan to meet up after the holiday. For. Fuck's. Sake. It turned out they lived in Bolton – bloody miles from Cirencester.

They seemed grateful for one of Mum's loaves of sliced bread, though, as they were also worried about the French food.

As if all of this wasn't bad enough – there was The Poncho.

'I crocheted it for you in holiday colours,' Mum said as she lifted it proudly out of her luggage.

'Are you fucking kidding me?' I wanted to scream, but I couldn't, because Mum had made it especially for me and I knew how wounded she would be if I didn't wear it.

The Poncho was the product of another of Mum's fads – one she was convinced would bring us in lots of money. I begged to differ. Unless Cirencester had suddenly transformed into the Wild West and was now teeming with bandidos sporting panpipes, I felt the market was limited.

I couldn't tell her, but it was also fucking horrendous. She'd handpicked yarns from the reduced basket in the Mays Sisters Haberdashery Shop in Five Alls Street. The shop was tucked away from the main drag and frozen in time. Nothing had changed since the sisters inherited it from their parents something like a hundred years ago. The yellowing film in the window was peeling and cracked. Some of the shelves were home to generations of spiders. Even the old bat who worked there had cobwebs on her. But it was one of Mum's favourite shops.

I wish I had kept a photo of The Poncho now. It was so hideous it had to be seen to be believed. It had tassels and clashing colours and it weighed a ton. Not something to wear in the searing French heat. A psychedelic chessboard, if you please, made by someone fucked on magic mushrooms.

'It's perfect, Dais!' Mum smiled dreamily at me whenever I wore it, which of course I did, to please her. She was so proud of it. But every time I did, a part of me died inside. I could hear the laughter of the other teenagers echoing around the campsite. I could feel fingers pointing at me. This was extra painful as I was just becoming aware of the opposite sex. And French boys were superfit. They ran their hands through their cropped hair and wore designer jeans and hung out with the Spanish and

Italian teenagers in the play area next to the bar drinking Coke or lemonade, or the odd can of cider if they managed to con the club barman. Some even smoked Gauloises.

I'd been practising my *Bonjour!* for precisely this moment. I had even fantasized about a teenage fumble with a Gaston or a Patrice or even a Sébastien. If not a fumble, then at least some French kissing. But I'd completely forgotten to factor in me. And Charlie. We had home-made haircuts (Mum used a bowl, of course) and the home-made fucking poncho. I tried making Charlie wear it, but he crumpled like a rag doll under the weight of it and I got in trouble with Dad for trying to kill him.

Please don't ask me why I never tried to 'lose' The Poncho, like I had done with so many other of Mum's home-made clothes. I think I kept hoping God would rescue me and send a flood so that it would be swept far out to sea, then I wouldn't feel so guilty.

My wish almost came true. Almost. After days of unbearable humidity, we were all woken one night by a tremendous thunderstorm. It was amazing. Biblical bolts of lightning zig-zagged across the sky, accompanied by terrific cracks of thunder. Charlie and I were thrilled and huddled in our sleeping bags to listen.

We were less keen when the pitter-patter of raindrops on the tarpaulin escalated to a full-on tropical storm. The rain was torrential. We watched on helplessly as the tent roof very quickly began to sag under the sheer volume of water, then gave up the ghost completely and collapsed.

This sent a torrent of water gushing through the middle. It was as if we were surfing the crest of a giant wave on airbeds. 'Hold on, kids!' Mum and Dad were shouting, and they sounded pretty panicked. This definitely hadn't featured in the welcome pack. Neither did the plague of toads that became our bedfellows, desperately trying to jump out of the fast-flowing river we were in danger of being swept away by.

When morning finally broke, the clouds had cleared and it was as if the storm had never happened. And it was still as humid. The odd toad croaked under our damp sleeping bags as we surveyed the debris.

Of course, in the devastation, The Poncho remained steadfast. But, thank God, it was sodden – the wool was so wet, and the colours had bled into each other. Now it looked like a bad Jackson Pollock painting. Dad struggled to pick it up from the small puddle of water where it had lain all night, but it had sucked up so much water it was a ton weight. Between us, we got it on to a hedge and spread it out to dry in the hot sun, where it stayed for a day or so.

Our last evening at the campsite was a fitting finale. There was a huge fair just a couple of miles away and it had the largest Big Wheel I had ever seen, with flashing lights and techno music blaring from speakers.

'Please, please can we go?' I kept begging. Mum and Dad finally caved in but, in the end, it was only Mum who agreed to take me up on the wheel. Dad gets sick just going up one floor in a lift, and they agreed that Charlie was a bit too young. I was so excited, hopping from one foot to the other, talking without taking a breath until Mum bellowed:

'For God's sake, Dais, *be quiet*!' But, as usual, I ignored her and carried on, until she threatened to take me back to the campsite.

The queue seemed to take for ever. I kept checking to make sure Dad and Charlie hadn't wandered off. I *so* wanted them to be part of this. In my head, I'd spot them in the crowd from the top and wave down.

Once we were seated and the safety barrier had been lowered, the carriage started to sway. I could barely contain myself. We travelled up, up and up further. We could see the campsite in the distance and the three pine trees swaying. The Mediterranean sparkled and stretched out to the horizon.

Dad and Charlie became like munchkins on the ground, but I was still waving at them furiously and I could see their tiny hands waving back.

'Dais . . . I think I'm . . .' Mum wasn't waving. Instead, her hands were gripping the safety rail of the basket and I noticed she was turning a funny colour.

'Dais, I don't feel . . .' Mum's face went a sickly shade

of green, then grey, then white. I watched in horror as she started to heave. At that very moment, the wheel creaked and yawned and then stopped.

Both Mum and I froze. We were at the very top, our basket rocking gently in the summer breeze. Panic set in. My knuckles turned white, like the colour of Mum's face, and Mum started frantically swallowing and gulping.

Then Mum was sick. A stream of projectile vomit exited her mouth and, in slow motion, her evening meal of escargots, steak frites and ice cream, together with a fair amount of red wine, hurtled through the air. I recoiled, but being forty yards off the ground, there was no place to hide as tiny speckled chunks of sick splattered my crop top.

'I'm so sorr—' she said sheepishly. But she didn't get to finish her sentence because she barfed again. The smell of the sick made me queasy and I barfed on her barf.

I looked down. The large crowd was below, looking up. They were smiling and waving, blissfully unaware that the projectile stream of vomit was about to hit. Dad knew it, though. Suddenly, I could see him bobbing around like a demented Weeble, shouting at the top of his voice, 'Get my wife and daughter off this fucking thing, you moron!'

Mum was still heaving and gulping, and so was I. I slumped into my seat, trying to pretend that this nightmare was not happening. A party of tourists who had been laughing down below had now gone quiet. Their shirts and shorts were covered in our dinner.

One German tourist who had taken the brunt of most of the red wine stomped towards Dad and poked him hard.

'*Schau mal! Schau mal!*' he kept shouting, pointing at his wine-stained T-shirt. He really was very annoyed.

By now Dad was spoiling for a fight. Being a devoted football fan, he carried with him all the humiliation the Germans had heaped on us for decades. He ripped off his T-shirt and squared up, hoping his tattoos would do the talking. When the German continued shouting, Dad danced around like a fucking nutter, yelling and gesturing like an extra on *Football Factory*.

'Come on, then, you sniggering bunch of Krauts – who wants to take me on?'

'*Fick dich, du Englische Hund!*' the tourist shouted back. I believe this roughly translates as: 'Go fuck yourself, you English dog.'

The Big Wheel started to creak its way back to life and slowly glide down. Now, I didn't want to be on the ground. I was more than a little concerned about meeting the German tourists. Thankfully, by the time we reached the bottom Dad was still shouting and gesturing but they were being led away by their driver and herded back on to their coach.

We walked home in silence. Each of us felt humiliated for different reasons. I realize now that I didn't even care that Mum had been ill or that Dad had tried to rescue us. Mostly, every time I got a whiff of sick from my crop top, I thought about how shamed I was by my parents, who, yet again, had managed to look like twats.

The only stroke of good fortune was that when we packed the car to leave I completely forgot about The Poncho getting crusty in the sun on the hedge and it got left behind. Mum was upset and promised to make a new one. I spent the entire journey home praying that she would forget.

Despite this horrendous experience, we did go on one more camping trip to France. It was as if we'd erased all the bad bits of Eurocamp from our minds.

This time around, it was a bigger family affair. Brothers, sisters, uncles and cousins piled into two cars filled to the brim with second-hand tents and assorted camping equipment collected by Mum.

The kids were roughly divided by age. Auntie Alison's kids Fiona and Lily were in their teens, like me, while my other cousins, Harry and Kitty, and Charlie were still young enough to be happy building sandcastles and splashing around in the pool.

The adults seemed more than happy to sit around, wine and beer in hand, with the excuse of watching over the younger kids. This left us girls free to roam the site, like the predatory teenagers we were – all eyeliner and heavy mascara, huge dangly earrings, crop tops and shorts so short they disappeared up our arse cracks.

We did not walk. We strutted. Arms folded, heads in the air, prowling the campsite for competition and giving any rival female in our path the evil eye.

Naturally, we gravitated towards the main attraction: a group of teenagers on motorbikes. I say motorbikes . . . in fact, what I thought were mean machines were about as powerful as Mum's Singer sewing machine. And the high-pitched sound they made was more like a constipated mosquito. I was so bloody naive . . .

But it felt so cool to finally be on holiday and welcomed by the in-crowd (or so we thought). No bowl haircut. Thankfully, no poncho. Just me and my bitches. It all felt very dangerous. Plus, my periods had started and so, unbeknown to me, my hormones were raging. The rebellious part of me wanted to leave childish things behind and catapult myself into the adult world, but a much bigger part of me was absolutely shit scared.

A couple of nights in a row we stayed out late – way past our curfew time. I should have known Mum was getting suspicious, but I deftly tried to swerve her stares. I figured I was a woman now and she was going to have to like it or lump it.

We carried on meeting up with the moped boys. Each

night a new barrier was broken. From Coke and lemonade we progressed to swigging the odd bit of cider. Some
light pecking progressed to some full-on tonsil tennis
and the kind of teenage fumbles I'd fantasized wildly
about when I was last in France.

One evening, just as the sun was going down on the
horizon, we were busy pretending to the moped boys
that we didn't actually have parents. We could stay out for
as long as we wanted. We were in an open field and I was
trying to light a cigarette without setting my fringe alight.
Suddenly, I saw a shadow out of the corner of my eye.

'Daisy? Daisy?!!'

Oh fuck. It was Mum. When I looked up, she was
stomping across the field in her Marge Simpson night-
dress and ankle boots. Fiona was off somewhere out of
sight and Lily was madly snogging a boy.

The cigarette dropped from my lips and I stood frozen, holding the lighter firmly in my hand behind my
back. I could feel Mum's temper rising with every step
she took closer. She was frothing like an Ibiza foam party.

'I didn't bring up my daughter to catch chlamydia on a
camping site!' she screamed. I got the full lecture about
girls with cheap reputations and a further run-down of
sexually transmitted diseases, none of which I honestly
understood.

The moped boys scattered like birds in fear of a hunter.
According to Mum, they were only after one thing and

we were on a downward slope which led to the Single Mothers' Unit and/or Hell. I thought it was a bit of an over-reaction, considering how innocent it all seemed.

Fiona, Lily and I got marched back to the tent. I was really quite pissed off. Mum had managed to humiliate me a second time, and in front of my cousins and several holiday crushes.

'From now on it's poolside with Charlie and the others,' she barked.

I had a face like a slapped arse for days.

When I think about it now, I can only thank Mum. As much as I had all the swagger and bravado of a girl becoming an adult, I was actually scared of getting into situations I couldn't control. Of course, this is not to say I didn't get into trouble later, but this time Mum did save me from myself. Thanks, Mum.

I've yet to forgive her for The Poncho.

# CHAPTER 7
# MATCHMAKERS

There wasn't much to do in Cirencester. Not for teenagers, anyway. But we never dreamed of being anywhere else. Instead, we learned to pass the time with what little we had. Whereas I was a wild child and craved attention – hard to believe, I know – Charlie didn't appear to have any personality at all. Now, I think he was just a dark horse.

He quietly busied himself with creative pursuits. One day I found him in his bedroom with his set of small green plastic toy soldiers. He had Mum and Dad's camcorder and he was filming stop-motion animations.

Charlie's directorial approach was very fucking pedantic. He carefully positioned one soldier, then pressed play, then did it again over and over with the soldiers in a variety of different positions.

It didn't help that he'd chosen the 1964 film *Zulu* to re-enact – great to begin with, but very, very long. Stanley Baker's part was played by a miniature that Charlie had painted pillar-box red. Michael Caine was the same colour. A forgiving audience would have overlooked the fact that Charlie's soldiers were vintage Airfix Second World War, not the troops in South Africa in 1879.

The four thousand Zulu warriors advancing on the British position were bloody tricky. But Charlie excelled himself by carefully sticking on small scraps of leopard-skin cloth he found in Mum's hoard of materials.

The camcorder was on hire from *Radio Rentals* at around £100 per month. Dad got it because he said he wanted a visual record of his family. God knows why. We were hardly photogenic.

'Got to get our money's worth!' he told us. There were home movies galore. Naturally, I threw myself into a leading role of watching TV while eating breakfast in my pyjamas, and telling Dad to:

'Fuck off and stop filming!'

Honestly, you could barely go for a piss in our house without Dad shouting, 'And . . . action!'

'Dad, I can't perform under that kind of pressure!' The prima donna was apparent in me from an early age.

The novelty soon wore off, though, and that's when Charlie's films took over.

Then, Charlie and I started making films together. At first, Charlie was a whizz with the technical stuff while I mainly scripted. Admittedly, the plot lines were a little thin.

One favourite was to set the camera up in the living room and grab each other in a headlock or throw each other around on the floor. Charlie would wear a pair of blue Speedos while I donned a sparkly leotard, finishing the ensemble off with square-toed, calf-length boots.

At the time, we were watching a lot of WWE wrestling. I would growl like Trish Stratus and Charlie would stare pensively like Kurt Angle. We re-imagined Smackdown classics for a Cirencester audience – which consisted of our parents.

Inspired by the cult TV series *Jackass*, we also captured a lot of our best pranks on the camcorder. Charlie filmed me pressing my tongue against a lit lightbulb. This ended in disaster – third-degree burns. And once I persuaded him to dissect a snail with a pair of tweezers.

'Don't worry. It's already dead!' I told him, as he looked quite nervous.

I lied.

However, our best work was filmed from Charlie's bedroom. We lived next to a B&B run by a God-fearing couple called Elizabeth and Stanley.

Elizabeth was a rather large lady and her living room was filled with pictures of Jesus hanging from the cross. We were always knocking on their front door and running away, or trying to break in.

I don't know where in the Bible Jesus said: 'Thou shalt not wear anything while sunbathing,' but Elizabeth spent whole summers topless in the garden soaking up the heat. She had saggy honkers and her areolas were the biggest I've ever seen. They were like fucking dart-boards.

At first, Charlie and I had an idea to land things on her tits from the window overlooking her patio. The set of toy paratroopers with parachutes that Charlie got given one Christmas worked quite well. However, we were disappointed when she didn't bat an eyelid.

Then we upped our game and set out to land mint Matchmakers on her areolas. I'd been given them for my birthday and I fucking hated them. We had a scoring system just like in darts, with a maximum fifty points for the inner circle and twenty-five for the outer. Bang on the nipple was clearly a bullseye.

'Cirencester? Are you ready for this? Let me hear you roar!'

Charlie got quite into the role of commentator. Mean-while, I did a mean Eric Bristow.

We landed our first Matchmaker and immediately ducked down below the windowsill so as not to be seen. But there was no shout whatsoever.

'Fucking hell! She's still not moving!'

We couldn't believe it. No amount of Matchmakers could stir Elizabeth; she just continued to snore on the sun lounger. We kept the camera rolling as the long thin strips of chocolate slowly melted and dribbled into her flabby creases. We'd wanted it to be a suspenseful who-dunnit, but Charlie and I ended up cataloguing *Matchmaker* under our experimental phase, a bit like Andy Warhol's *Empire*. The tape got mislabelled as *It's a Wonderful Life* and when Grandad pressed play on the VCR he got quite a shock. Weirdly, he didn't turn it off straight away.

Charlie and I definitely bonded more as teenagers. We also discovered a mutual love of plaster, which brought us even closer together.

Don't ask me how it started, but the plaster in Dad's study was breaking loose from the wall, and I began eating it. It was fucking fantastic, like a savoury meringue. Every time I went there, I'd take another scoop, but I was careful to pat the wall down after so it didn't look obvious. After a while, Dad started to cotton on that something wasn't quite right.

'Daisy?'

Oh fuck.

I walked into Dad's study to find him with his finger stuck in the crumbling hole. The study used to be a nursery and it still had remnants of Peter Rabbit wallpaper. Dad was frowning as his finger hovered around Mrs Tiggywinkle's arse.

'What the fucking fuck is this, Dais?'

Dad could be very sweary when he was angry.

'I don't even know how that happened!' I said. He had such a nerve, accusing me like that. But the hole was looking suspiciously bigger.

'It's Charlie!' I lied.

'Charlie?' When he got dragged in, he denied it too. Fuck.

Dad said he'd leave no stone unturned in getting to the bottom of Plastergate. I was scared, but not undeterred.

Not long afterwards, I edged the door open, hoping to sneak in another mouthful. Suddenly, from behind the door I heard someone furiously scrambling around.

'What are you doing?' I said, standing there with one hand on my hip and my eyebrows raised.

Charlie was sat at Dad's desk, casually pretending to work on the computer, but his cheeks were puffed out like Alvin and the fucking Chipmunks.

'Gotcha!' I thought.

The problem was, when Dad did find out, the punishment seemed far too severe. He tried to ground me for a year, but he could obviously never stick to that. In fact, Dad's punishments were always ridiculous and never fitted the crime.

There was the sponsored swim, which wasn't even the worst of my crimes – but the punishment was fucking nuts.

I'd seen the swimmathon announced on *Blue Peter*. Richard Bacon and Konnie Huq had made it sound so exciting. Without skipping a beat, I sent off for the introductory pack and sponsorship form. This money was going to help children in war-torn parts of Africa. My heart melted when their sad faces flashed up on screen. Charlie and I didn't have a lot, but these kids didn't have a pot to piss in. I could save them! I could be a hero!

This sudden burst of altruism quickly evaporated when I realized I actually had to do some swimming. A full fifty lengths of the local pool.

No. Fucking. Way. I panted like a Labradoodle in heat just going up our stairs. Seriously, I couldn't be arsed.

But I really enjoyed gathering in all my sponsorship money. I raised £20 from teachers, aunties, neighbours. *Everybody* knew how Daisy was going to save starving children one lap at a time . . . if I'd bothered to turn up. And without mentioning it to anyone, I spent all the money.

I would have got away with it, but I'd already sent my sponsorship form back to *Blue Peter* and announced how much I'd raised. Ridiculous schoolgirl error. What were you thinking, Daisy? When the letter turned up to ask where the cheque was, Dad was waiting for me.

'You've deceived *Blue Peter*. You've deceived your sponsors. You've deceived us. You've deceived those poor children. And most of all, you've deceived yourself.'

All right. Calm down, mate, I'm hardly double agent Kim Philby, I thought.

Dad angrily whipped out his cheque book and made out a cheque for the sum of £20 to *Blue Peter*.

'This time, Daisy, but never again . . .'

This was a lie, as Dad's cheque book would make a guest appearance in several more Daisy-made disasters.

'Those poor, desperate people, and you're just swaggering about spunking the whole lot on Dipdabs and *Just Seventeen* magazines.'

Christ, he went on and on.

For weeks afterwards, I felt tortured. But Dad wasn't done yet; he made it worse. The fucker forced me to re-arrange my trip to see PJ & Duncan play at Cardiff Arms Park. I'd adored the pubescent pop combo ever since 'Let's Get Ready to Rumble'. I had tickets for my birthday and I'd been allowed to take two friends with me.

Dad said I was still allowed to go, but now I wasn't allowed to take anyone. WTF? I was absolutely incandescent with rage. Breaking it to my friends was totally humiliating. Instead, Dad drove me there and sat beside me, arms folded and with a face like a blobfish.

I'd rather have taken along a fungal infection than have to share my first ever PJ & Duncan gig with Dad. Around me, other teenagers were busting out perky dance moves with their baseball caps jauntily swivelled backwards. I wanted to die. I hung my head in shame and shuffled. I could feel the looks of revulsion. So embarrassing.

At the end, he led me out by the collar and we drove home in silence.

The oddest punishment was when Dad found out I hadn't been eating my packed lunch. He prepared it for me every morning. In fairness, the menu was limited. Two slices of white bread with salad cream. Not even Hellmann's mayonnaise. Salad cream. Every fucking day.

The sandwiches accumulated at the bottom of my bag, wrapped in cling film, until they went mouldy and ruined my French textbook. Then flies got in and laid eggs and it got filled with maggots. I was too busy filling my face with crisps and chocolate bought from the school canteen with money stolen from Mum's purse to even notice.

It all came to a head when a letter came home from the French teacher telling Mum and Dad they needed to buy me a new textbook. Dad stood in the garden with my upturned bag raised above his head like fucking Godzilla. Hundreds of maggots wriggled on the grass below.

'Why didn't you just say you didn't like the sandwiches?' he bellowed as a backlog of white bread tumbled from my bag like rabbits from a magician's hat. 'I could have put Marmite in them!'

I can't abide Marmite.

The punishment? Confiscation of my CD player and all my music, which included all my albums by Boyz II Men, Take That, Westlife, New Kids on the Block and, most importantly, PJ & Duncan.

Yup. That's right. All my favourite boy bands.

I had a strop on for weeks. Ground me, but don't fuck with my boy bands, I thought.

He looked very fucking satisfied.

I would have my revenge.

It came in the shape of the Internet Boyfriend. Only, when it started, I hadn't set out to hurt anyone, least of all Dad. It had all the unintended consequences of Cupid's arrow puncturing a lung. The chubby-winged cherub had an ethernet connection. It was never going to end well.

I would often take myself off to play on Dad's computer. The box-room-cum-study was quiet and I could play Minesweeper without any interruption. When I'd exhausted all the levels, I got bored and joined an online AOL message board.

Some of the girls at school had boyfriends, but so far I'd attracted zero interest. But online, my problems were solved. I could interact with boys without actually having to be in the same physical space as them.

I received some early interest from a boy in Manchester. This happened far more quickly than I had imagined, but it may have been down to my profile picture being an image that I'd ripped off Google of the supermodel Eva Herzigová. I reckoned I bore more than a passing resemblance to her in a certain light.

My profile also said I was seventeen. I was fourteen.

Admittedly, I felt a bit guilty about lying, but I was also getting to quite like his attention.

'I love your profile,' he commented.

'Thanks! All my own work . . .'

We did all the getting-to-first-base chit-chat. His name was Keith.

'What do you do?'

'Oh, just a bit of modelling. Clothing companies like Gap and Benetton,' I replied casually.

'No way! Doesn't surprise me, though. You look amazing in your picture!'

'Yeah, just missed out on a leading role in *Hollyoaks* . . .'

'You serious? What happened?'

'The director loved me, but unfortunately he thought I was too attractive for the part.' I finished off that post with a sad-face sign.

'No way!' he replied, again.

'Yeah. I was gutted . . .'

'*Coronation Street*'s filmed near me. Maybe you could get a part in that?'

'Maybe. But my agent is scouting around Hollywood at the moment . . .'

'No way!'

Keith seemed quite gentlemanly. He didn't even ask for a tit flash or snatch shots. Surprising, really, considering I'd just been paid a gazillion for the shoot for Wonderbra. Online dating was much more innocent back then.

'What do you look like?' I asked him.

He had neglected to post a profile picture of himself.

'Do you know the footballer Michael Owen?'

Did I know him? Fuck yeah! I'd salivated over the Liverpool striker since Euro 2000. His inability to shake off a hamstring injury in the run-up to the tournament only made me want him more. A champion with vulnerability.

'Well, I look like him.'

He said he was seventeen, which was exactly my fake age. We fitted together like David Seaman's hand in a goalie's glove.

After around a month, we decided to dial up the heat on our burgeoning romance. I stole my dad's mobile phone and sneaked it up to my bedroom. Dad had a brand-new phone and a new provider, Orange – a company just starting out at the time.

'It's great to hear your voice . . .'

'And yours . . .'

'What are you doing?'

'Oh, just having some downtime between shoots,' I purred seductively.

I was spreadeagled on my bed, still wearing my school uniform.

'And you?'

'Oh, just chilling.' He had quite a high-pitched voice for a Michael Owen lookalike.

On paper, Keith was my soulmate. He loved boy bands. I loved boy bands. He hated Tesco Value Jaffa Cakes and only ate the branded variety.

'Really? Wow. I'm exactly the same!'

'My favourite film is *The Green Mile* . . .'

'No way! That's mine too. Spooky!'

Our love was meant to be. I stopped feeling guilty about lying on my profile because, underneath the shallowness of outward appearance, we had a lot in common. I convinced myself that our attraction wasn't skin deep. If we ever met, then he'd see beyond my massive nose and nerdish disposition.

At school, I began writing his name in Tipp-Ex on my pencil case. It was covered in Keith. And I boasted to all my mates that I had a boyfriend.

'Nah, you're lying, Dais . . .'

They didn't want to believe that I was attractive to the opposite sex.

'Yup, and you'll get to meet him soon . . .'

At the time, this wasn't true. But it did plant a seed in my head that maybe we could see each other face to face. That would prove to everyone that he was real.

'Do you want to come down to Cirencester?' I asked him tentatively.

'Yeah!' He sounded very enthusiastic.

He planned to get to Cirencester on the National Express bus. And he asked if I minded if his mum rang my parents so she could let him go. This seemed odd for a seventeen-year-old, but he did still live at home, so maybe his mum was a little over-protective. And seeing as I lived at home too, I agreed.

His mum rang my dad on his mobile. Beforehand, I'd told Dad that I'd been talking to a boy as we'd been writing to each other as pen pals as part of social studies lessons at school. It was to encourage diversity through connecting with people from different backgrounds. Surprisingly, he swallowed it.

Granted, I don't think he was properly listening. He'd been somewhat preoccupied, as bills had been arriving from Orange and I'd been casually chucking them in the boiler cupboard. The orange writing on them had turned red. Every day, he'd been bawling down the phone to Orange, alerting them to the error.

'How can you even call yourselves a company when you've sent me someone else's bill?' he kept repeating.

Weeks went by. I thought it best not to mention my phone calls to Keith.

Dad's blood boiled every time Orange got mentioned. I felt sorry for the customer service assistant. However, I felt convinced the company would concede sooner or later and refund him the money. It gave me a false confidence to continue using his phone.

Now, my conversations with Keith centred around his impending visit.

'I can't wait until you come. I'm counting down the days.'

This was not a lie. I did have a calendar pinned to my bedroom wall that I was marking large red crosses on.

'Oh my God, I can't wait to kiss you . . .'

'Me neither . . .'

'I can't wait to cuddle you and be in each other's arms.'

'Me neither . . .'

'How will I recognize you at the bus station?'

Keith said he would send an image of himself before he left so that I could download it and bring it with me.

The day of Keith's arrival drew closer.

'You haven't sent the image yet,' I reminded him.

He only had a Toshiba PC and he said his image had been very slow to upload as an email attachment. We spoke again just before he boarded his connection at Milton Keynes and he promised he'd sent it.

Phew! When I checked, he had. I double-clicked. The image was there, but instead of it flashing up, a spinning pinwheel of death appeared on Dad's screen. I waited patiently. Finally, gradually, Keith's face was revealed. I could see his hair, but his forehead just got longer . . . and longer . . . and longer . . .

'Dais, we need to leave now if we're picking up your pen pal!'

Dad was calling from downstairs. He was right. I'd been sorting the technical hitch out for hours. Keith's bus was due in at 4.30 p.m. I quickly pressed print and hoped the picture would come out in time.

'Come on, Dais!' Dad was getting quite irate now.

'Hold on. I'm nearly ready!' I shouted enthusiastically.

*Shit.* Keith's forehead was so fucking huge that the printer hadn't even got to his eyes.

'Dais . . . Don't make me call you again!'

'OK, Dad, I'm coming.'

The printer was still chugging away. *Fuck.* I ripped the paper off and hoped to God I could identify Keith by a mop of mousy brown hair and his ginormous forehead.

On the car journey there, I was more than a little nervous. I pictured Michael Owen jumping down from the bus, running his hand through his lightly gelled hair in slow motion. His eyes would meet mine and my heart would pound out of my chest like Jim Carrey's in *The Mask*. We'd throw our arms around one another and Dad would have to prise us apart.

Dad drove up to the car park while I sat clutching the picture of Keith's forehead. When the bus pulled in, Dad said he'd wait while I walked to the terminus to collect him. The tops of my legs felt wobbly as I made my way across the tarmac.

I looked up expectantly as one boy made his way down the steps.

I peered into the bus, hoping someone else might appear. No one was behind.

The boy looked dreamily past me into the distance.

'Daisy?' Eventually, he realized I was the only person waiting. I did not look like Eva Herzigová. Keith eyed me up and down, obviously crestfallen.

'Keith?' I answered hesitantly.

Keith did not look like Michael Owen. He was very short. His hair was frying-pan greasy and his face was covered in cystic acne. I physically recoiled. I didn't want to hug him. As a last-minute compromise, I held out my right hand to shake his. And that was the other thing . . . instead of holding out his left, he manoeuvred round awkwardly and offered me his right. He had no left arm. Nothing. Just a stump.

I didn't have a fucking clue what to say. At no point during our months-long phone tryst did he think to mention this. On the one hand, I felt a pang of sympathy for him. On the other (non-existent) hand, it was irksome because I'd planned a game of mini golf as an icebreaker. Arsehole.

From the outset, it was patently obvious that Keith had all the sexual magnetism of a tree sloth. And he didn't fancy me one iota either.

When I say we didn't talk to one another, this would not be an over-exaggeration. It was the longest weekend of my entire existence, like doomscrolling on Twitter for days.

Keith slept on the bottom bunk in the bunkbed in my

room. I legged it to the top before he got back from the bathroom and pulled my covers right up to my neck. I lay awake listening to the low drone of his snore for hours.

On the Sunday night, Mum and Dad offered to take us out for pizza. Pizza? This meant spending time with Dad, who would undoubtedly grill Keith on our marathon letter-writing friendship.

I spent the whole afternoon sick with worry. Because Keith and I hadn't spoken, I hadn't filled him in on the epic pen-pal lie. Dad had by now found out that his phone bill had been racked up to £1,000 and was still blaming Orange. Whenever the conversation edged in that direction, I batted it in another.

'The margherita here is my favourite . . .' Deftly done, Daisy. Deftly done.

'So, Daisy says she's got to know you through the school exchange . . .'

Fuck. Fuck. Fuck.

Keith didn't even attempt to play it smart.

'The what . . . sorry?'

'The pen-pal exchange. Says you've been writing for months. Nice to get kids together like this.'

'The pen-pal exchange? But we met online and we've been talking on the phone to each other for hours.'

*Oh, Keith. Mate! No! You utter fuckwit!*

'No . . . no . . . no, Keith. We've been writing. I've kept all your letters.'

I stared at him very intently.

'But I've never written a letter to . . .'

Keith looked utterly confused. When I looked over at Dad, I could see him silently working it out.

'Your phone number doesn't end in 654, does it?'

'Yes!' said Keith. 'How do you know that?'

The moment the penny dropped, Dad's mouth turned up slightly and his eyes narrowed.

We dropped Keith off at Swindon bus station. I contemplated getting on his National Express bus with him, but decided I would rather perish at the gates of hell than spend another moment with this tosser. Besides, I'd never seen anyone leap on to a bus so fast in my life. His relief was palpable.

'*Daisy* . . .' I could hear the naked fury in Dad's voice when I got back into the car. He was a dormant volcano of rage preparing to spew out the *biggest bollocking ever*. It would see me grounded, random pleasures confiscated, and I even got slapped with a long list of household chores that included cleaning out the shitty budgie cage. This, in my view, was excessive.

'Dad . . . It isn't what you think,' I said, my voice shaking.

Who the hell was I kidding?

# CHAPTER 8
# SOUPED-UP RENAULT CLIO

In 2002, my life changed completely. I wanted to go to college, but having left school with two GCSEs – an A star in drama and an A in English – I didn't think this would ever be enough. In every other subject, I got a U, which was the universal sign for Utterly fucking Unconcerned. To say that I was not cut out for academia was the understatement of the century.

That summer, I put all of this to one side. Up until then, I'd not really had many boyfriends. Obviously, there was the crap Michael Owen wannabe, but we did not exchange bodily fluids – or anything. In fact, once the National Express disappeared into the sunset, I never heard from him again.

I was beginning to realize I was drawn to complicated men.

I started dating a goth called Jamie. He bled angst. My dad hated him.

'Dais, Marilyn Manson's here to see you.' Dad couldn't hide his contempt.

Every time Jamie turned up, Dad said it couldn't possibly be Halloween every fucking day. I did try to add a little colour to Jamie's life, but he saw everything in black and white. Plus, he hated Mum's animals. Cat hair shows up really badly on dark-coloured clothing. I don't know why I continued to go out with him. I think we bonded over a shared love of alcohol.

We hung out in the park together with bottles of vodka stolen from home. When Dad found out, he banned me from seeing Jamie altogether and gave me an ultimatum: if I continued to see him, I wouldn't be allowed to go to the after-school acting classes I'd always done. Dad had paid for me to go every Tuesday throughout school, and I took to them from a young age like a duck to water. There, I felt a freedom I never found anywhere else. I simply belonged.

'It's the only thing I love in life,' I pleaded with Dad.

'Listen, Dais. It's drama or The Damned. You choose.'

Fortunately, I was able to prolong the relationship by a few weeks, but only because I found Mum's sleeping tablets. I crushed them up and put them in Mum and Dad's tea. This allowed me to sneak out of my bedroom window undetected and meet Jamie under a dead tree.

While being drawn to the dark side was interesting, goths were a bit over-sensitive for my liking. I needed a man who was 'dangerous'. Enter Lee. I met him at the local chip shop and was immediately drawn to him when he wolf-whistled at me from behind the wheel of his souped-up Peugeot 106. His pale white arm was draped casually over the side of his white car, while badly painted-on flames licked around its headlights.

'All right, love? Fancy a spin?'

I wasn't sure. Lee looked like a bizarre cross between Dean Gaffney and the Jules Rimet World Cup trophy. Danny Zuko he was not. His massive ears and grubby hoodie with a cannabis leaf on the front dwarfed his wiry body. But I was no Sandy, either. I had started rocking a new look.

I had not long discovered fake tan. But I quickly developed tanning dysmorphia. Whenever I looked in the mirror, I never thought I was mahogany enough. And the more tan I applied, the more streaked it became, and it also came off in patches. By the end of the summer, anyone could have mistaken me for a rhino freshly rolled from a mud bath.

Then there was my hair. I say 'my hair', but it wasn't actually mine. I had long, blonde clip-on extensions textured like Barbie's that I washed with fabric conditioner in the bath. I reckoned I looked like Reece Witherspoon in *Legally Blonde*. In truth, I was more of a buxom Debbie McGee channelling David Dickinson.

I stuffed so many socks down my bra I'd give Pamela Anderson a run for her money. Although sometimes I was in such a rush it looked like I needed urgent medical attention. Cleverly, I managed to give my tits added drama by painting eye-shadow above my cleavage in a fake sweetheart line. From the front, my norks looked like *Baywatch* buoys. If I turned sideways, they were more of an ocean ripple. I thought I was the fucking bomb.

Lee was from South Cerney, one of the villages on the outskirts of Cirencester. For him, town was the metropolis. It was like hitting the strip in LA or cruising down Sunset Boulevard. His pimped-up Peugeot 106 narrowly cleared the road with its lowered suspension and bumper extension. There were woofer speakers on the parcel shelf.

We nodded our heads in unison to UK garage classics, bass pumping, tinted windows open.

'Yo, whassup?' I'd nod coolly to passers-by. These were made up of a gaggle of blue rinses exiting the tea shop and some Japanese tourists up by St John the Baptist church.

'Shall we go on a proper date?' Lee asked one day. So far, our meetings had consisted of several laps around the market place and a shag on the back seat parked up on the outskirts of a field.

'A proper date?' I got quite excited.

'Yeah. Castle Combe . . .'

'Castle Combe?'

Castle Combe was a sprawling Gothic manor house that doubled as a race circuit on weekends. Odd place for a date, but I was always up for new experiences.

The date was a disaster. It consisted of Lee meeting

his mates at a Max Power event, the Mecca for wannabe men with modified passion wagons.

There were Ford Escorts groaning under the weight of poorly fitted body styling and Vauxhall Novas spray-painted in neon pink.

They lined their cars up and walked around each other's alloy wheels admiring the hub caps while engines revved and exhausts farted out acrid smoke.

'What should I do?' I asked Lee. I felt like a fucking spare part.

'Join the other girls. Loads of girlfriends are here,' Lee said dismissively.

I looked along the line of cars.

Girlfriends were there. But they didn't look in the mood for chit-chat. Some had bikini tops on and thong-type bottoms and they'd spread-eagled themselves across the car bonnets.

It was a potent mix of motor and minge. But not one I was going to be easily sucked into. Not with my mahogany tan looking so uneven . . .

'I'll just wait in the car,' I told Lee. I sat on the back seat pouting and smoking fags until all the petrolhead yakking was done.

Sometimes a reporter from the *Max Power* magazine could be seen working his way along the line with high-brow questions for the girls such as 'Do you play the pink oboe?' or 'Do you flick the bean?' If they were lucky, they got their picture printed beside their answer. I was never asked, but for the record it was a 'never' for the oboe, and an 'all the fucking time' for the bean.

Later that year, Lee took me to another Max Power event at Weston-super-Mare. It was freezing. You could have hung adjustable wrenches off my nipples, and I stood, arms folded, with a face on me like a pranged tailgate.

That year we drove endlessly. We weren't eighteen yet so there wasn't anywhere for us to go. Often Lee and his mates would park up outside McDonald's, wind their windows down and chat down the line while us girlfriends sat in the passenger seats, staring out blankly.

I counted myself as one of the lucky ones. Lee had a DVD player in his Peugeot 106, so I entertained myself with *Fast and Furious* on a loop. Or I'd play DJ by taking charge of his CD wallet.

'What do you want to listen to?'

'Let's play Big Brovaz. When the bass line drops, these guys be catching my flow.' Who did he think he was? Fucking Tupac?

Lee was a man of few words. More so when he started smoking skunk. Jesus, he was boring. Nevertheless, seeing him filled an emotional hole, even though I felt his interest waning.

Months went by. I contemplated dumping Lee, but I couldn't be arsed. Then, one day I picked up my *Max*

*Power* magazine, which I read religiously, from the news-agent's. The cover story was about a Nissan Micra and had the headline: THROBBING PURPLE MONSTER. I flicked through. Suddenly, Lee's Peugeot 106 beamed out at me. Draped across the bonnet like a bad hangover was Shelley. Fucking Shelley with tits she didn't have to eye-shadow.

Shelley was a girl from Cirencester who had been hanging round us like a rank-smelling Magic Tree air freshener.

'Do you flick the bean?' She'd answered brazenly that she didn't need to. And, apparently, she didn't just play the pink oboe, she'd mastered a whole fucking orchestra, complete with guest harp. I was absolutely livid.

My indifference to Lee vanished instantly. There was no way on God's earth I was going to let Shelley pimp my ride and not even look remotely apologetic.

In a concerted effort to win Lee back, it took me all of three seconds to formulate a plan. I was turning eighteen soon, when I would get my inheritance from Gran and Grandad, which amounted to £500. A mate of a mate was selling a Renault Clio so I made a call and went to view it. I couldn't drive.

The car was metallic bogey green, small and a bit bat-tered, but it had new exterior styling to die for. A massive bumper had been attached. When I ran my hand along it, it wobbled slightly. I remember thinking this was odd, but it was a fleeting thought.

I asked if I could see under the bonnet. Lee and his nerdy mates always said things like that. Stroking my chin masterfully, I twiddled with some levers.

'Engine fluid topped up?' I dropped in casually. I had not a fucking clue what I was talking about.

The car sat outside Mum and Dad's for days. Only Mum was insured to drive it as I hadn't passed my test. By that time I had my provisional licence and had taken one test, but I'd panicked and braked over-enthusiastically at a pedestrian crossing. Except I didn't brake. My foot jammed on to the accelerator, almost killing an old dear who was shuffling across. The examiner yelled, 'No! No! No!' and his face lit up like the Belisha beacon light. It was an instant fail.

This technicality aside, I was thrilled to have a new car – especially one that wouldn't look out of place at any Max Power show. I had visions of me nonchalantly rolling down my window, clip-on Barbie hair extensions fluttering in the breeze. I'd nod and whack up Nelly's 'Hot in Here', bass pounding from my super-super-super subwoofers.

'Daisy, is that you?' Lee would get a semi on just looking at my slatted grille.

'What's up, L?' I'd smile like he'd missed out on the fuck of the century.

Sadly, this never happened.

One afternoon, Mum said we had to pick up Great Auntie Joan from the hairdresser's. She was getting a perm and it was taking hours and she didn't want to stand at the bus stop and ruin it.

Mum's car was in the garage for a service, so we had to use mine. The bumper had now been exposed to the elements for several weeks and it was clinging on to the undercarriage with Super Glue, one end swaying like a sloshed teenager in an anti-binge-drinking ad.

The metallic bogey-green paint was flaking from the driver's door and the tail light looked like it was about to do a runner.

Great Auntie Joan was grateful for our assistance. I gave up my passenger seat while she clambered in. She was only around five foot and her pastel-pink perm balanced on her head like a fluffy mass of candy floss.

'Errr . . . nice car, Gill . . .' she said.

'It's Daisy's,' Mum replied, embarrassed.

'Just waiting to pass my test!' I chipped in eagerly.

'Hmmmm . . .' Great Auntie Joan's tone was disapproving. And I noticed that when she turned my way to talk, she looked quizzically at me. I'd gone a tad overboard with the fake tan the night before.

We pulled up to the junction by the kitchen and bathroom showroom. The conversation had lulled and Mum broke the tension by playing Abba's 'Dancing Queen' very, very loudly.

The lights lingered on red and we waited for them to change. It took for ever. In my peripheral, I clocked a gleaming vision in white pull up beside us. I'd recognize those dodgy painted-on flames anywhere. Shit. Shit. Shit.

I didn't want to look. I couldn't look. This was not how this moment was supposed to pan out. Momentarily, I glanced up and saw Lee staring in, jaw dropping. Mum was bobbing along and singing to Abba at the top of her voice. Great Auntie Joan's pink perm towered bewilderingly above the leatherette trim covers. I sunk lower in my seat.

Beside Lee was Shelley. She was popping Hubba Bubba out of her mouth and her large hoop earrings glistened in the afternoon sunlight. Her lip curled into a sneer when my eyes drifted up to meet hers. Fucking great, I thought. I'm being eyeballed by Crystal Tits to fucking 'Dancing Queen'. Humiliating.

I was insanely happy when I heard a few months later that they'd split up. Apparently, she discovered that Lee had cheated on her and she hit him with a frying pan, like something out of a *Tom and Jerry* cartoon. *Badoink!* By now I was struggling to fathom how Lee was such a flange magnet.

Thankfully, by then I'd moved on. But, with hindsight, my new boyfriend, Jake, was a whole different level of complicated.

Jake worked behind the bar of our local. He was a good few years older than me. Having been a former MI5 officer who'd left the intelligence service after a diagnosis of terminal lung cancer, he seemed hideously over-qualified for the bar job.

Naturally, Jake appealed to my inner empath. He was both manly and fragile – a cross between 007 and an injured budgie. I hung on his every word. I was hope-lessly in love with him, and so naive.

'It wasn't the lung cancer that ended my career,' Jake confessed to me not long after we started seeing each other.

'Oh? But it is terminal, isn't it?'

'Sadly, yes, but I could have continued at MI5 in a desk job . . .'

Jake hung his head and shuffled awkwardly.

'Is there something you're not telling me, Jake?'

'Yes . . .'

'OK. Well, trust is really important to me in a relation-ship.'

After the whole Lee-cheating-on-me-with-Shelley heartbreak, I was feeling very bruised.

'I know, Daisy, that's why I want to be honest with you.'

'What is it?'

Jake explained that his lung cancer had been only the official reason that his Bond-esque existence had been suddenly curtailed.

The truth was far more sinister. In fact, he'd been gathering intelligence on a cocaine smuggling ring. It had involved some undercover work, but along the way he'd succumbed himself. His habit had spiralled out of control. He'd become unreliable at work and ended up in prison after smuggling in a million pounds' worth of coke for personal use.

'How did the police find out?' I asked.

Jake hesitated. He was clearly embarrassed.

'Promise you won't tell anyone, Dais?'

'Promise . . .'

'I was transporting it in a Tesco carrier bag, but I hadn't realized it had a hole in the bottom. The trail of white powder led right to my front door.'

I tried to stifle a laugh. Of all the ways to end a high-flying MI5 career! It did seem a very silly mistake to make.

As the weeks wore on, more of Jake's dodgy past emerged. After coming out of prison, he'd worked as a pizza delivery guy on Manchester Road in Swindon. He'd been shot at several times on his moped and was lucky to be alive. Once, a bullet had ricocheted off his helmet.

Manchester Road is quite a rough area in Swindon.

To stay in business, the pizza parlour had taken the unusual step of sending staff out in an armoured vehicle. Jake was under strict instructions never to deliver pizza to anyone's front door. Instead, he had to phone the customer and have them collect their thick-crust Hawaiians from a hatch on the side.

'Really? Weren't you terrified?' I asked.

'Yeah, but when you've done bird, you feel invincible.' I did love Jake's edgier side.

He even had a VW Scirocco, which he called his *Knight Rider* car. It was sleek and black and sexy, and he'd gone to the effort of recording the theme tune from the 1980s cult classic on a loop and played it whenever he picked me up.

But he had a softer, creative side too. One that had cost him dearly. I felt outraged on his behalf over the Bart Simpson saga.

Jake had visited Birdland wildlife park in Bourton-on-the-Water, and he'd graffitied a picture of a Bart Simpson lookalike on a wall before *The Simpsons* ever existed. When the show's creator, Matt Groening, had a holiday near there a year later, he'd seen it and based the character of Bart on it.

'Oh my God. You are losing out on all this money!' I said to Jake.

This was particularly galling, as Jake had asked me to move in with him. He wanted me to pretend to be his dependant so he could qualify for a council flat. I thought he could have had a mansion with the kind of money *The Simpsons* would have made him.

I could barely watch *The Simpsons* after that. If it came on, I'd storm out of the room. It made me very cross to think that someone's creative talent could just be stolen and trashed like that.

And, of course, I told all of my mates.

When I repeated some of Jake's stories, often some of the details and the timelines didn't quite stack up, but I dismissed it. When you've led such a whirlwind life, it's easy to get things a bit confused, isn't it?

And he did say he thought he may have suffered post-traumatic stress disorder after the pizza job . . .

One night, he was due to pick me up from a house party. But he was really late. By the time he eventually put in an appearance, I was furious.

In fairness, Jake was very apologetic. And he seemed pale and shaken up.

'What's happened? Tell me.'

'I'm not sure how to . . . I . . . I . . . hit a sheep on the road,' he said.

'Oh no! Did it die?'

'Not just the sheep, Dais. It's bad . . . *really* bad . . .'

'How bad is *really* bad?' Jake was making me feel very anxious now.

'I swerved, but my bumper caught the tail end of the sheep. It bounced off the windscreen of a minibus full of schoolchildren . . .'

It was 1 a.m. on a Sunday.

'What were they doing out so late? And on a week-end?'

'Dunno. School trip, I think,' he replied, a hint of irritation in his voice.

'So what happened?'

'The minibus swerved off the road. Everyone's dead, Dais. It's absolute carnage.'

It did seem very strange that the road traffic police had let Jake go so soon after he'd punted a sheep across a road, which then hit off the windscreen of a minibus packed with schoolchildren on its way back from a mystery school trip around midnight on a Saturday night . . .

I asked Jake to drop me home, turning up the local news on his stereo, eager to hear what was being reported.

The headline story was about a petition to prevent the introduction of pay-and-display parking around the market in Cirencester.

Also, a historic monument had been restored to its full glory after a fundraising effort by church elders.

And the most dangerous tribute band in the world, Guns not Roses, had announced a gig at the Corn Hall.

I didn't mention the minibus incident again, and he didn't bring it up either. I don't know why I didn't split up with Jake there and then. I guess I desperately wanted to believe he was the damaged hero he made himself out to be.

But it was the beginning of the end.

The last straw came when I paid for us both to go on an all-inclusive week's holiday to Zakynthos with money I'd saved from my first job after leaving school. One sun-drenched afternoon at four o'clock, Jake announced he was going to the pool bar for a couple of drinks. I stayed in our room. He didn't return until three the next afternoon. His explanation? He'd fallen asleep under a bush. I never found out whose bush.

# CHAPTER 9
# WORKING NINE TO FIVE

D umping Jake came at a cost. Up until then, I'd enjoyed the luxury of sharing his council flat in Cirencester.

We had a deal. If I bought food and cooked, I could live there free of charge. But I was a terrible cook. Really terrible. Minced beef sautéed with tikka masala sauce courtesy of the Chicken Tonight sizzle-and-stir range was cooking, as far as I was concerned. Jake always wanted to eat at work.

Because he was doing shifts in a bar job, he often didn't come home until after midnight. This was brilliant because, after a hard day's work, I had time to myself. Just me, some Beefy Chicken Tonight, a bottle of lemon Bacardi Breezer and back-to-back episodes of *Footballers' Wives*. Pure bliss.

I'd left school, so I needed to earn money. This was to tide me over until I got to college to pursue my dream of being an actress. Dad was still paying for me to take private lessons. I knew it was a real stretch for him but, honestly, it was the only thing I looked forward to.

No college wanted to accept me. Applications to the most prestigious colleges cost £30 a pop, so I limited myself to three. The Royal Academy of Dramatic Art (RADA) looked *amazing*, and it was where all the top actors went: John Gielgud, Kenneth Branagh, Sheila Hancock, Diana Rigg, to name just a few.

Even Joan Collins! Move over Joan – Daisy May Cooper is the new Alexis Colby in town, I thought. I didn't even get an audition.

Next up was the London Academy of Music and Dramatic Art (LAMDA), which also boasted a fair few success stories. If a posho like Benedict Cumberbatch could go there, so could Daisy May Cooper. Two GCSEs from Deer Park comprehensive might not have looked *that* impressive on paper, but wait till they saw me perform. I'd knock their fucking socks off.

LAMDA had no places, but suggested I pay for a summer-school course. The fee was £1,000. It was a non-starter.

The Bristol Old Vic Theatre School was my last attempt. It also failed.

I was devastated. Mostly, I felt a weird sense of emptiness, like someone had sucked every last drop of hope from me. When I think about it now, by finishing school and leaving home, I'd also lost my biggest fanbase. I'd spent years farting about, entertaining my family and my mates in class.

'Don't laugh, it'll only encourage her.' Everybody said that.

But now, I had no audience.

I saw an advert at the Job Centre for a junior sales assistant in the homeware section of a department store and wondered whether this might fill the void. For reasons that will become apparent, this well-known retail giant will remain nameless.

This is a customer-focused role.
Applicants must be warm and charismatic and proactively approach every customer, delivering a true retail customer experience.

Please apply by submitting a CV and attaching a cover letter.

Pay: £4.20 per hour

Full time: 40-hour contract

I'm sooooo warm, and very charismatic! And I could tell immediately that the store supervisor, Janet, spotted this when I rocked up for my interview.

'Can you try and sell me this?' she beamed. She was wearing a perfectly ironed uniform with a pencil skirt and her hair was tied in a neat bun. She guided me over to the kitchen accessory range.

'This?' I asked with a hint of incredulity.

'Yes, that's right,' she said, pointing to a mug tree on display.

It's a fucking mug tree. Don't people just buy one if they need one? Go with it, Dais. Go with it.

'Er . . . It's sleek, it's pine and it caters for all six of your mug needs?' I gave it my best shot, but I wasn't sure I'd completely nailed it.

'Wonderful, Daisy! We'd like to welcome you into our retail family. When can you start?'

My heart swelled with pride. I was taken aback that I'd got a job so easily. My first since leaving school! Yes! Yes! Yes!

For the first few days, I was *on fire*. I even ironed my uniform. I was shifting ice-cube trays and Tupperware like it was going out of fashion. Janet said if I carried on like that, then I could be winging my way on to the Employee of the Month pinboard in the staffroom within a few months.

A few months? Jesus . . .

I was good, and I knew it, but keeping any enthusiasm up for shifting fucking toasters and clothes horses *for a few months* was going to be hard.

In my interview, Janet had made a special point of saying that the company nurtured every member of staff's individual talents. Perfect. I had so many ideas to make the job more interesting.

I decided to adopt a different character for different types of sales. That way I could keep my hand in with my acting and earn some dosh at the same time. What could possibly go wrong?

For the garlic presses, I feigned a delightful French accent.

'*Bonjour, monsieur*, can I interest you in this press of *garlique . . . oui?* It is so stylish and cute that *mesdemoiselles* will *j'adore* you.'

I dropped the double-cheek kiss after several abortive attempts.

Bread bins screamed out for a Yorkshire twang delivered with my chest puffed out and a no-nonsense stance.

'Is it pricey? Is it 'eck as like. This bread bin 'ere won't cost you nowt more than £9.99.'

The days flew by.

For Sabatier kitchen knives, I took inspiration from the TV chef Gordon Ramsay.

'Look, pal. Do you want them? Standing here while you make up your fucking mind is doing my head in. Fucking useless. They're sharp. They're on sale. What more do you want?'

One angry customer ended up throwing a knife block in my direction. Bit of an over-reaction, I thought.

In the end, Janet said Homeware wasn't really working out for me and that I might be more suited to Womenswear. She said she could see the future crown of

Employee of the Month slipping from me. Disappointment spread across her face. I could not give a rat's arse.

In fact, I was starting to think that work fucking owed me. Every fibre of my body hated being there. It was such hard graft. On my feet for eight hours a day, having to smile endlessly at members of the public who were largely rude and ungrateful.

Clocking in and out felt like being trapped in some Kafkaesque nightmare.

'Oh, you *really are* a nine-to-five girl!' one assistant as perky as Wendy Richards in *Are You Being Served?* called out to me. I was in the queue, poised to punch my clocking-out card. Snide bitch. Evidently, she wanted to climb the greasy pole of Home Appliances. At £4.20 an hour, I wasn't doing unpaid overtime for anyone.

Having CCTV cameras trained on us all the time was an infringement of civil liberties I could not stomach. Except it was common knowledge that most in the store were dummies. They didn't record a thing.

This was an opportunity I could not pass up.

Loads of Levi's jeans languished in the stock room. Whenever I could, I pulled the security tags off them and bagged them up. Then I arranged for a mate to pick up a bag while pretending to buy something. She'd exit unchallenged and we'd sell them and split the profit.

I would like to say to anyone even remotely tempted to copy this: do not try this at home, kids. It is absolutely not my finest moment and I'm not proud of it at all. But, as I say, I was eighteen and I thought work owed me a living.

Word quickly got round that there was a thief working in the store. A memo was sent down from on high. No one ever met the top managers, but they occupied the rooms at the back of Bridal Wear. Random bag checks would now happen. It would be instant dismissal for any member of staff caught. This didn't worry me in the slightest.

I figured that Security knew I was the thief. I'd had several warnings about the state of my uniform, which I'd stopped ironing, and my don't-give-a-fuck attitude. And I was always being told off for gossiping behind the till. I was a target, but they would have a hard time proving it.

I threw my bag open enthusiastically whenever asked. I practically begged for it to be rummaged through, knowing that I'd smuggled out three pairs of vintage 501s only hours earlier. I felt like Pablo Escobar heading up a denim cartel. If they wanted to bring me in, they needed to be more cunning than that.

One security guard called Tanya was in her fifties and built like the Michelin Man. She always sneered knowingly whenever I approached.

'Let's be 'aving you, sunshine,' she'd say, like she was auditioning to be an extra on *Silent Witness*.

'Sure. Wonder what you'll find . . . a nine-tog summer duvet? An exercise bike? A Blu-ray DVD player?'

I relished rubbing Tanya's nose in it.

Nothing gave me more pleasure than the day she pulled out my wallet, my house keys, my notebook, a box of extra-absorbent tampons and my Boots No. 7 make-up bag. She opened the last item under the fluorescent lighting and spun the contents round in her fingers as the clocking-off queue behind me backed up.

'What in God's name is this?' She frowned.

'They sell it in Lifestyle and Athletics. I must have slipped it into my bag by accident.' I smiled and winked.

Of all the shit they sold in Lifestyle and Athletics, an electric-blue Rampant Rabbit dildo was definitely not on the EPOS system.

'Go on! Give it a go! I've given it a wipe-down . . .'

Tanya looked like she hadn't had an orgasm since 1980.

'Erm . . . It's OK, Daisy.' She recoiled slightly, staring, mystified, at its five inches of insertable length and vibrating clit-stimulation bunny ears.

Honestly, I never went to work without my Rampant Rabbit. A *ménage-à-moi* in the ladies' loos to the lilt of in-store soft rock was far more pleasurable than listening to a posse of assistants discuss the new range of support bras.

After that Tanya was a lot more careful when she rifled through my bag.

Just as I was at the top of my game heading up the denim crime syndicate, I fucked up badly. Really, really badly. I'd just come back after diddling Miss Daisy on my break to find a queue had formed around the till in Outdoor Clothing and Footwear.

Fuck. More twats to smile inanely at.

At the time, we had insane targets to sell customers store cards. And I mean *insane*. If we didn't sign up our weekly quota, our bonus got cut. Some of the girls were ruthless. It was like watching Helen Mirren in *Prime Suspect* forcing a confession from a total innocent. Most people didn't even know what they were signing up to. You'd hear old dears ask:

'Is it like a Tesco Clubcard? Do I get points?'

And a bonus-hungry sales assistant would reply:

'Yes, it's just like that. Tick here and here. There's loads of benefits. Twenty-five per cent off your purchase today if you sign. Signature in this box, please.'

Most of the time, I was brutally honest with customers. Which is why I rarely hit my target. The interest on these cards was something ridiculous, like 29 per cent. Imprinted on my brain was one woman who had bought a blouse for £18.99. Six months later, she realized she'd racked up a bill of £500. She pleaded with the manager and said she'd not known how store cards worked. She'd been mortified.

This month, I needed the bonus. Just need to shift a

few more, I thought. I put my head down and worked my way through the conveyor belt of customers. Out of the corner of my eye, I could see Janet circling like a vulture.

'Would you like to open a store card with today's purchase, madam?' I didn't even look up at the next customer.

'No, thank you.'

'Are you sure, madam? There's twenty-five per cent off today's purchase and a whole range of in-store benefits that you can enjoy as a member.'

'No, thank you.'

'It's excellent value and payable in instalments to spread the cost if you're holding out until pay day.'

*Just tick the fucking box, love. I need my bonus!*

I looked up. Her slightly pinched, angular face looked down at me. She had beady eyes and her skin was immaculately soft and powdered. She looked vaguely familiar. Maybe I'd helped her out in Womenswear before?

Two broad-chested men stepped up beside her.

'Nothing to pay for thirty days, and you're automatically entered into our prize draw. First prize, £500 worth of vouchers to spend in store; second prize, £100 off your next purchase; third prize, free fried breakfast for two in the restaurant on the fifth floor.'

*Just tick the fucking box.*

Then, off to one side, I caught a glimpse of Janet

grimacing and shaking her head. Strange. I looked around to see if anyone was behind me. No one.

I continued with my sales pitch.

Janet was now pretending to garotte herself with her right hand. Why the hell is she doing that? I thought.

I looked up. The two broad-chested men seemed quite pissed off, and the customer was now doing an impression of an English thoroughbred chewing a wasp. Oh, how I longed to be back in the Ladies with my Rampant Rabbit.

Suddenly, Janet swept across the floor like a banshee and stopped me mid-flow. Quite fucking rudely, actually. She seemed flustered and a little sweaty.

'Your Royal Highness. I'm so sorry. Would you like to come with me and pay at the till at the back, where it's a little quieter?'

*Your Royal Highness?*

Without further ado, Janet whisked the party of three away. I began mentally scrolling through the House of Windsor. I only really knew the Queen . . . and Princess Diana, but she was already sadly departed . . .

'How could you?' A few moments later, Janet stormed across the lingerie department, heading in my direction. She was spitting feathers.

'How could you?' she kept repeating.

'How could I what?'

'How could you even think of hard-selling Princess Anne a store card?'

'Princess Anne?'

'Princess Anne!'

No matter how much I argued that the pressure on me to meet my target was to blame, my days were numbered. The final straw came when I got moved to the food hall. That Christmas I got caught smashing Lindt Chocolate Santas in the stock room and writing them off as damaged so I could eat them. In fairness, lots of us did it, but management were just waiting for an excuse to get rid of me.

Fuck. Back to the Job Centre.

Within a few months I'd got sacked from Costa Coffee for scoffing Danish pastries. The one with the fat blob of custard in the centre was my favourite.

There was also a short spell in a salon. I started out washing hair, until my hands crumpled like corrugated cardboard. One of the few times I was entrusted with a perm, I fucked off outside for a fag . . . which morphed into another fag . . . which dovetailed into an extended fag break. The woman under the dryer demanded a refund on account of her looking like Edward Scissorhands.

However, the best job by far was in the label factory. As it turned out, I was the only girl in the team. The work was so simple it hurt. Peel one sticky label off a sheet and stick it on to a clothing tag. Again and again and again. No wonder the workers there were absolutely insane.

DAISY MAY COOPER

DOB: 01-08-1986

EDUCATION
2002-2004 Swindon College
QUALIFICATIONS
National Diploma Performing Arts BTEC

1997-2002 Deer Park School
QUALIFICATIONS
GCSE Drama A*
English Lit A
English Lang B
History C
Social Care GNVQ Pass
IT GNVQ Pass

EMPLOYMENT
2004-2005
I started as a sales assistant, and within 6 months I was promoted
to Young Fashions Manager. This role involved sales, promotions,
ordering of stock, cashing up, opening up, e.t.c.

Short and sweet – my CV.

Big Geoff had a thick West Country accent and a belly overhang Rab C. Nesbitt would be proud of. He was always trying to sneak in porn on his mobile while sitting at his work station, big butts and bukkake being two of his favourite genres. Nathan was a skinny twenty-something stoner who barely ever spoke. He drew a crowd as a club DJ by night, which was impossible to believe. And there were a few others, who all passed the time moaning about their wives.

It was like being back in school. Everyone was so bored I could make people laugh again. There was loads and loads of banter. Best of all, I could bring in mono-logues and rehearse scripts that were bound to get me into some drama school, somewhere.

I was also sacked from this job.

Technically, it wasn't my fault. Big Geoff had sug-gested that I sit with my arse cheeks nestled within the forks on the warehouse forklift truck, just for a laugh. He was one of the few licensed to drive it and he reckoned he could elevate me up to the top rack of the industrial shelving unit. I bet him he couldn't.

He could. And he left me on the shelf with my legs dangling.

For a while, he and Nathan stared up at me, pissing themselves. Then, they left. I had to call out for a man-ager to manoeuvre me down. Apparently, I was a risk to health and safety.

I was dreading telling Mum and Dad. I knew money was tight at home and I would be just another problem.

'Dad, I'm going to get sacked from everything.'

'Something will come up, Dais. Don't worry,' he said, bringing up another game of Solitaire on his computer.

I think Dad understood. He's always been a frustrated performer at heart, and a massive fucking narcissist. By that time, he'd also started living out his martyr complex by organizing grassroots kids' football matches. I regularly found him in the living room shedding a tear to *Coach Carter* on DVD.

His job as an electronics salesman wasn't going very well. Work wasn't guaranteed for ever, he said, and he was tunnelling his way out. However amazing kids' football was, it was probably not going to tunnel him very far.

Fortunately, for many of my short-lived careers, I was still living in Jake's council flat, but in the light of the shock revelation that he was an absolute fucking fantasist, I returned to Mum and Dad's.

This made me doubly determined. I had to make it as an actress. I had to. What did I have left?

I told Dad about the LAMDA summer school. It had been gnawing away at my brain, but I knew Mum and Dad didn't have the cash.

I think I lied and told Dad that once you'd been to the summer school, you were pretty much guaranteed to pass the audition at the next intake.

'Is it what you really want, Dais?'

'It's the only thing I want, Dad!'

'OK, love, we'll see what we can do.'

Mum and Dad agreed to pay for the course on a credit card.

It was a month-long Shakespearian acting course. And the accommodation was in a super-posh part of London: Kensington. I felt like Dick Whittington leaving Gloucestershire for the bright lights of the capital to seek my fortune.

And South Kensington was sooooo cosmopolitan. And so was the course. I was probably the only English girl on it. It was jam-packed with rich Americans, flown over for the summer. Or Europeans. I didn't care. I launched myself in and soaked it up like cheap white wine on a shag-pile carpet.

There were classes on voice projection and movement. I loved prancing around in mad pantaloons and pretending to sword-fight. There were games and dance classes and improvisation lessons. And some evenings we went to the theatre. We even got bussed up to Stratford-on-Avon to see an RSC production of *Macbeth* and got to hang out with the cast afterwards.

This is my destiny! This is where I belong! The life of an actor will be like hanging out in South Kensington every fucking day . . . right? All those months of shitty

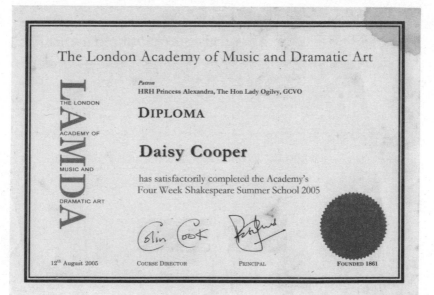

The London Academy of Music and Dramatic Art

*Patron*
HRH Princess Alexandra, The Hon Lady Ogilvy, GCVO

## DIPLOMA

## Daisy Cooper

has satisfactorily completed the Academy's
Four Week Shakespeare Summer School 2005

THE LONDON
ACADEMY OF
MUSIC AND
DRAMATIC ART

LAMDA

12th August 2005

COURSE DIRECTOR

PRINCIPAL

FOUNDED 1861

jobs back home faded from the rear-view mirror of my mind. There was no going back now. Destination: fame . . .

Even now, acting is better than any drug I've ever done – the adrenaline of snorting coke, the contentedness of smoking weed, the utter euphoria of ecstasy all rolled into one. When I'm up on a stage, I don't want to be anywhere else in the world.

I had no idea then, but reality was about to hit me like a ten-ton hammer.

# CHAPTER 10
# SHEPHERD'S BUSH

Eurgh . . . I haven't thought about the time I lived in Shepherd's Bush for donkey's years – in fact, I've tried very hard not to. Even seeing it on a Tube map makes me so anxious I want to barf my guts out. I was eighteen when I moved there and thought I fucking knew it all. It turned out that Shepherd's Bush was going to teach me that I didn't know jack-shit.

I knew that if I wanted to follow my dreams of becoming an actress, I'd have to move to London, so when I got a phone call from Mariah, a Portuguese girl I met at the acting workshop in London, asking if I fancied house-sharing with her and her two mates in Shepherd's Bush, I jumped at the chance.

I'll be like Joey Tribiani in *Friends*, just hanging out with mates and rocking up to auditions, I thought. Yeah, it'll be a fucking ball. Mariah's boyfriend was a club promoter. I'd be rubbing shoulders with the London elite in no time, probably get invited to tons of A-lister parties, maybe even get a picture of me stumbling out of Chinawhite in *Heat* magazine. Sadly, it turned out he just worked in a nightclub collecting empties and wiping tables and, as it transpired, I had all the smart street-cred of Paddington-fucking-Bear.

Dad drove me up in the Ford to London to view the house. It was on a side road right near Queens Park Rangers football ground. Dad was shitting himself.

'Fuck, can't park here.'

'Why not?'

'The car's gonna get keyed.'

'What? Why?'

Dad gestured towards the Fulham FC air freshener dangling from the rear-view mirror.

'I'm a target, Daisy. Rangers fans hate Fulham.'

'Well, just take it down.'

'Can't. They've already clocked me.'

He pointed at two lads on BMX bikes chatting by a postbox.

'Dad, I honestly don't think they give a shit. They aren't even looking at the car.'

'They'll rob the stereo out of spite. You don't understand football fans, Daisy. It's war. Me having this air freshener is the equivalent of Nelson going up to Napoleon and pissing on Empress Josephine. I'm on their territory and, as far as they're concerned, I'm mocking them.'

Dad took down the air freshener and shoved it into the glove compartment.

But he still wouldn't get out of the car, not even when the lads had cycled away. He was convinced they were going to come back. We ended up parking in a shopping centre, half an hour's walk away, and paying ten quid an hour. Fucking ridiculous.

When we finally walked into the house, it was like walking into the gates of hell. It was a cold, damp shell of a squat. The wallpaper was peeling from the wet walls. The tiny kitchen looked out on to a minute concrete square of a garden which looked as though several bodies had been buried under it. Four metal-framed beds (they looked like traps from the film *Saw*) were gathered in the one room. It was like a 1920s hospital ward.

'We'll all be sharing this room. It saves on rent.' Mariah's face was perfectly still, her expression giving no sign that four grown people sharing one room was anything but perfectly normal.

Great! No privacy . . . I'll have to wait it out if I ever want to masturbate.

Dad saw the horrified look on my face.

'I think it's great, Dais. You want to be an actress. You need to be in the metropolis to make it to the big time.'

'I can't wait for you to meet the other girls. You're gonna love them,' Mariah said.

Against every instinct, I moved in, and met the other girls sharing the flat . . .

And I fucking hated them, and they fucking hated me.

I can't remember their names – I think my brain has blocked them out – so let's just call them Polly and Sue.

Polly was a nanny for a family in Primrose Hill during the day. She and Mariah worked as bar staff in a nightclub in Leicester Square until the early hours. They used to brag about a con they used on the customers. They would put a napkin on silver dishes when they gave people their change but hide the notes underneath it, just putting the coins on top. The drunken customers only saw the change, not the notes, so the girls made a lot of money from their 'tips'.

They were always bringing blokes back to shag. Polly would often go straight to the club after finishing her nannying job, and the three of them would roll in at four in the morning. I wouldn't have minded too much – but we were all sharing a room.

I learned the Portuguese for 'Fuck me harder' quite quickly. It was the only thing that any of them ever really said in that room, and they said it repeatedly.

I would often take myself to the tiny box room. It was full of suitcases and a large clothes rail that could only fit in the room diagonally. I'd sleep under it on the floor, hearing the three of them getting 'porked out' through the Ritz-cracker-thin walls.

Nothing was *ever* private. I was taking a bath one day when Sue walked in like John Wayne, pulled her trousers and pants down and began to fish a tampon out of her foof. She had forgotten to take it out before sex. Did I need to know that? Honestly. There are boundaries.

I figured out the girls hated me pretty quickly. They would talk to each other in a lot of angry Portuguese, but I knew they were talking about me because the word 'Daisy' was thrown in every now and again.

It was probably because I was shite at housekeeping. Really shite, and I had no idea that I had to do shit like mop floors, empty bins and clean stuff. I didn't know how to use a washing machine either, so I washed my knickers in the sink and left them to dry on the sides of the bath. It clearly upset the others, because I'd walk into the shared bedroom to find my pants had been passive-aggressively shoved into a bubble-lined envelope on my bed. On the envelope someone had drawn a giant question mark in eyeliner, which I assume means 'WTF?' in all languages.

Polly had a thing for eating raw bacon out of the packet. She would dangle it in her mouth like a seagull swallowing a hot dog. She had a stomach of steel, Polly . . . and she terrified the shit out of me.

One day I was sat on the sofa, eating Wotsits and watching *Homes under the Hammer*, when Polly came storming in and switched the telly off.

'When are you going to get a job?' she barked.

'Soon,' I mumbled, at the same time trying to blow Wotsit crumbs from my jumper so I didn't look like a complete A-class slob. I failed.

'And,' she carried on barking, closer to my face now, 'it's your turn to pay the electric.'

Fuck. Does living in a house mean you have to pay electric? I thought it just came with the rent . . .

I didn't have a fucking clue about paying bills, and I was living on the very last tenner of the money I'd saved while working back home in the department store.

'Don't worry, I've got a job interview lined up for tomorrow,' I said.

After trawling the jobs section of *The Stage* for auditions, I'd finally found one that looked promising. It read:

## !!EXOTIC DANCERS REQUIRED!!

Paying up to £500 per week

No experience necessary

Outgoing and vivacious personality

Fucking brilliant!!!

My problems were solved! I can dance a bit. My shapes on the dance floor have been commented on. Exotic dancing? Is that like with fruit on your head, like Carmen Miranda in her Calypso Queen get-up? Yes, dear readers, this was the first image that flew into my naive brain on reading the advert. Talk about a Tellytubby living in fucking La-La Land.

I called the number and spoke to a guy called Tony who sounded like he had just smoked an entire pack of

Rothmans/Players, as he kept coughing mid-sentence. Tony told me that the audition would be held at 9 p.m. in a club called Sophisticats in central London and that I was to wear evening dress.

Evening dress? What did he mean by evening dress? The only evening dresses I've ever come across are the ones that you wear to your secondary-school prom. Is that what he means? That must be what he means.

That day I scoured the charity shops of Shepherd's Bush, wishing Mum was around to help. She's a whizz in charity shops. Eventually, I rocked up to one that looked slightly dodgy, with grimy windows and a sign that read 'S VE HE WO BLES FOUNDATION'. Save the Wombles? It didn't seem legit, but there were enough people scrabbling through shit – videos of old *Carry On* and *Doctor in the House* films and loads of oversized Sports Direct mugs – that I felt safe enough to enter. I rummaged through the endless musty clothes on the rail.

The bloke behind the counter sauntered over.

'What yer after, love?'

'An evening dress,' I said.

'Some new stuff just come in . . . d'you wanna look out the back? It's proper quality. Silk and all.'

He led me to a back room, an old kitchenette that stank of stale coffee. There was a lightbulb swinging from decidedly dodgy wiring. He pointed at an open bin bag full of clothes.

The clothes looked like the entire wardrobe of an eccentric elderly lady and the smell led me to believe she'd probably died in them.

'Expensive stuff that . . . designer stuff.'

Yeah, if you consider Bon Marché a fucking designer.

Finally, after all my rummaging and trying not to be sick from the overpowering scent of cheap talcum powder and moth balls, I found a purple floor-length gown with spaghetti straps in a size ten. (Yes, I know what you're thinking, but I really was that thin once.) There was a small stain on the front and it looked and smelled a little bit like vomit . . . the old lady had obviously overdone it on Smirnoff Ice and Doritos at the last tea dance.

I can wash that puke out in no time, no problem, I thought, then give it a good Febreze.

'How much?' I asked.

'Tenner.'

'There's a puke stain on it.'

He looked pissed off.

'Fiver, then.'

I gave it to him, which left me with just a fiver to top up my Oyster card.

I dolled myself up as best I could in the dim light of the bathroom mirror, hoping the blusher and lipstick didn't clash. I got a train into town at about seven. I was way too early and I had a couple of hours to kill, so I just wandered around Oxford Circus in my stupid ball gown, looking like Miss Havisham from *Great Expectations*. When it finally got to quarter to nine, I made my way to the club. An Eastern European girl with platinum-blonde hair dyed to within an inch of its life and wearing a mini skirt was smoking a fag outside. She gave me a funny look.

'Arrrre yooou lost, darrrrling?' she purred.

'Is this Sophisticats?'

Her eyes widened and something akin to a smirk grew on her face.

'I'm here to see Tony?'

She nodded towards the door, hiding her smoky laugh by licking coral lipstick from her teeth.

'Thanks.'

'Good luck, darrrrlinng.'

I held my dress as I walked down some stairs carpeted in leopard print. A waft of stale ash and old beer billowed upwards to greet me.

The double doors at the bottom of the stairs opened out into an empty nightclub. The overhead lighting was on – they hadn't opened yet. A bartender refilling the optics glanced up to look at me.

'Is Tony here?' I asked.

The bartender gestured with a tea towel at a balding middle-aged man sat in a VIP booth facing the stage. He was so greasy that the strip lighting lit up his bald head like a mirror ball.

'Tone, someone's 'ere for yer.'

Tony was wearing sunglasses indoors and had thick gold chains on both his wrists. He looked like a character from *Grand Theft Auto*.

Tony looked over his shoulder at me as I stood there in a fucking prom dress like a wilting flower. My feet were killing me. My shoes were far too tight and I was beginning to regret the impulse to 'borrow' them. There would be hell to pay later. Tony turned back around to the stage and continued his conversation with the DJ.

'Play it again.'

The DJ interrupted the silence of the empty club with an obnoxious dance track that was deafening. I could feel the bass of the shit song throbbing through the sweaty walls. The disco laser lights were pale against the harsh overhead lighting.

After thirty seconds of my ears bleeding out, Tony waved his hand for the music to stop.

'That's the fucking one.'

'Fucking told you it were,' the thin DJ replied.

Another girl came through the double doors. She was dressed in jeans and a strappy T-shirt. I felt fucking ridiculous.

Tony turned to look at us, or as much as his fat neck allowed him to.

'If you two wanna use the dressing room to get changed and then come back out again in five.'

The girl nodded. I had not a fucking clue what was going on. Wasn't I already dressed?

He pointed to the girl.

'You Susan or Daisy?'

'Susan.'

'Right, what's yer stage name?'

'Jessica or Jessica Rabbit.'

Tony scribbled the name down on the back of a beer mat.

'What track you wanna dance to?'

'"Ghetto Romance" by Damage,' she replied.

'Yeah,' shouted the DJ. 'I got it.'

Tony nodded.

What the fuck was this? Was there something I had missed? How did Susan know what the fuck was going on and I didn't?

Then I looked up to the stage and saw the pole.

Oh . . . my . . . God . . . it was a fucking strip club.

Tony then pointed at me.

'And you? What's your stage name?'

I froze in absolute horror and said the only name that came to my head.

'Louise . . . or Louise Redknapp.' My voice trembled.

*Daisy? Why the fuck did you say that?*

Louise fucking Redknapp. Wife of footballer Jamie fucking Redknapp. Of all the names in all the fucking world, you chose that. Dais, this is a new fucking low.

Everyone smirked and the barman dropped a pint glass behind the bar. It bounced off a rubber mat.

*Just kill me. Kill me, kill me, kill me. Kill me now.*

'Song?'

Oh fuck, I thought I'd be dancing to the fucking calypso with fruit on my head.

Is there any way I can walk out? Maybe if I just started backing out the door they wouldn't see me? No, I can't. My fucking feet are nailed to the floor and I can't move.

'Same.'

'All right then, girls. Go freshen yer fannies up and I'll see yer in five.'

*This cannot be happening. This cannot be fucking happening.*

Tony ushered us into a dressing-room, and I could not believe my eyes.

It was long and narrow and full right to the end of naked women. Some were putting bronzer on their fannies, some were oiling up their tits. All I could hear was hairdryers, all I could smell was Charlie Red and Impulse, and all I could see was a sea of tits and fannies. Giant tits and tiny fannies. I looked down at my two bee stings and the massive gap there was between them and the bust of the dress.

I felt like I was going to throw up all over the fucking prom dress. This dress was definitely cursed.

One of the girls, who had the most giant honkers I've ever seen, eyeballed my dress and burst into cackling

Dad had many sleepless nights when I was a baby as Mum's horrible floral curtains that looked like monsters gave me night terrors.

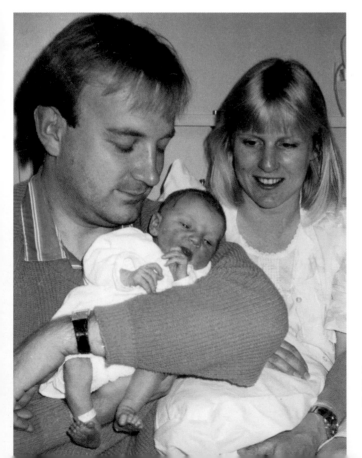

Charlie not long after he was born – look how fucking ugly he is!

Shortly after this family snap was taken, Dad caught me trying to shove a bar of soap down Charlie's throat.

Mum cut my hair around a pudding bowl. I'll never forgive her.

The stupid hats are to disguise the fact that me and my cousin Katherine (*left*) had cut our own hair with fabric scissors for her birthday.

Daisy
Reading
Diary

My first attempt at forging a school report.

Me on some boring holiday . . . somewhere . . .

Coming last in sports day as per usual.

Me and Charlie the day after I forced him to dissect a live snail.

Early signs of my narcissism.

Uncle Trevor (*left*), who plays Len in *This Country*, and Dad (*right*), looking like something out of *Men Behaving Badly*.

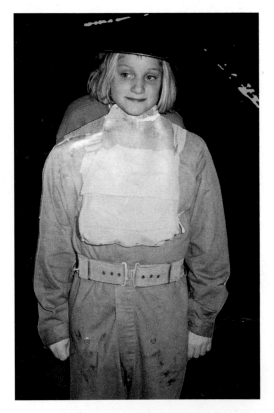

Me behind the worst cardboard cut-out at a shitty mining museum.

A taste of things to come? I have drawn myself in an identical T-shirt to the one I wore on *Doc Martin*.

Buzz, our dog, would later star in our very first Kerry videos.

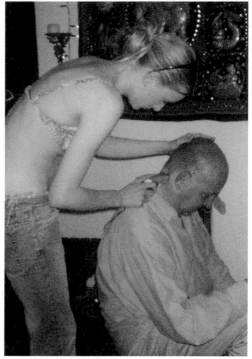

Shaving Dad's hair. We had no money for a proper barber.

Living the dream on holiday with my first earnings from running my denim crime syndicate. Note the expensive fags on the table.

Mum often wanted to take nice pictures of me and Charlie to send to our grandparents. I always tried to be sultry, hoping they would show their fit next-door neighbour. Charlie never wanted to pose with me.

laughter. Another girl with a thong pulled up to her bloody armpits stifled a giggle.

Susan, or 'Jessica', whipped out a tiny silver latex dress that barely covered her flange.

Oh right, that's what he fucking meant by 'evening dress'.

There was a knock on the dressing-room door. It was Tony.

'You girls wanna watch or not?' he barked. The naked women all filed out of the dressing room. One girl with gigantic tits walked past Tony as he held the door open.

'Give us a suck on them tits, Chrissie.'

'Fuck off, Tone,' she snapped.

He slapped her on the arse.

'Prick tease.'

I watched through the door as all the girls sat in chairs and booths in front of the stage.

No . . . no . . . no . . . this couldn't get any worse. They aren't going to be watching, are they?

Yes. Yes, they were. It was like a fucked-up version of *Britain's Got Talent*, except it wasn't like that *at all*. In this nightmarish version, I was being judged on how quickly I could give a bloke a boner by a ton of bitchy naked women who all looked like Victoria Silvstedt. Suddenly, the opening bars of 'Ghetto Romance' boomed on the speakers and the DJ took the mic.

'Please welcome to the stage . . . Jessica Rabbit!'

Jessica (aka Susan) shimmied past me and jumped on to the stage like a gazelle. She was a fucking pro. She attacked the pole . . . thighs first. Upwards, downwards, upside down. She swung from that pole like a fucking macaque, and in a way that was so sexy and elegant she could have given a nun an orgasm. I watched in awe.

But this feeling quickly evaporated as she came to the end of her routine. Then I just felt my heart bungee-jump from my chest into my gut. This was it. I felt like I was walking to my execution.

Jessica walked off the stage to a frosty, silent reception. The girls obviously thought she was good but they didn't want to show it.

'Ghetto Romance' started up again . . .

Oh fuck!

'And welcome to the stage, Louise . . .' The DJ looked closely at the beer mat he was reading from and tittered: '. . . Redknapp?'

There wasn't even a laugh from the naked judges. Just utter confusion. I felt my legs trembling beneath me as they started to walk up the steps to the stage. Every part of me was shaking so much I looked like one great big vibrating dildo in a prom dress.

The music was playing . . .

'"Just another Friday night . . ."'

Oh fuck.

I'm not doing anything.

I'm just standing by the pole, staring at the audience. I'm not moving.

I'd heard once that 'to get over nerves of public speaking', you had to imagine that the audience was naked. But my audience *was* already naked, and I wasn't speaking, I was fucking stripping. My nerves were out of control.

Come on, Dais . . . you've got to do something. *Just do something!*

OK . . . I'm grinding on the pole now . . . Yeah, that's ummm . . . yeah, bit difficult . . . prom dress isn't really helping me get my thighs on the pole. I'm being cock-blocked by my own dress. Right . . . fuck . . . just pretend the pole is some really hot bloke you've always fancied. That's it! Imagine it's Christian Slater in *Heathers*. Oh, fuck yes . . . OK . . . I can do that . . . Might just take these spaghetti straps down . . . show my tits . . . OK . . . tits are now fully out of my prom dress, but the prom dress is still on, as I can't reach the zip at the back. OK. Maybe just swing 'em about a bit. Yeah . . . yeah, just swing 'em. OK . . . Beginning to get the hang of this . . . OK. Don't mind me. Just swinging them around. OK, so I can tell there is still, like, a minute of the song left and I've already got my tits out. That was meant to be my big climax. Now what? Oh God . . . I'm snogging the pole . . . I'm doing it . . . I can't stop doing it . . . just snog the pole until the end of the song. Maybe sort of touch your nipples at the same time? OK . . . so . . . The music stops. I swivel round as best I can and look over at the DJ, who has now stopped the record mid-flow. Silence falls like snow. Deadly and cold. I'm now just hugging a pole with my tits out.

OK. Dais, stop snogging the pole. Just *stop*.

I finally come to my senses and stop.

Oh God. I catch a glimpse of my naked judges, and they aren't laughing. They look absolutely fucking horrified.

Maybe I can save this if I just pop my tits back in my dress and walk off sexily.

Instead, I trip over my dress walking down the stairs and turn to look back over my shoulder . . .

. . . and wink.

What

the

*fuck*?

Why did I just wink?

I went back into the dressing room. Susan was sitting in a chair, grooming herself in one of the mirrors. She obviously hadn't watched my performance.

'How did it go?' she asked, pulling some lumpy mascara from an eyelash.

'Awful,' I mumbled.

Then Tony burst into the dressing room.

'Susan, you wanna start Monday?'

'Yeah, sure.' She slid her vest top on over her perfect boobs.

'I'll give yer a call tomorrow.'

'OK. Great. Cheers.' And with a smile as wide as the Amazon, Susan left.

Tony then turned to me.

'Er. Yeah. It's a definite no for you.'

Without saying a word, I walked as fast as I could out of the dressing room, through the club and up the leopard-print stairs, trying not to trip up over my stupid dress. The humiliating events burned into my brain like a series of Technicolor images, spinning round like some awful kaleidoscope.

I found myself at Bond Street station, waiting for my Tube home. The platform was empty. The dress, the horrified faces, the music – everything I did was on replay in my head. I felt sick. I could have thrown myself in front of the oncoming train.

'Yeah, it's a definite no for you' was ringing in my brain, over and over.

How awful. How fucking embarrassing. I felt lower than dog shit. I promised myself I would keep this secret to the grave. I even disposed of the dress the very next day, as if to eliminate the entire event from ever having existed. I made a solemn vow. I would never tell a soul . . .

. . . until a few years later, when I ended up telling Romesh Ranganathan on his show *In Cafés with Comedians*. The confession went viral and ended up getting over 16 million views on YouTube. Fucking typical.

*The Stage* was to be the source of many a humiliating audition. I even very nearly ended up auditioning for *Babe Station* after seeing it advertised in the back pages. I got the Tube to Camden but chickened out at the very last minute. Thank fuck I did. I may have been desperate for money, but keeping seedy old blokes on the phone for as long as it took them to have a wank was a step too far, even for me. Instead I ended up getting a credit card – full of hope and promise that I would carefully manage the payments once I had got a foothold on the stage, in film, on TV – whatever! Just *something*.

# CHAPTER 11
# BRIAN, BO' SELECTA! AND THE MISSING MONOLOGUE

**T**he next advert for an audition I found in *The Stage* read:

ACTING SHOWCASE

*Be part of an acting showcase in front of an
audience of agents and industry professionals!*

Auditions 1 p.m. this Saturday
Hackney Baptist Church
Please prepare a monologue.
Duologues also accepted.

Yes! *Yes!* YES! This was exactly what I had been look-ing for. This was my big break. I believed that if I just got in front of the right people, I would be able to get somewhere with my acting career.

I turned up at the village hall and was surprised to see that not many people were queuing up outside. There were only about twelve of us and it was now one thirty and the doors were still locked. Suddenly, a young girl in her twenties ran to the front of the queue with a set of keys.

'Oh gosh, sorry. Sorry to keep you waiting, everyone. I'm Tasha, by the way! Thank you all for coming.'

Everyone walked into the empty wood-cladded hall. There were banners all over the walls which children had obviously made at Sunday school. They were mostly drawings of Jesus Christ made from little screwballs of multicoloured tissue paper.

Tasha sprinted to the other side of the hall and started to push a trestle table across the room. An eccentric-looking woman in her sixties wearing what looked like an Elizabethan velvet dress, her veiny, pale breasts trying to escape the bodice, popped out from behind me and squinted through bi-focal glasses – they made her look like a character from *Bo' Selecta!* – then glided across the floor to help Tasha move the table. I think she thought by helping Tasha she would pass the audition.

The table screeched over the newly varnished floor.

'If you all want to grab some chairs,' Tasha shouted, 'and make a circle around the table.'

Everyone grabbed a chair, bar a man in his forties in an electric wheelchair who made a weak joke about not needing one. Everyone laughed uncomfortably. Tasha opened a satchel and put some paper and pens on the table and sat behind it.

'So, I want to thank you all again for coming. As I said before, I'm Tasha. So I want to explain a bit about the showcase. Next Saturday, we will be holding a showcase for industry professionals at the Piccadilly Theatre. This is a wonderful opportunity to get an agent and I know for a fact that we have a very famous casting director coming to watch.'

There was a murmur of excitement in the circle. I could see Bo' Selecta! turn to her male companion, who was also in his sixties and also wearing what looked like Elizabethan clothing. She clapped her hands in excitement at him.

'To begin with, I'm going to go round the circle and get your names and email addresses. Then we'll do a few games as a warm-up, followed by each of you presenting your monologue or duologue for the group.'

Tasha went around the circle of twelve and everyone gave the details she'd asked for, except for Bo' Selecta!, who insisted on giving us a run-down of every single play she had been in since the seventies.

'My name is Margery Bathurst. My father was a tailor, Savile Row, and my mother was a dancer. I toured the country with the Rag and Bones theatre company from 1984 to 1991. I was Gertrude in *Hamlet* for the Bexhill-on-Sea players . . . I also write my own plays.'

Then it was Margery's male friend's turn. He looked like a recovering alcoholic. He told the group his name was William but that he was known in the industry as Bill. Then he told us that he'd had a walk-on role in *Emmerdale* in the eighties. He spoke about it like he was Laurence Olivier.

At least, for once, it wasn't me completely humiliating myself.

When the last person gave their name and email address, Tasha jumped from her chair.

'OK, everyone, we're going to play a game called Grandmother's Footsteps.'

She grabbed another chair and put it at the very end of the room. She got out her keys and placed them on the chair.

'Does everyone know how to play?'

Bo' Selecta! put her hand straight up. Then very loudly interrupted Tasha. Fuck me, this woman was annoying. Worse was the theatrical tone she used to recite the rules.

'One person is chosen to be Grandma. That person then has to face a wall by the chair, away from the other players. When the game starts, all the other players have to try and sneak up on Grandma without being seen or heard and grab the keys. At random points throughout the game, Grandma can turn around. All the players have to stand completely still. If Grandma sees any player move, she sends them back to the start. I may as well be Grandma, to show you all how it works.'

She walked up to the chair and faced the wall. The game started and we all had to creep up on her and try to grab the keys. She turned around and everyone froze except the man in the wheelchair. He had tried to stop it in time but there was a one-second delay.

'*Him!*' Bo' Selecta! shouted. 'The one in the wheel-chair!'

'My name is Brian.'

'Brian! I saw Brian move. Back to the start, Brian.'

Brian looked a bit pissed off but made his way back.

Bo' Selecta! turned again but then immediately turned back.

'Brian! I saw him move!'

Brian hadn't even got back to the start yet.

'Just let Brian get back first!' Tasha shouted.

It was like dealing with a group of toddlers.

Bo' Selecta! turned to face the wall again and we all started to creep up on her when she turned around, once more calling out Brian's name. Again, there was a delay before Brian's wheelchair came to an absolute stop.

Brian was now absolutely furious.

'I can't help it! There's a delay on my wheelchair! I'd rather just sit this game out, Tasha, if you don't mind. I came here to do my monologue, not to be humiliated for my disability.'

'Are you upset with me?' Bo' Selecta! started squawking from the other side of the room.

Brian ignored her. It was like watching a car crash in slow motion.

'I'm sorry, Brian,' she continued. 'It's just that I didn't want it to seem like I was positively prejudiced by letting you cheat.'

'I wasn't cheating! Are you taking the piss?!'

By now, the atmosphere had turned really frosty, especially as Bo' Selecta! walked over to Brian and patronizingly patted him on the shoulder.

'We're sensitive souls, us actors . . . makes us good at what we do.'

What an absolute twat.

It was time for our performances. Brian went first and proceeded to do a comedy monologue from the play *The Boor* by Chekhov. Tasha smiled along and wrote down some notes on a piece of paper. Everyone tittered in all the right places, and I could see this was massively pissing off Bo' Selecta!, who needed all the attention, all of the time. It was no surprise that she volunteered even before Brian had finished his last sentence, so eager was she to do her duologue with Bill of *Emmerdale* fame.

They did a duologue from *Macbeth*. It was awful. Bill did a hammy version of Macbeth and Bo' Selecta! did an even hammier version of Lady Macbeth. I could see that Tasha was very unimpressed.

Bo' Selecta! even took a bow in front of her audience. She was so fucking chuffed with herself.

Now it was my turn to do my monologue. I felt like Susan must have felt at the strip club. I knew exactly what I was doing this time. I was a pro at this. This was in my fucking blood.

I did a funny speech from *The Lieutenant of Inishmore*,

an Irish play by Martin McDonagh about the IRA. My accent was a bit on the dodge, but I was praying that this monologue would be enough to get me in front of the industry professionals. I was born to do this. Acting is in my DNA.

After we had all done our audition pieces, Tasha said we would hear later that evening via email whether we had been successful.

I sat in an internet café in Leicester Square all afternoon, paying £1 an hour to refresh my emails.

Oh God, I hope she took my email address down properly . . . What if Tasha had written a 'dot com' instead of a 'dot co dot uk'? Or worse, maybe I simply wasn't good enough.

Oh God, what if my instincts about myself were wrong? What if I couldn't act? I've chased my dreams all the way to London and, if I can't become an actor, then I'm fucked, because I can't do anything else – well, apart from fold towels nicely.

Suddenly a message pings into my inbox. It's from Tasha Gibbons . . .

Subject: SHOWCASE

Hi Daisy

Thank you so much for auditioning today. I am delighted to tell you that you have successfully made it into our showcase line-up.

To appear in the showcase, all I ask is that you pay £120 to cover the cost of the venue. The showcase will take place next Saturday at 1 p.m. Please arrive for 11 a.m. for a tech rehearsal.

Address is attached.

Congratulations again

Tasha x

I almost skipped home that night. Yes . . . I *can* act, and this is my chance to shine. No one can ignore my talent any longer.

That week I practised my monologue until the words didn't make sense any more and at night, in the tiny box room, I drowned out the Portuguese girls shagging with thoughts of all the industry professionals who would be knocking on my door.

I called Mum and Dad to tell them the wonderful news but, instead of congratulating me, they seemed a little suspicious . . .

'Why are they asking you to pay a hundred and twenty quid?'

'To cover the venue.'

'That seems a bit strange. If they think you're talented enough to be in the showcase, why are they asking you for money?'

Dad's tone was now starting to piss me off.

'I told you, to cover the cost of the venue . . . it's at the

Piccadilly Theatre. Dad, it's one of the biggest theatres in the West End.'

'I thought you said it was a "fringe" theatre *in* Piccadilly.'

'Well, at the audition, Tasha did say it was *the* Piccadilly Theatre. There are probably two stages . . . maybe it's a smaller one that they have for fringe performances.'

Silence from Dad.

'Why can't you just be happy for me?'

'I am, Dais. I just worry, that's all.'

'Dad, I'm fine.'

'And you're sure it's legit?'

'A hundred per cent.'

'OK. Well, me and Mum are really proud of you, honey.'

You wouldn't be quite so proud if you knew that I had auditioned as a pole dancer in a strip club the week before, I thought.

'Thanks, Dad . . . I really think this is my chance.'

'I'm sure it is – you're going to blow them away. I love you.'

'Love you too, Dad.'

'Er, Dais, before you go . . . You haven't got a credit card out in your name, have you? Someone from a credit company phoned here saying you'd missed a payment.'

Oh shit. The credit card. Yes, it was pretty much maxed out already and no, I hadn't been keeping up with payments, as I had promised myself.

'Of course not, Dad . . . Must have been some other Daisy May Cooper. I'm still living off my savings.'

My savings went months ago.

'Well, that's all right then. Good girl. Good luck . . . so bloody proud of you.'

It's fine, I told myself. I can pay off some of my credit card with the first job I get off the back of this showcase.

The day of the showcase rolled around quickly. I made sure I got there early so I had enough time to prepare. I walked into the grand Piccadilly Theatre. It was beautiful. Romantic red carpets, grandiose art deco interior, the smell of popcorn . . . This is where I belong, I thought. I am meant to be here. I approached the woman at the box office.

'Can I help you?'

'Yes. I'm here for the showcase.'

'Showcase?'

'I'm one of the actors starring in the showcase.'

She looked utterly confused.

'The only thing we're showing is *Guys and Dolls* . . . It's the only show we've had on for the last three years. Are you sure you've got the right theatre?'

My heart was starting to sink. My stomach was sinking lower.

'Oh, right . . . It's just that I was told it was at the Piccadilly Theatre?'

'Do you have an address?'

I handed her a crumpled piece of paper. She took it from me and googled the address on her computer.

'Right . . . so . . . um . . . this is bringing up an address for a pub?'

'A pub?'

She drew a map on a Post-it with a biro.

'Yes . . . if you go out of here, turn right . . . keep walking straight, and you'll find the pub on your left. It's called the Nag's Head.'

The Nag's Head? A showcase in a fucking pub? This didn't sound good.

I left the Piccadilly Theatre with a heavy heart, and the further I ventured out of Piccadilly Circus, the more nervous I became. The map was taking me down some seedy backstreets; one door I passed had a sign that read 'FEMALE, 23, MASSAGES'. I headed towards the Nag's Head pub sign, walking past overflowing bins filled with the lukewarm remains of abandoned KFC buckets and discarded doner kebabs. A waft of stale piss and vomit filled my nostrils.

I eventually found the pub. It was a tiny, run-down shit-hole. The red, patterned carpet looked like it had absorbed over thirty years of spilt ale. Barely any light came through the small, dirty windows and a jar of pick-led eggs on the bar had turned green. A frail old man with a long, dirty beard and a leather waistcoat sat at the bar. He was sipping from a pint of ale and on the table in front of him sat two empty glasses of froth . . . it was eleven o'clock in the morning.

'Downstairs,' snapped the barmaid, pouring another ale for Old Father Time.

Downstairs, I found Tasha arranging some chairs in a line. The only thing that made it even remotely look like a theatre was the stage lighting that hung from the ceiling. There was no stage, and not even a carpet, just an uneven stone floor. Tasha beamed at me.

'Ah, Lucy! You found it then!'

'Daisy,' I corrected her.

'Ah yes, Daisy . . . sorry.'

Wow . . . I must have made a real impression on her at the auditions.

'The dressing room is just through there if you want to start getting ready . . .'

I pulled aside a thin, stained curtain to find the rest of the cast getting ready in what was clearly the pub's stock room. It was filled with beer barrels and boxes of Walkers crisps. A thought crossed my mind. Everyone who was at the showcase was here, except Brian. The audition can't have been that fucking ruthless if pretty much everyone that had auditioned was chosen. Even fucking Bo' Selecta! was here. I thought I'd seen the last of that twat. She was putting on some heavy make-up and looking into a small mirror balanced on top of some crates of J2o. She and Bill were wearing dressing gowns over their costumes. Fucking dickheads. Tasha walked in.

'Could someone help me put the refreshments out? Going to do a spread upstairs for after the show. Thought it would be nice for you guys to network with the bigwigs over nibbles and drinks.'

'I would, Tash, but I've got to get into the zone,' Bo' Selecta! replied, not taking her eyes from the mirror. 'Oh, one thing I should mention. Bill and I aren't going to do Shakespeare for our duologue any more. We've written our own thing . . . much more current. Do you want to read our script before we go on?'

Tasha smiled politely. 'I'm sure it's fine,' she said.

'I used to write radio plays, don't you know?' Bill chimed in. 'In '78 I won the Playwright Newcomer Award for my play *Ashtray*.'

Tasha ignored him.

'I'll give you a hand, Tash,' I volunteered.

'Cheers, Lucy.'

'*Daisy*.' Christ. It's not that difficult to remember my bloody name.

Upstairs, Tasha handed me a carrier bag full of Tesco Value nibbles and guacamole dip, then started putting plastic wine glasses on the table and filling each up only a couple of centimetres with a bottle of cheap red wine.

'Fuck . . . so nervous about him coming . . .'

'Who?' I asked.

'John Burdett . . . He's the casting director for *Emmerdale*.'

My eyes lit up.

'Holy shit. That's amazing!'

'Between you and me . . . He's only sort of coming for me.'

I was confused. What did she mean, 'Only coming for her'?

'I wrote to him asking to audition for a part in *Emmerdale*, and he said he would only see me if I'm in a proper showcase, so I organized this.'

'Are you doing a monologue?'

'Yeah, of course. Oh God . . . Look how nervous I am.'

She held up a hand, but it wasn't really shaking; there wasn't even a fucking tremble.

'Who else is coming?'

'Just him, I think, but I don't think any of the actors will notice, as the stage lights will be so bright we won't be able to see the audience.'

I was fucking furious. On so many levels. Dad had been right – what an absolute scam. This entire thing had been organized purely so that Tasha would be seen by this casting director. Everything was beginning to make sense. Everyone who auditioned had got through. All because it had to look like a legitimate showcase to this casting director. And, naturally, Tash needed everyone's cash to pay for the venue. I was absolutely raging. Fucking incandescent. What a cow. She'd given everyone false hope. She'd given me false hope. I eyeballed her. She was totally oblivious to my evil stare.

'Your monologue was really good,' she said, but I was too cross to feel flattered. 'He'd better not give you the part.'

She was cutting a piece of Brie with a plastic knife and did a quick impression of the killer in *Psycho*, stabbing the cheese and laughing.

I pondered things. If she was feeling threatened by me, maybe my monologue *was* good? Maybe this casting director *would* give me the part instead? I'd be pretty good as a Dingle.

Suddenly there was loud banging on the pub window. It was Brian, in his motorized wheelchair.

'I can't get my wheelchair into the pub,' he mouthed through the window. 'The door's too narrow.'

'Shit,' Tash mumbled. She clearly hadn't thought about wheelchair access. We stared at Brian in silence through the window.

'You'll have to help me,' Tasha pleaded.

'Help you how?'

'We're going to have to carry him downstairs.'

'In his wheelchair?! It will weigh a ton, and the stairs are far too narrow . . .'

'OK . . . fuck . . . just let me think.'

She opened the pub door to reveal an extremely pissed-off Brian.

'Where's the disabled entry? Is it round the back?'

'Um . . . slight cock-up on that front, I'm afraid.'

'What do you mean?'

'Um, so the plan is to leave the wheelchair outside and . . . er . . . um . . . carry you down the stairs on to a chair?'

He stared at her.

'Are you fucking joking?!'

'I'm afraid not, no . . .'

'This is appalling.'

'I know, I'm so sorry, Brian . . . I'm happy to refund you the £120. I was assured that the venue had disability access.'

'I never said that!' the barmaid barked.

Tash, clearly embarrassed, very patronizingly bent down to Brian's level.

'I'm so sorry, Brian. I'll refund you an extra twenty quid on top of the hundred and twenty.'

Brian sighed. 'If you have to carry me . . . you have to carry me.'

*What?!*

'Are you sure you don't want the refund, Brian?' I piped up.

*Brian. Mate. Take the fucking refund. It's a scam.*

'No. No. This is my one and only shot, and if I don't

get any industry interest, I'll give it up for good, but I have to at least try . . .'

Tasha guiltily averted her eyes. My heart broke. This guy was talented, too.

'We don't even know if any industry people are even going to show up, Brian.'

Then Tasha chimed in.

'Well . . . We do. We have one, for sure.'

I glared at her. How does this bitch sleep at night?

'Where am I going to leave my wheelchair? I don't want it to get stolen.'

Tasha grabbed her wallet out of her jeans, took out a tenner and handed it to me.

'Could you just nip to the hardware shop and get a chain and a padlock? Meanwhile, I'll grab Bill and ask for his help.'

I glared at her again.

I ran from Soho all the way to Tottenham Court Road to find a chain and padlock. My lungs were so tight I could barely breathe. They ended up costing over twenty quid, so I paid the tenner cash and had to fork out the extra myself, going over my overdraft on my bank card. When I finally made it back, just Tasha and Brian were outside. No Bill.

'Where's Bill?'

'He can't carry him because he's got a dodgy back. You're going to have to do it with me.'

'Fuck.'

'We haven't got much time.'

Brian chained his wheelchair to a lamp post outside the pub.

'OK, you go that side, I'll stay this side. Brian, put your arms around our shoulders and, on the count of three, we'll lift together.'

'OK.'

'Brian, you ready?'

'Yep. Ready.'

'OK. Here we go. One . . . two . . . three . . . lift!'

He weighed the same as a fridge freezer and was just as solid. He was grabbing my neck so hard I couldn't breathe.

As we made our way to the basement door, we found it had closed.

Tasha screamed at the barmaid, 'Open the fucking door!'

'I'm halfway through pouring a pint,' she sneered.

'I can't hold him for much longer,' I croaked, choking on my own words.

'Back to the chair!' Tasha shouted.

We reversed out of the pub door and dropped him on to the chair just in time.

My back was twisted like a fucking pretzel. How the fuck were we going to manage this?

'How long have we got?' I puffed to Tash.

She looked at her watch. 'About seven minutes.'

'I've got an idea. If you take Brian's arms and I take his legs, we can take him down the stairs.'

Tasha ran into the pub, propped open the basement door with a bar stool and ran back out to join us.

'OK, I've got his legs. You got his arms?'

Tasha nodded. 'On the count of three.'

'One . . . two . . . three . . . lift.'

Just as we started navigating the basement steps, a thought rushed in like a wave. I was walking *backwards* into this stairway death trap; I felt for each step cautiously with my foot, one step at a time, all the while holding on to Brian. It was agonizing. Time seemed to stand still. I was starting to buckle under the weight. We were only two steps down.

'We're going to have to . . . put you down . . . Brian . . . otherwise, I'm going to . . . fucking . . . drop you,' I panted.

I was taking most of the weight. Tasha wasn't helping much at all.

We placed Brian down on the second step.

'I fucking hate asking you this, Brian, but is there any way you can go down the steps on your . . . er . . . bum?'

'Not really, no . . .'

'OK. Well, Tash, you're going to have to really help with taking the weight and we are just going to have to do it a couple of steps at a time . . .'

'I *am* taking most of the weight!' she snapped.

The barmaid shoved her head into the basement doorway. 'Some bloke here for the showcase,' she said.

'Tell him we're running two minutes late,' Tasha called back.

Maybe it was the thought of finally being scouted by an industry professional, but a superhuman strength suddenly came over us. I might have been carrying a bloke twice my weight backwards down some narrow steps, but this was not going to stop me from getting my shot at stardom. With every muscle and sinew screaming, we carried him down like a Roman emperor and sat him on a chair in the audience.

Wiping the sweat from her forehead, Tash put her hand out for a high five, but I ignored it, pretending it was too dark to see. Silently, I stood beside Brian's chair, holding on to it to steady my shaking limbs, catching my breath and waiting for a 'thank you' that never came.

A shout from Tash broke my reverie.

'Cast!' she shrieked. Bo' Selecta! and the others emerged from the stock room to the basement stage floor like a bunch of circus freaks. Tash stood facing the chairs in the harsh beam of the stage lights. She squinted to the cast, who gathered in the dark in front of her.

'Our audience has arrived!'

There was excited murmuring from the cast. Tash pulled a piece of paper from her back pocket while blowing upward to cool her sweaty face.

'Here's the running order. Remember who is before you so that you know your cue to come on stage. And, opening the show, is Daisy . . .'

Huh! Finally, she had remembered my name.

'What? *No!* You can't make me open the show. I haven't had time to get changed!'

Tasha sighed an overly dramatic sigh. She was trying to make out that I was being difficult. Cow.

'Fine, you can go second to last.'

That was great; it gave me thirty minutes to prepare . . . plenty of time.

'Right, so first up is Katya, then Brian . . . Then the duologue from Bill and Margery . . . then, Daisy, it's you and, last, me. OK. Everybody into the dressing room. I'll let the landlady know she can bring him down.'

'Hang on – what am I going to do?' asked Brian. 'Is someone going to bring me on, or what?'

Tasha went over to Brian, who was sitting where we had left him, looking a little stranded.

'Katya . . . give us a hand.'

'What are you doing? Where are you moving me to?'

Tasha and Katya dragged Brian on his chair in front of the lights and placed him upstage left.

'I think you're just going to hang out here until it's your turn, then you're going to wait here until the end.'

'Brian . . . what's your last line? So I know what the cue is for me and Bill,' asked Bo' Selecta!

Brian ignored her. He was going a funny colour.

'I'm going to have to sit here, on the stage, all the time? During everyone's performance? Are you serious?'

'Look, Brian, we really don't have time to debate this.' Tasha was irritated now.

'I died once in the first scene of the first act and I had to lie dead on stage for two hours,' Bill said, stroking his moustache. 'Now that's what I call dedication to the actor's craft.'

'Fuck's sake . . . can't fucking believe this,' Brian muttered. He was enraged.

'Right. Everyone back into the dressing room, bar Brian. Good luck, everyone.'

Everybody scrambled into the storeroom, while Tasha called upstairs to bring down the director. Minutes later, Bo' Selecta! moved behind the curtain to peer at their audience. Her big, lumpy arse stuck out, preventing anyone else from getting a peek.

'The bigwig has landed!' she whispered loudly.

Katya was up first but it was clear that nerves had got to her and she was trembling like she'd just seen a ghost. Her monologue sounded pretty flat to me. 'She's smashing it,' whispered Bo' Selecta!, giving us a double thumbs-up sign. 'Looks like Brian's bringing the mood down, though. His face looks like a smacked arse.'

In case I haven't made it crystal clear by now, Bo' Selecta! really hated Brian.

Tasha tapped me on the shoulder.

'I'm going to put my headphones in and listen to a bit of Tchaikovsky to get myself in the mood for my performance. Don't let anyone disturb me, will you?'

Pretentious twat. I shook my head.

'Just give me a tap on the shoulder to let me know when you're heading on so I know my cue.'

'Sure.'

Tasha walked to the corner of the storeroom, sat on a large barrel of London Pride, shoved her headphones in and stared at the wall.

I got changed into a tracksuit, with Bill staring at me blatantly, in that old-man-in-a-dirty-raincoat way.

'Bill. Do you want to do a line run?' Bo' Selecta! asked, trying to get his attention away from me.

'No, I don't want to get stale,' Bill replied, still ogling my tits.

When Katya walked backstage she was clearly disappointed with her performance.

She sat down on a box of Walkers and began sinking slowly as the box caved under her weight. It seemed to suit her mood.

Brian began his monologue. It sounded great and I thought I heard the bigwig titter. Annoyingly, I couldn't see a single bloody thing, as Bo' Selecta! was still blocking the view with her giant arse.

'Oh God . . . Brian's dying out there,' she whispered.

She *really* fucking hated Brian.

I tried to rehearse my lines in my head, but it was getting hard as Bo' Selecta! carried on whispering loudly to Bill about how bad an actor Brian was. But if you didn't already think the events that led up to this were fucking mental . . .

Brian finished and next on were Bo' Selecta! and Bill. Still in their dressing gowns, they gave each other a good-luck hug, parted the curtain and walked on to the stage.

I moved to the curtain to watch their performance.

Bo' Selecta! began.

'Welcome, ladies and gentlemen. My name is Margery Bathurst, and this is my husband, Bill.' Fuck me, this woman loves the sound of her own voice. 'And today we are going to present a duologue from a play we have written called *Red-light District.*'

*Red-light District*? This is going to be gold.

'I'm going to be playing the part of Peggy, a brothel madam and dominatrix.'

*What the* . . . I could not believe what I was hearing.

'And Bill is going to be playing the part of Tony, a depressed playwright suffering from writer's block.'

Brian was still on the stage, and in full view. He looked very pale.

Bill and Bo' Selecta! whipped off their dressing gowns. Bill was now stark naked bar a thong. Bo' Selecta! wore tight fishnet stockings that pushed the cellulite in her thighs through the diamonds of the netting, a red corset like a sausage skin, a red feather boa, a see-through red thong that failed to hide a bush of sprouting white pubic hair and . . . an enormous black strap-on dildo.

Brian was now a pale shade of concrete.

To the best of my memory, this is the dialogue they performed. Some of these lines I will *never* forget . . . no matter how much counselling I have.

## Red-light District

By Bo' Selecta! and Bill

TONY (a man in his sixties) is sitting on a chair.
PEGGY (a woman in her sixties) enters, wearing a
     strap-on dildo. She handcuffs TONY's hands
     behind his back.
Peggy: What's it today, Tony? Do you want it up the
     arse?
Tony: Not yet . . . let's build up to it, Peggy.
*(Peggy takes off her feather boa and dangles it over Tony's face)*
Tony: Mm. That feels good.
Peggy: How's your playwriting coming along?
Tony: I've got writer's block.
Peggy: Maybe this will help?

*(Peggy pulls her corset down to expose both her breasts. She undoes Tony's handcuffs and places Tony's hand on her left breast.)*

Tony: Mmm.

Peggy: Now, isn't that helping with your writer's block?

Tony: Getting there.

Peggy: Do you want it up the arse yet?

Tony: I want you to fanny-fart on my face first.

*(Tony lies on the ground, Peggy squatting over his face)*

Tony: That's it! Fart on my face . . . fart on my face.

At this point, Bo' Selecta! grinds her hips above Bill's face and makes a farting sound with her mouth. Brian's face is in his hands.

Tony: That's it, Peggy! I know what I should write about – I should write about you! I'm going to call the play *Peggy*!

*(Tony jumps to his feet. He grabs Peggy passionately and they snog with tongues)*

Readers, I kid you not. The snogging with tongues went on for about a minute and was more disgusting than the fanny-farting. Poor fucking Brian was stranded there, helpless, and absolutely traumatized. The sound of their saliva smacking will never leave me.

*(Tony pulls away and looks into Peggy's eyes)*

Tony: *I love you, Peggy!*

Peggy: I love you too, Tony.

Tony: Now fuck me up the arse, Peggy. Yes. Yes.

    Ooooooh.

*(Tony bends over and Peggy goes to put the dildo in his arse)*


'Peggy' and 'Tony' froze in a weird, fucked-up doggy position to mark the end of the scene.

My mouth was agape. I needed to wash my eyeballs in TCP.

And I could see it in his face, Brian had given up any will to live.

Bo' Selecta! and Bill jumped to their feet and took a very theatrical bow in front of a silent – or, should I say, stunned – audience. Taking the silence as a recognition of the brilliance of their performance, they swept the audience with their arms, like it was a Royal Command performance at the Palladium. *Fuck*. My cringe radar was through the roof . . . But instead of walking off the stage, Bo' Selecta! decided she didn't want to step out of the limelight.

'Thank you so much, ladies and gentlemen . . . This is now the end of the showcase.'

What?

What the fuck is she doing?! She's ending the show-case *now*? Shit. This is not happening to me.

Tash and I hadn't even gone on stage yet.

'Please do join us upstairs at the bar for refreshments.'

I couldn't believe my ears. I jumped across the stock room to Tasha, who was still sitting facing the wall with her headphones in. I pulled one of them out of her ear and she turned around in a panic.

'My turn to go on?' she asked.

'No. She's just ended the show!' I blurted.

'What do you mean?'

'Fucking Margery! She's just done the speech about the showcase being finished and "Join us for refreshments upstairs."'

Tasha jumped to her feet.

Bo' Selecta! walked through the curtain, beaming, her big black dildo bouncing up and down with every step.

Tasha looked on in horror – she had been far too busy getting into the zone to have any clue about what had just gone on – but she had bigger things on her mind.

'You ended the show?'

She was so fucking happy with herself. So was Bill, who shouted in his booming lovey, flowery and slightly edgy voice, 'Well done, everyone. Superb show.'

Tasha exploded. '*Me and Daisy haven't been on yet!*' It was like a scream in a murder mystery.

Bo' Selecta! froze. Was it dawning on her that she might have made a boo-boo? Her smile faded.

'Oh . . . Oh dear . . . I totally forgot you two were going on . . . um . . . Oh, dearie me . . . so sorry. So sorry. The adrenaline got to me . . . want me to go out there and say there are two more acts?' Anything less sincere was impossible to imagine.

Tasha shoved Bo' Selecta! out of the way and ran through the flimsy curtain to find only traumatized Brian, still stranded on stage.

'Where is he?' she shrieked at him.

'He left.'

'*He left?!*'

Bo' Selecta! had followed her out and Tasha turned and pointed at her.

'You are a fucking stupid twat.'

Bo' Selecta! seemed to crumple. Even the bouncing dildo started to droop.

Tasha ran up the stairs and I followed her.

'Which direction did he go?' she yelled at the barmaid.

'Dunno,' she replied, pouring yet another pint for Old Father Time, who was still the only customer.

Tasha ran on to the street like a police detective in an ITV drama when the suspect they are chasing has given them the slip. An episode of *The Sweeney* played in my head – me and my dad had been watching re-runs. Tasha was running up and down the street, weaving in and out of people to find the scout. When she finally realized that the bigwig really was gone, she fell to her knees and howled the word:

'FUCK!'

An angry cyclist swerved to dodge her, shouting over his shoulder, 'Stupid bitch!'

I sat down next to her. Tasha broke down in tears. Hopeless at first and then angry tears.

'Where is she? I'll fucking kill her!'

I restrained her with an armlock I had seen on *Baywatch*.

'Just calm down . . .'

She was still struggling, and she elbowed me in the tits, which hurt and pissed me off.

'*Just fucking calm down!* Do you have his number?'

'No . . .'

These were the days before we had internet on our phones.

'OK . . . what was his name?'

'John . . . John Burdett.'

'Wait here.'

I pegged it to the Piccadilly Theatre as fast as I could and, elbowing my way through the crowd of people queuing for the matinee of *Guys and Dolls*, slipped into the box office.

The same lady was at the desk.

'Hi . . . sorry . . . I don't know if you remember me,' I panted.

She looked up and smiled.

'Oh, yes. Hello again. Did you find the pub?'

'Yes, thank you. Great directions! But now I need

another favour, and I know this is a really odd request, but I was wondering if you could help me again . . . it's an emergency.'

'Has something happened? Do you need me to dial 999?' She picked up the phone next to her.

'No . . . no . . . nothing like that . . . I was wondering if you could possibly google someone for me on your computer?'

She raised an eyebrow.

'Please, his name is John Burdett . . . He's a casting director. I need his number. It really is an emergency.'

Her eyebrows softened and she started to type into her computer.

'OK. I've found his website. Burdett and Boyle Casting.'

She wrote down the number on a piece of paper and gave it to me.

'Thank you!' I shouted over my shoulder as I ran out of the theatre. 'May the god of karma repay you tenfold!'

I typed the number into my phone as I sprinted back to the pub. It started ringing and then a woman picked up the phone.

'Good afternoon, Burdett and Boyle Casting. Jenny speaking. How can I help you?'

'Is it possible to speak to John Burdett?'

'He's out of the office, I'm afraid. Can I ask who's calling?'

'He doesn't know me. My name is Daisy. He was at a showcase I was about to perform in at the Nag's Head. And it's very important that I speak to him.'

'Can I pass on a message?'

'It's difficult to explain. Can you pass on his mobile number?'

'I can't do that, I'm afraid.'

'Is there any chance you can call him and tell him the showcase ended too abruptly and there were still two more acts he had to see, me and Tasha, and he came especially to see her for a part in *Emmerdale*.' I ran out of breath.

'I'll call him on his mobile now. What's your number? I'll get him to call you as soon as I've spoken to him.'

By now I had reached the spot where I had last seen Tasha. She wasn't there. I walked into the pub.

'Is Tasha here?' I asked the landlady.

'Ain't seen her since she ran out with you.'

Bo' Selecta! and Bill were sitting with the old drunk, hanging on to every last word. They must have thought he was the industry bigwig. Stupid twats. Her fawning over him while Bill stood by paying for the drinks made it like some weird *ménage-à-trois*.

I went outside and waited for fifteen minutes. John was never going to fucking call, and who would blame him, after that performance? Tasha had gone. She probably thought I would ask for my hundred and twenty quid back and had done a runner.

I didn't see her again until many years later. She popped up in *Casualty* with some sort of head wound.

I got the bus back to Shepherd's Bush, pretending to swipe my empty Oyster card, and collapsed into my makeshift bed in the box room. Mum and Dad had left several messages. I couldn't bear the thought of what they would say: 'Told you it was a scam.' 'Why didn't you listen to us?' I switched my phone to silent and stared at the ceiling.

*Fuck*, I thought.

I'd left my bag of clothes in that fucking storeroom.

Was I ever going back there to get them?

Then another thought popped into my head.

Fuck. Fuck. Fuck.

*Brian!* He was still in the basement.

# CHAPTER 12
# THADDEUS-MOTHAFUCKING-TOOGOOD

The last audition I attended while living in Shepherd's Bush was also advertised in *The Stage*. The Portuguese bitches were now seriously twisting my melons, and I was stony broke. I needed something, *anything* . . .

**\*\*\* CASTING \*\*\***

Seeking cast for blockbuster film
by Universal Pictures

Audition will consist of an
improvisation workshop

Saturday 10 a.m.

Holy Trinity church hall

Islington

Universal Pictures? A blockbuster film? Fuck me, that's amazing. My first legit audition ever. And what's more, it's improv, and that's my biggest strength. I had done loads in my drama lessons. Wow! I wonder what the film is about. Images ran through my brain like a movie trailer – *Saw*? *Psycho*? The last blockbuster film I had seen was *Titanic*, and hadn't Kate Winslet been a complete unknown? (I assure you, there was nothing ironic in my thought process.) Imagine following in her footsteps. Fuck, Daisy. This could be the real deal.

When I turned the corner to the church hall in Islington, I was met with a queue of over two hundred people that snaked into the next street. Yeah . . . this is definitely fucking legit. Hadn't they done these open auditions to find the *Harry Potter* lot? I was trembling with excitement and desperate to show them what I had to offer. The only problem was keeping my enthusiasm going while queuing for such a fuck of a long time. It started raining. Quite hard, actually. Some people left the queue to buy umbrellas from the corner shop, only to find that they had lost their place on their return. I held my denim jacket over my head so as to not ruin my make-up. I desperately needed a piss as well (it felt like I was holding in one of those giant horse pisses you do first thing in the morning), but I was determined not to leave that queue. Crossed legs. Scrunched-up insides. Whatever it took. I was *not* going to lose my place.

Every half an hour the queue moved up a bit, which made it easier to see what was going on. A guy in the doorway of the church hall was writing people's names on white labels and sticking them to their chests. Thirty or so people at a time were being allowed in. On leaving, the hopefuls were guided towards one of two guys, one with a clipboard and the other one with no clipboard.

It was grim. And quite brutal. The people who had made the cut were happy, obviously; those who hadn't were back to a life on the dole. One stunning girl who was the spit of Alesha Dixon came running out with a piece of paper, screaming, 'I got through! I got through!' She jumped into the arms of her boyfriend like a koala hugging a tree and he spun her up into her arms. Then she and her boyfriend paraded past the queue, his arm over her shoulder.

'Congratulations!' I shouted, I didn't mean it, of course. I was jealous as fuck.

'Aww, thanks . . .' she replied, wiping a tear from her eye.

'So what did you have to do in there?'

Yeah, that was my *real* motive. Hey, I can do subtle.

'Um. Well, like a group of you go in and, basically, you have to pretend there's a fire.'

'A fire?'

'Yeah.'

'Are they nice?'

'Yeah, they're lovely . . . Thaddeus is an absolute sweetheart . . . you'll really enjoy it.'

'Who's Thaddeus?'

'The director.'

'What stuff has he done?'

'I think this is his first movie . . . he used to be music producer for the Black-Eyed Peas.'

'Really?!' . . . Fuck.

Her boyfriend was smugly beaming at her.

'You got any tips for me?'

'Yeah . . . just try and be as real as possible.'

'Well . . . Congratulations again.'

She sauntered off down the street and very loudly phoned her mum while her boyfriend held her bag.

'Mum! I got through!'

 I could hear a faint scream from her mother.

Behind me, a very pretty girl wearing heavy black goth make-up, a Morticia Addams dress and biker boots tapped me on the shoulder.

'Your label is sticking out of your top.'

'Oh shit, cheers.'

'I'm Amy, by the way . . .'

'I'm Daisy . . .'

'Did she say we have to improv being in a fire?'

'Yeah.'

'Did she say how many they take through from each round?'

'No . . .'

'Do you want an E?'

'Sorry . . . what?'

A mate took these and I entered *Just Seventeen*'s modelling competition. I never heard back . . .

Me with Charlie after school. I'd just
discovered fags, booze and boys.

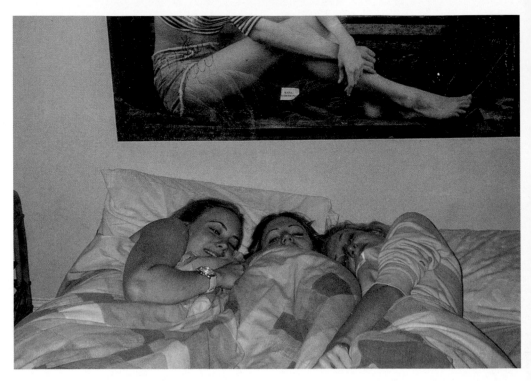

Me and my best friends and cousins Lily (*left*) and Fiona (*middle*).

Fiona (*left*), Lily (*middle*) and me (*right*). Hungover with the munchies after a night out trying to pull squaddies at Fairford Airbase.

Me (*left*) performing in *Joseph and the Amazing Technicolor Dreamcoat*.

Lily (*left*), Fiona (*middle*) and me (*right*) trying to catch crabs in Weymouth harbour after a night of catching crabs in the local nightclub.

Me (*right*) at my school prom pouting like I've had botched plastic surgery.

Me (*right*) and Fiona (*left*) wearing matching Rude tops getting ready to ride in pimped-up Clios with boys.

Hello children.
I have taken it upon myself to warn you all.
When I was your age I wish someone could have
done the same to me and all the other
kids who were is Class 3B.
But its all too late for us now, but its not for you.
dont let what happend to us
      happen to you......

I will start from the Begging....

Timmy Tugface

I once knew a young boy called Timmy,
who liked to pull funny faces,
he pulled them in school and in the street.
he pulled them in all sorts of places.

his mother grew very
                worried,
And sat Timmy Down to say,

"If the wind changes
while you are pulling faces,
you will stay forever
that way!"

Timmy

Weird, fucked-up and creepy stories: no wonder my teachers were worried.

But Timmy didn't listen,

But Timmy didn't care,
he kept on pulling faces,
so the people would stop and stare.

BOO!!

One day he thought it would
be funny,
he had a brilliant plan,
To pull a very ugly face,
and scare the life out of his Gran.

Timmy

My portfolio pictures to be an actress . . . or possibly a prostitute . . .

IMG_3792.JPG    IMG_3793.JPG    IMG_3794.JPG    IMG_3795.JPG    IMG_3796.JPG

IMG_3809.JPG    IMG_3810.JPG    IMG_3811.JPG    IMG_3812.JPG    IMG_3813.JPG

IMG_3814.JPG    IMG_3815.JPG    IMG_3816.JPG    IMG_3817.JPG    IMG_3818.JPG

IMG_3819.JPG    IMG_3820.JPG    IMG_3821.JPG    IMG_3822.JPG    IMG_3823.JPG

IMG_3831.JPG    IMG_3837.JPG    IMG_3838.JPG    IMG_3839.JPG    IMG_3840.JPG

My RADA headshots . . . so cringe.

'Do you wanna drop an E with me? Makes me more confident in auditions.'

She flashed a couple of pills in a see-through baggie.

Was she fucking insane?!

'Nah. Thanks. I'm all right. Cheers, anyway.'

She rolled her eyes, took both of the pills out of the baggie, tipped her head back and swallowed them.

Fucking nutbag. Who the fuck drops a pill, let alone two, before an audition?

I looked at the queue. It was still ages to the front and I was getting even more desperate for a piss. My bladder was starting to burst at the seams. I looked behind me. Loads more people had joined the tail end of the queue. I couldn't leave it now.

I turned to Amy. The rain was starting to make her eyeliner and white foundation run. She didn't seem like she gave a fuck, though.

'Is there any chance you could hold my place in the queue while I go for a piss?'

She shrugged.

'Sure.'

I sprinted down the street, looking for a pub or a McDonald's. I found nothing but fruit-and-veg shops and estate agents.

Fuck . . . if I didn't find a toilet soon, I was going to fill my flares with piss . . . not that you'd notice. The bell bottoms had soaked up the puddles like a sponge and my wet socks were squeaking around in my shit Lonsdale trainers.

After lots of running around, I saw an empty cemetery. Well, not really empty, but you know what I mean. No one seemed to be about, so I found a more or less secluded spot behind a giant oak tree, undid my flares and took down my pants. In case any of you have relatives in a churchyard near Holy Trinity Church in Islington, I was respectful enough to make absolutely sure that I was not pissing on or near any gravestones, I promise.

The relief as I started to piss was like my very own ecstasy high. But then I felt something touch my bare arse. Don't worry about it, I muttered to myself. Must just be a stray blade of grass – ignore it. Just keep going. But then I felt it again. I turned around to see a giant Afghan hound that had more than a passing resemblance to Cher and her big hair, with its nose up my arse. Obviously drawn by the scent of my dehydrated coffee piss. A dog like this doesn't just wander around a cemetery on its own. Where the fuck is the owner? I tried to bat the dog away with my hand, but it was drawn to my wee like Snoop Doggy Dogg to a bottle of Cristal.

'Mouse!' I heard a woman shrilly call. The dog lifted one ear slightly. Shit. This dog called Mouse – stupid name for a fucking Afghan hound; anything less mouse-like was hard to imagine – and me and my pissing antics were about to be discovered.

'Fuck off, Mouse.' I tried to push the dog's nose away from my arse, but it refused to be told. It was as if my arse and the dog's nose were magnetized.

The biggest problem was, I couldn't stop going. It seemed I'd held on to this wee for so long, it hadn't just filled up my bladder but also a reserve tank somewhere. I clung on to the tree and pushed as hard as I could, like a tap turned on full.

'Mouse! Where are you?'

The dog, significantly aroused by my bare arse, was now trying to mount me.

I finally came to the end of my piss and pushed it off with one hand, then jumped up and zipped my trousers.

Seconds later a woman in a see-through mac and wellies appeared from behind the tree.

'Mouse! Darling boy! There you are!' she shouted. 'So sorry if Mouse was bothering you,' she said to me, putting the dog on the lead. She then turned to address the dog again. 'You naughty boy!'

I could only hope that she had mistaken me for a mourner.

'Don't worry, no problem.'

Your dog just tried to fuck me, but whatever.

They walked away, Mouse tugging on his lead to come back to me.

I locked eyes with him. He stared back, then thought better of it and went on his way. I'd better ace this audition, I thought, otherwise all I'm going to remember about this day is some hairy brute trying to get his end away.

I ran back as fast as I could. The queue had moved quite a bit since I'd left it a few minutes earlier and it looked like we'd be in the next group to go in.

'Thanks for holding my place, Amy.'

'Aww – it's nice to have you back.'

Amy was definitely a lot warmer than she had been before. Her pupils were the size of fucking saucers – she looked like a barn owl. She was also moving her weight from one leg to the other and grinding her teeth. Fuck . . . she was coming up already.

'Next thirty, please!' the guy at the door shouted. We started to file in.

I was just pleased to be out of the rain.

'Amy,' Goth Girl said to the guy.

As he wrote down her name on a white sticker, she said, 'Can I have a hug?'

Somewhat confused, the guy hugged her, and she left a giant white face print on his black bomber jacket.

We shuffled into the hall and were greeted by a row of attractive women sitting behind a table. In the middle of them was a guy in his late forties with sunglasses on. He looked like a cross between Flava Flav and Don King.

As we filed through, he gave us all a wide grin and welcomed us in.

Everybody gathered in front of him like contestants on *The X Factor*. We were all shivering and soaked through.

'Raining out there? Huh? Coz a lotta you girls are *wet*!'

He laughed hysterically at his own innuendo.

'Dammit! I'm a funny mothafucka.'

I swear a lot, but the number of times this man said the word 'mothafucka' was unreal. He seemed to use it for every verb, noun and pronoun.

'Let's see what Thaddeus got here then, huh?'

He also liked to refer to himself in the third person *a lot*.

'So let Thaddeus introduce himself. I'm Thaddeus-Mothafucking-Toogood.'

The women on the panel giggled. He tugged on a huge gold chain that hung around his neck and swept his hand up towards the top of his afro.

'Anyone heard of the White Peas?'

There was a murmur of assent. I heard Amy guffaw and looked across at her. She was absolutely fucking out of it. She was beaming at a stained-glass window and rocking from foot to foot.

'I said, has anyone heard of the White Peas?' Thaddeus shouted.

This guy was definitely a showman – actually, he was more of a show-off. His eyes darted around the room for reassurance that we were all looking at him.

'Yes!' everyone shouted back, as if he was some sort of pantomime dame. Amy's 'Yes' came a couple of seconds behind everyone else's.

'You wanna know who produced those mothafuckas? Thaddeus-Mothafucking-Toogood. That's who.'

Amy let out a big 'whoop-whoop'. My immediate thought was that she was fucked. But no, Thaddeus just leaned his head back and laughed.

'Who's this little honey? I like you. What's your name, girl?'

'Amy.' Christ, she could barely keep still.

'Amy . . .' He laughed again.

'I like you, girl . . . I'm gonna watch out for you . . . Thaddeus-Mothafucking-Toogood gonna watch out for you.'

'Can I have a hug?' she slurred.

'Shit, yes, you can, my girl . . . You come to Daddy, girl.'

Oh God. Amy stumbled over to Thaddeus and almost tripped over a soaking loose bootlace from one of her biker boots. Her make-up, smudged halfway across her face, gave her the appearance of a pissed-up Casper the Friendly Ghost.

'Come give Daddy some sugar, girl.'

Thaddeus didn't get out of the chair and Amy hugged his shoulders awkwardly from behind. She then tried to sit on his lap. Oh fuck, it was so embarrassing and awful.

'Whoa! Watch it, girl. Steady on! You're gonna make my bitches jealous,' he said, eyeballing the women sitting next to him.

Amy stumbled back to her place.

'You need some water, girl?' Thaddeus looked concerned.

Amy nodded. She was now gyrating her hips seductively to the sound of silence.

'Right. Listen up! I'm making a mothafucking motion picture and I'm looking for T-A-L-E-N-T, ya'll hear me?!'

Everyone nodded.

'I said, *ya'll hear me?* I want you to imagine there's a mothafucking fire . . . a disco inferno . . . you hear what I'm saying to ya'll?'

Amy started singing the 'Disco Inferno' lyrics 'Burn, baby, burn,' to herself; she was very off key.

'So, what you bitches do?' He pointed at me. I froze.

'I'm talking to you, Blondie?'

'Um . . . scream?' I muttered.

'That's right, bitch . . . you scream.'

He then pointed to a short timid girl wearing glasses.

'What about you, Four-eyes?'

The poor girl was trembling. I could see the brain fart that was about to come out of her mouth.

'Scream?'

'Blondie just said that, bitch, be original!'

'Um, writhe?'

'*Writhe?* What you writhe for, bitch?'

She started to stammer.

'If . . . if . . . if you're on fire, you'd be writhing because you're on fire . . . trying . . . put out . . . writhing to put out the flames.'

'This bitch gotta point!'

A guy in his twenties put up his hand. Thaddeus ignored him. He was obviously only interested in the women.

'OK, so when Thaddeus-Mothafucking-Toogood shouts "Fire!" you bitches gonna act like da whole place is on *fire*. Ya'll ready for this?'

Everyone took a deep breath and nodded.

'OK, you mothafuckas . . . *Fire!!!*'

Everyone started to scream. I had nothing to lose so I dropped to the floor and shrieked and rolled and writhed. I gave it everything I had. I shook my legs furiously and patted my jeans, screaming hysterically as if they really were on fire. I could see Thaddeus looking at my name badge. I looked like a fucking twat, but I knew I was killing it.

Suddenly, the fire alarm sounded, piercing every eardrum in the place. Amy had only gone and pressed the fucking fire bell. Some people stopped to see what had happened, but others were still acting, thinking that the fire alarm had something to do with the improvisation.

Thaddeus shouted over the noise of the siren at her.

'What the fuck? What y'all do that for?'

'You said to act as if it were a real fire!' she shouted back.

Thaddeus nodded approvingly. And clapped. The alarm was still shrieking through the hall.

'Yes, I did, girl . . . I'll see you on set. Adam, turn that damn fire alarm off and get that girl's details.'

She got through?! What the fuck? For turning on a real-life fire alarm?

'And Blondie?!' he hollered over the screeching bell. I stopped and looked at him. He was definitely looking at me. I pointed to myself and he grinned. 'Yeah, you, you're through too. Adam, get her details.'

The bell was still going when I gave Adam my phone number. He handed me a piece of paper. As I walked out reading it, two fire engines came screeching down the road and pulled up outside.

Congratulations!

Welcome to the Da Block family

We will be in touch in the next couple of days

Walking down the street past the other hopefuls still waiting in line, I didn't really feel in the mood for celebrating. The whole thing had felt really unprofessional. But maybe Hollywood was like that? How would I know?

I decided to hold fire – I smiled a bit at my own joke – on telling Mum and Dad, until I'd found out more.

When I got back to the shitty flat, the Portuguese girls were waiting on the sofa for me. Oh fuck . . . what was all this about?

'You haven't paid this month's rent,' Polly hissed at me. Shit. I hadn't.

'I'm getting it . . . I'll have it by the end of next week.'

'Nah . . .' Sue chimed in, 'by the end of *this* week.'

Fuck, it was Wednesday already. Mariah looked down at the floor, embarrassed. She was the one who had suggested I move in with them.

'You gotta job yet?' Sue spat the words and narrowed her eyes. Christ, an image flashed in – at that moment she looked just like Nagini in *Harry Potter*.

'Yes. I got signed up for a Universal Pictures blockbuster today, and you can kiss my arse when I'm walking on that red carpet for my premiere – you twat.'

'Hmm.' She grunted and switched on the telly. I went back into the box room. I couldn't take any more of listening to them slagging me off in Portuguese.

Later, I headed out and stopped at an internet café that was selling slices of cold pizza. I paid a quid for an hour on the computer and the first thing I googled was 'Thaddeus Toogood'.

The first result that came up was a shop called 'Toogoodtobetrue Thaddeus Bear Store' in Tooting.

'Daisy owes rent on room' was an understatement. I needed this role so badly.

Then I googled 'Music producer of the Black-Eyed Peas' and the only names that came up were David Guetta and Frederic Riesterer. Which was odd, as they were both French – one was a DJ and the other a composer. Something didn't feel right. I had a really uneasy feeling about it, but I was determined to believe this was *it* – my big breakthrough. Surely I was due a bit of success now after all the shit I'd been through.

The next day I received a phone call from Adam.

'So, Thaddeus is inviting all the cast to his apartment this afternoon, to run you all through the script.'

'Great . . . That's so exciting.'

'Yeah . . .'

'It is Universal Pictures who are making it, right?'

'Yeah. Yeah.'

'As in *the* Universal Pictures.'

'Yeah . . . as in *the* Universal Pictures.'

'Wow!'

'I'll text you the address. See you later, Daisy, and congratulations.'

Thaddeus's apartment was in Acton. I'd have to walk for forty minutes to get there. I had no money left.

The front door needed a lick of paint and the neighbourhood seemed a bit run-down. Weird, but maybe it was nice on the inside. When I buzzed the intercom, no one answered. Eventually I was let in by Adam. The smell of weed hit me immediately.

Thaddeus and a couple of other guys were sitting on blue bean bags on the floor in front of a record player on a broken faux wood TV cabinet. At first, it was hard to see in the dim light, but gradually my eyes adjusted, and I started to see the empty beer and cider cans everywhere, the old pizza boxes covered in mould stacked in a corner – tidy smackheads, I thought – and chocolate foil wrappers. It was not a flat, or even an apartment. It was a fucking squat. This place was sapping my will to live.

On the record player, 'Five on It' by Luniz was playing.

Two girls in boob tubes stood in the corner of the room by a radiator, freezing in the draught coming through the window, their arms crossed. One of them was the Alesha Dixon girl. I smiled at her, but she didn't recognize me. Amy was sat on the windowsill next to the cactus, smoking a joint and nodding along to the music. Thaddeus clocked this.

'Hey!' he shouted at her.

She looked slightly more with it this time around.

'Ya know, I worked with these mothafuckas.'

'Who?' Amy croaked after taking a big drag.

'Luniz, bitch.'

'I love this song,' she exhaled.

'Dem mothafuckas was nothing till they met me.'

Silence. I thought it was probably a good opportunity to make him aware I was here.

'Who da fuck are you?'

Everyone laughed. How embarrassing.

'Daisy . . . from the audition yesterday?'

He pointed at me, a joint between two fingers, and squinted.

'Oh yeah . . . that's right, Blondie . . . Ya'll was good, Blondie.' I smiled weakly. 'Now ya'll here, I can tell ya'll about my movie, *Da Block*.'

He beckoned to the Alesha Dixon lookalike and the girl next to her.

'Come over here, bitches, sit down.'

Alesha sat awkwardly on the floor. She was wearing a very short skirt and trying to keep her legs together so no one would see her cooter.

'Blondie. Sit!'

What? Am I a dog now? But Jesus, I did sit down. Not even my mum could make me do that. Or Mrs Pasternak in Primary 4.

We all gathered around him like a fucked-up version of *Jackanory*.

'*Da Block* . . . OK. So, you bitches ever heard of *Romeo and Juliet*? Imagine that, but set in the Bronx.'

Oh Christ, how fucking unoriginal. Absolute fucking rip-off. Didn't he know about Leo DiCaprio's *Romeo and Juliet* then? This guy was full of shit. He wasn't a director. He was just a master bullshitter. All I could think about was how I was going to get the fuck out of there. Tactics, Daisy, tactics.

Adam got up from his bean bag and stepped over Alesha to head towards the hall.

'Romeo is a part of a gang, ya'll hearing me,' Thaddeus continued. Suddenly we heard Adam shout from the bathroom.

'Holy shit!'

Thaddeus stopped.

'What is it, brother?!'

'Come look at this!'

Thaddeus got up, muttering, 'mothafucker,' under his breath.

'Holy Jesus! Holy Mary Mother of God!' Thaddeus screamed.

There was silence when he stormed back into the sitting room.

'You bitches, on yer feet.' Everyone stayed sitting on the floor.

Thaddeus looked pissed off.

We all jumped up and he frog-marched us to the bathroom.

The smell of raw sewage hit my nostrils straight away. The hallway was soaked with piss and shit and bits of shredded toilet paper.

'One of you bitches just blocked my goddam macerator with this!' he yelled, pointing to the enormous turd poking out of the toilet basin. It was really enormous. And God knows I've done some in my time. The way it was balanced on the back of the toilet bowl made it look like it was trying to escape.

'Which one of you'se did it? Cos I can tell you now, as Jesus is my witness, the disrespect you've shown me . . . Hell's teeth! No! No! 'Fess up! Which one of you gone and pooped this out the pipe?!'

'I only just got here!' I pleaded.

'True . . . true . . .' He nodded at me. 'Yeah, Blondie's innocent.'

'Well, it wasn't me!' Amy protested.

Thaddeus walked up to her and eyeballed her like a drill sergeant.

'I don't trust *you*, Goth Girl . . . Yer all the same. Vegan and shit and all. Only some crazy mothafucking rabbit diet could have caused this.'

Adam pointed to Alesha, 'I saw her go to the toilet.'

Fuck me. This was turning into an Agatha Christie.

'I only went in to check my make-up.'

'Well, I'd be surprised if someone as pretty as y'all gone done a monstrosity like this, but stranger things have happened, ya'll know what I'm saying?'

Thaddeus started to pace around the sitting room.

'You mothafuckas wanna get into show business? Doing a crap the size of King Kong in *my* toilet?! That ain't show business!' As if doing a crap *anywhere* was showbusiness, I thought.

Alesha started towards the door.

'Nuh-uh!' He waggled a finger at her. 'Ain't none of you leaving till one ya'll 'fesses up. One of you is paying for a damn plumber, cos I'm not!'

This was surreal. I was being held against my will because someone wasn't confessing to doing a gigantic turd. This was bloody unbelievable – I *auditioned* to be here. I'm in some god-awful nightmare! This is fucking mental!

I thought about all those hopefuls queuing to audition just yesterday – if only they knew how lucky they were not to be trapped in this flat, ankle deep in shit and piss, literally and metaphorically. Gosh, such long words, Dais, maybe you did learn something in school.

'Ya'll gonna wait here.' Thaddeus grabbed his phone out of his jeans pocket and punched in a number.

'I'm calling my friend Patrick.'

'Patrick?' Adam asked, stepping over a bit of shitty toilet paper to the only corner of the hall that wasn't covered in sewage.

'Patrick's a mothafucking human lie detector, ex-army. He'll get to the bottom of this with his ways and means.' Part of me wanted to laugh at this, but I was too scared.

We waited in silence for Patrick to arrive. Well, *we* were silent. Thaddeus paced back and forth, ranting and raving as though he were dancing on hot coals. After an absolute age, we heard the entry phone and Thaddeus buzzed Patrick in.

Patrick was old, fat and bald and, at a rough guess, in his sixties. He was wearing Doc Martens and had a tattoo on his arm of the English flag, and another on his face. Accompanying Patrick was an Alsatian by the name of Genghis. Patrick was finding him a tad difficult to control. The dog wasn't aggressive, just an unruly pain in the arse. He almost dragged Patrick into the flat, straining on his collar. Genghis sniffed one bean bag then went over to the other, cocked his leg and did a piss. Oh well, what's one more piss? I thought as I sat watching the trickle of dog piss wind its way to meet the other trickle of seeping piss in the hallway.

When I look back on this now, I cannot believe we all

stayed. I have no idea why the fuck I stood there. Why we all stood there. Maybe we were all clinging on to some vague hope that Thaddeus really was making a blockbuster film for Universal, he was just an eccentric director. Tarantino is a fucking nutjob – maybe all Hollywood directors are? And just maybe the reason he stays in this shitty flat is by choice? When I think about it, the sad thing is, I was happy to stand there and get accused of doing a massive shit, because that was better than admitting that I had been well and truly conned. Thaddeus-Mothafucking-Toogood was a nobody, despite his pompous name. I had wasted my time at that audition. It had all been for nothing. And worse, much worse, I'd have to walk back to the Portuguese girls with my tail between my legs and admit that I still hadn't found a fucking job.

Thaddeus had a great deal of charisma, flair and confidence, and I'd never come across that before. Looking back now, maybe it was just the American accent, but more than anything . . . I stayed because he was selling me a dream.

Patrick stood by the door and took a good look at each one of us. For fuck's sake, what was this fucking screwball going to do? Interrogate us using water torture? Inject us with truth serum? Hook us up to some sort of Jeremy Kyle lie detector?

After about a minute of scrutinizing us, he pointed to the quiet girl standing next to the radiator.

'Her,' he said casually. 'She's got her hand over her mouth. Which means she did it but she doesn't want to admit to it.'

Thaddeus looked at her with utter disgust and muttered, 'Hmmm. I thought so.'

'That all you want, Thaddeus?'

'Yep . . . Thanks, Patrick.'

'No problem.'

And with that, Patrick walked out the door with Genghis and left.

Baffling.

What an anticlimax. That was it? That's how quickly he could tell? And she wasn't even protesting it; she just had her eyes on the floor. So, it was her? I really felt for the poor girl but still, on long weekends away with new boyfriends I could hold on to a shit for fucking days, just to save myself the embarrassment of blocking the toilet with a big turd. But, seriously, of all the times . . . of all the places . . . for her to just pull down her cacks and do a dump *here*, *now*. How long had she been saving that up for? And she didn't seem bothered about having left the evidence, she didn't even try to conceal it. If I do a fart at the in-laws, I can guarantee you I'll have all the bathroom taps running, the air freshener out and I'll be pulling my cheeks so far apart you won't hear a squeak. Good grief, what she did was just sloppy.

What upset me most was how disappointing it was

that I didn't get to see more of the colourful characters of Patrick and Genghis. They swanned in and out of my life like salmon sashimi on a Yo! Sushi conveyer belt. I really thought they would have more prominence in this anecdote, but alas no. Patrick walked in, Genghis pissed on a bean bag, Patrick pointed to the girl and they left.

In light of this new information, Thaddeus was pacing some more and shaking his head. I honestly think he thought he was in an episode of *Line of Duty*.

'Thaddeus-Mothafucking-Toogood offers you Hollywood, and you repay Thaddeus with this?!' He gestured down the hall to the shit.

'I suggest you all leave,' Thaddeus went on. 'I am really mad right now.' He opened the door and we all filed out into the hallway, except for Adam and Amy. She seemed quite at home on his windowsill, getting fucked on drugs . . . classic Amy. I was desperate to talk to Alesha and the silent shitter, but the girls were so quick out the door they almost left a smoke trail behind them, like in a Bugs Bunny cartoon. I made my way home, still trying to process it all.

The next day I woke up to a text message from Adam.

'Hi, Daisy. Thaddeus wants to do some screen tests today. Please come to 181 Timbrells Road, Acton for 11 a.m.'

It was a different address. A studio somewhere? In Acton? How likely was that? My gut was telling me not to go, especially after the massive dump shenanigans yesterday. But I fucking went anyway, terrified of missing out on what could possibly be my big break.

The address brought me to a barber shop on Acton High Street. An A4 piece of paper was tacked to the door. It read, 'Closed for filming'. Thaddeus was sitting in a barber's chair. Thaddeus and the barber glanced at me as I walked in, then Thaddeus completely fucking blanked me and continued to hold court.

'I knew Puff Daddy when he was Biggie's mothafucking bitch.'

He glanced into the mirror like David Brent, desperate to get the attention of Alesha and, rather surprisingly, the girl who had blocked the toilet with her huge dump. They were sitting on the sofa behind him. I couldn't believe the 'Silent Shitter' had turned up. How did she have the audacity? Was I the only one who remembered the trauma of yesterday's events?

'Puff Daddy ain't shit . . . Remember that shooting in the club with J.Lo? I was there! Mothafucka so scared of getting into shit. Fucking pussy tried to make me hold his gun,' Thaddeus continued as the barber applied shaving foam.

Then a bloke who looked like Ian Beale emerged from the back room holding two giant camera cases. He knelt down on the floor and started screwing a boom mic together. This was the first time since the audition that anything had felt legit. Meanwhile a bald bloke was using gaffer tape and black card to block out the light from the shopfront window.

'Ladies. If you want to get ready for the screen test, the bathroom is through there.' He pointed to the coloured plastic strips hanging in the doorway.

Alesha stood up and started walking. Silent Shitter and I followed her to a dingy back toilet. The cubicle was covered in chipped yellow tiles . . . cracked and brown-stained with piss. The toilet bowl was so unclean it looked like what I imagine a wormhole in the universe would look like.

No sooner had the door swung shut on the three of us than Alesha blurted out, 'I think it's a porno . . .'

'What the fuck?'

'Look, I'm not one hundred per cent, but Amy turned up before you did and she did a runner. She overheard them earlier talking about a sex scene, so she told them she needed to pop to the shop to get a bottle of water and hasn't come back. I don't want to stay long enough to find out.'

Alesha climbed on top of the white plastic toilet seat to get a better look at the window.

'What are you doing?!'

She didn't answer.

'You weren't seriously thinking of getting out of that window, were you? You couldn't get a fucking Dachshund's bollocks through there! Let's all just say we need to go to the shop . . . Tampons . . . let's say we need fucking tampons . . . no bloke can argue with that.' Panic was coursing through my body and I was practically shouting.

'Blondie!' Thaddeus's voice boomed through the MDF door and we all froze. The bathroom door was ripped open and a clean-shaven Thaddeus stood in the doorway. He eyeballed all three of us.

'None of you mothafuckers blocked the damn toilet again?'

We shook our heads.

'Good. Blondie, you're up . . .'

He turned on a sixpence and we slowly followed him back into the darkened barber's shop. I could just about make out the Ian Beale lookalike holding a camera on his shoulder. Close by him there was a large bright spotlight balanced on a stepladder entangled with extension plugs facing the barber-shop mirrors. The boom operator was leaning on his boom mic like it was a solid object, his face lit by his phone.

'Stand on the X!' Thaddeus's voice boomed from behind the camera like the mighty Oz.

I looked at the floor and walked slowly over to the wonky gaffer-taped X. Oh fuck . . . was this a porno? What had I got myself into now? I'm not going to have to suck anyone's cock, am I? Panicking now . . . because I know myself well enough to realize I'll probably end up doing it out of sheer politeness. I looked into the black void, desperately seeking Alesha and the Silent Shitter. I saw a slither of light appear behind the giant silhouette of Thaddeus. It was the door opening. Alesha and Silent Shitter were doing a fucking runner without me. Fuck, fuck, oh God. I'm going to get fucking gangbanged . . . this is worse than the fucking stripper audition. Thaddeus seemed unconcerned – which was more than a little strange, I thought.

'OK, Blondie . . . The part you're gonna play is a crack addict called Crystal, cos your mumma named you after meth. Look into the camera and try and sell me some drugs . . .'

I squinted at the spotlight . . . and raised my hand like I was in Year Five at fucking primary school.

'Sorry. Can I just ask a quick question? Please.'

'What the fuck is it?! I gave you the mothafucking character bio. Don't tell me you're fucking method . . .'

'No . . . It's not that, it's just, well, ummm . . . I'm not going to have to suck anyone off, am I?'

Silence.

'What da fuck you talking 'bout, Blondie?! Why da holy hell do you wanna be sucking someone off?! I know there's method . . . but bitch, you taking it to another level.'

'So . . . It's not a porno . . . ?'

'Hell no!'

More silence . . . bar a few sniggers from the camera man and the boom operator. Oh God, I wanted to die . . . *again*. I'm the cat with nine lives . . . with each death more humiliating than the last.

'It's just . . . um . . . one of the girls said . . . that you asked Amy to do a sex scene.'

'A sax scene. Bitch told me she could play the motha-fucking saxophone, but she went to the store to get some H2O and never came back, so I'm assuming she's a lying ho and does not play the fucking sax. What da fuck wrong with your English, huh? You all is twisted as fuck!'

'Sorry . . . about that. Misunderstanding on my part . . . um . . . do you still want me to do the crackhead thing . . . for the camera?'

'Whatever.'

I took a deep breath in. This would have to be the performance of a lifetime to make up for accusing Thad-deus of making a porno film. I got into character . . . took a deep breath . . .

'Do you want some drugs? I've got meth, crack . . . more meth –'

Thaddeus interrupted.

'That's enough! We'll be in touch.'

I stood in embarrassment and a horrible memory rose to the surface. The utter mortification I felt when I pissed on the gym mat in PE doing squats. On a scale of ten, that was about a six or a seven, but this – this flew right off it.

'You can go now,' Thaddeus barked.

I walked through the darkness to where I thought the door was. I didn't see the stepladder in the murky light and tripped over it, falling on to the door and sliding down to the floor.

'Jesus Christ, girl! Don't ruin my set!'

I found the doorknob and stumbled out into the bright daylight, blinking madly and feeling as though I had been in the darkness for ever. I walked as quickly as I could to the nearest safe space I could find and cried. Well, howled, really. Once I had calmed down a little, I realized something. I had to admit defeat now. I pulled my mobile phone out of my pocket and called the house phone. Dad picked up.

'Hello?'

'Dad. Dad,' I sobbed. 'I want to come home.'

# CHAPTER 13
## RADA

I know, I know what you are thinking. This chapter is called RADA and this is supposed to be the point where all my dreams come true and I get my *big* break. RADA, dahling . . . the place young wannabes put up with *anything* in the hope of making it.

And I had been trying to get to RADA for an absolute age . . .

I cringe when I think about this now, but I was so desperate to be discovered that not long after I arrived home from Shepherd's Bush I pulled myself together and created my own stand-up character. Open-mic comedy nights happened all over the Cotswolds: 'I'll get scouted that way!'

Er . . . no . . .

To get scouted, Dais, you need to be *funny*. My character, 'Tracey', wasn't. She was a straight rip-off of the hilarious flight attendant Pam Ann created by Caroline Reid. Tracey did jokes about bingo wings and run-ins with frequent flyers with bad altitude. It was base. It was crap. I played hotels and working men's clubs to the sound of old men clicking pool balls across green baize. I died a thousand deaths.

One gig I fixed up was in the back of a pub in Cheltenham. Mum got over-excited and invited our new neighbours. The warm-up guy introduced me. I rocked up on stage. I froze and got a few lines out. I wasn't booed. I wasn't even heckled. But tumbleweed rolled slowly through the double doors and across the room. Every time I looked to Mum for reassurance I saw her heart quietly breaking. She was clearly embarrassed and the new neighbours avoided us after that.

Weirdly, it taught me a lesson. If I was unsure of my routine, the audience would be unsure too. If I wasn't confident, the audience would never trust me enough to laugh with me.

On stage, a little voice in one ear became a fuck-off massive gremlin.

'You don't know what the fuck you're doing, do you, Daisy May Cooper? What on earth is going on with your hands? Do you actually know what your next line is? Well . . . do you?'

This gremlin would come back to haunt me at RADA.

In the other ear, I could hear Dad's voice.

'You're on stage. You're doing it. It's great. It's better than not doing it. Keep going, Dais. Keep going!' Dad was so ridiculously encouraging – to the point of being in denial. He never once told me I was crap. And Tracey the rip-off flight attendant was *really* crap.

In fact, Dad always reminded me of the father of the serial killer Jeffrey Dahmer. I saw him being interviewed once. Lionel Dahmer's son butchered seventeen people, yet he was relentlessly upbeat about Jeffrey as a kid.

'Was there any inkling your son was a mass murderer?'

'Bit shy, maybe. But he was normal.'

'What about the roadkill he dissected? The animal bones in buckets?'

'Oh, that was just Jeffrey. He had such a keen interest in science. I thought maybe he'd make a great surgeon . . .'

Dad's encouragement did keep me applying for RADA, though. That year I applied again, and I got so close. Reaching the third round of auditions was so gruelling. Four thousand applicants battling it out for twenty-eight places. I failed. Again.

Fuck.

'OK, so you're going to pick yourself up and reapply . . .'

Dad's voice, again.

Could I? I gave it one last shot. In 2006, I got through to the third round for a second time. A monologue from the intense psychological drama *Iron* got me a place in the fourth and final round. I played the part of a female murderer much like I play the character Kerry Mucklowe I'd create for *This Country* ten years later.

April 30th, 2007

Dear Daisy,

I am very pleased to confirm my verbal offer of a place on the Three-Year Acting Degree Course beginning on Monday September 24th, 2007.

The offer is based on your eligibility as a Home Student to receive an award through the Conservatoire for Dance and Drama from the Higher Education Funding Council for your annual fee.

You will be required to pay the student mandatory fee contribution which, in the 2007/8 academic year, is set at £3070 and to cover your term time living costs in London. You are eligible to apply to your LEA for means tested assistance towards the payment of the mandatory student contribution and for a student loan to contribute to your term time living costs. Bearing in mind London costs, it is realistic to assume that these will be a minimum of £9500 per year depending on where you live, with an additional £200 -£400 required in the third year to cover entry into Spotlight and photographs and general correspondence to agents and casting directors.

Patricia Myers, the Registrar, will contact you to discuss your funding position. In the meantime, please do not hesitate to telephone me if there is anything that you wish to discuss.

Congratulations!

Yours sincerely

Nicholas Barter
Principal

At last I could stop stalking RADA.

Fuck. Getting closer was more stomach-churning than failing. Maybe I *could* do it? Maybe I wasn't an abysmal excuse for a human being after all?

On the day, Mum rang me to tell me the principal of RADA had called. I was at another crap boyfriend's house. A tingle of excitement spread up from my toes. I screamed down the phone. This was it! This was success! I'd skip in, crack off an acting degree. Agents would be *begging* me to be on their books. The Coen Brothers wouldn't leave me alone, belling me up for their next hit film. Yes! Yes! Yes!

I would need a student loan to get me through, but that was no biggie. I'd be earning that back in spades when the industry knew what I had to offer.

Mum rang the administrator. Were there halls of residence I could stay in? Yes! Bonham Carter House, right next door, but I'd have to find accommodation for the first week to cover my induction. I scoured the internet. Hotels were so expensive in London. Eventually, I found one I could just about stretch to. Marble Arch. £400 for five nights. Could I afford it? Not. At. All. I shut my eyes, clicked and booked.

May as well limber up for the high life. And the room looked *amazing*. It boasted a skyline view over London. Maybe I could sneak in a bottle of Chardonnay from Tesco and sip it on the balcony? Meg Ryan in *Sleepless in Seattle* – eat your heart out.

2 Friday 123-243

08 Daisy gets digs by RADA.

09

10

11

12

13

14

15

16

17

When I got there, the staff were sooooo friendly. Unbelievably helpful. And the room? OMG! The king-sized bed was piled high with fluffy cushions. A TV rose up automatically from the end of the bed. Oh . . . and round the corner there was a living room! Hadn't expected that! A leather sofa hugged one wall and framed a lavish dining table. The en suite bathroom was head to toe in marble, and on the balcony I had my very own jacuzzi, complete with water fountain. Just looking at it made me desperate for a piss.

I called Mum and Dad.

'How's your first night, love? Exciting, huh?'

'It's *amazing*, Dad. Everything I've ever wanted.'

'So pleased for you, honey. It's the start of something big.'

'I hope so, Dad!'

'So proud of you, Dais!'

Five nights flew by. Admittedly, the induction at RADA was a bit boring: forms to fill out and health-and-safety bollocks. Every evening, I pirouetted up Oxford Street like I was dancing on air. I knew I had to make the most of this before halls!

The great thing was, I didn't even have to sneak wine into my hotel room. Literally, I got a call from reception on the hour to ask if I needed anything. Then, a butler appeared to deliver my order and check back to see that everything was to my satisfaction.

Honestly, I was pretty sad to leave.

'Miss Cooper. I hope you enjoyed your stay.'

'Loved it so much. Thank you. I'll definitely be coming back.' I smiled dreamily at the concierge.

'Oh, that's great to hear. The excess on your bill is £3,000. How would you like to pay?'

'Sorry . . . what?'

'Three thousand pounds. We accept all major credit cards.' He slipped across a leather wallet so I could discreetly pop a card into it.

'Are you fucking kidding me?' I barked. His lips pursed disapprovingly.

'The room is £400 for five nights! Which I've *already paid*!'

'No, Miss Cooper . . . £400 is the deposit . . .'

I tittered nervously – moments before my whole body shut down. My face drained of all colour, like a swamp.

'Can I use the phone, please?'

My financial crisis was deep. Deeper than if the Great Depression and the global financial crash had spawned a lovechild. Mum was still trying to get me some help from the college two weeks later:

'I'm terribly sorry. My daughter's student loan got spunked on a penthouse suite overlooking Hyde Park.' Explain that one . . .

What made things more disastrous was that Dad had been made redundant from his salesman's job and he'd

Thursday, June 21, 2007    www.wiltsglosstandard.co.uk

# Dream now a drama

by
**Emma Tilley**
Cirencester

A CIRENCESTER student has realised her lifelong dream of earning a place at the prestigious Royal Academy of Dramatic Art (Rada).

Daisy-May Cooper, 20, of Chesterton Lane, will be following in the footsteps of the most celebrated actors in the world who trained at Rada including Joan Collins, Oscar-winning MP Glenda Jackson, Sir Anthony Hopkins, Kenneth Branagh and Rada president Lord Attenborough.

Daisy-May, who was one of 34 people out of over 2,000 to be offered a place, said: 'Ever since I was little I wanted to be an actor and I have been auditioning for Rada for a few years now.'

Daisy-May has been involved in the theatre since the age of 10 and even performed a Shakespeare piece in front of thousands at the Cheltenham Festival.

The talented actress has been involved with stand-up comedy in the last few months and has performed gigs at the Laughing Horse

in Wimbledon and Monkey Business in Camden Town, London.

After her time at Rada she hopes to go into either the theatre or comedy.

She said: 'The auditions were really tough and there were four stages to get through. I even changed my audition piece at the last minute because I thought it was better than my original idea and they told me it was fantastic.'

• Daisy-May is now on a fundraising mission to pay for her expensive living costs while she is in London.

Registrar at Rada Patricia Myers said: 'I urge anyone who is in a position to offer financial assistance to this talented local young woman to do so in the knowledge that they are investing in the theatre of the future.'

Any individual or business able to help Daisy-May can contact her on 01285 640139.

Drama student Daisy-May Cooper wgrp0678h07

Clothes show is just the fashion for shopy~

been trying to find another. Money was so tight for them. I felt stupid and guilty. How could you do this, Daisy? How could you? I wanted to die.

In a bold – possibly fraudulent – move, I rang the local newspaper and put out an appeal for funds. My picture appeared under the headline DREAM NOW A DRAMA. But no one wanted to see homegrown talent succeed *that* much, it seemed.

I remember one comment that appeared under the story in particular. Farmer_Trev_879 had written: 'She'll never be an actress with a nose like that.'

In the end, RADA agreed to a loan. Very fucking annoyingly, the hotel wouldn't budge an inch, even though I argued, quite convincingly I thought, that the £400 had appeared in large letters on the website and my eye had naturally been drawn to it.

From the off, the registrar at RADA hated me. She'd stuck thank-you cards of her grinning wildly with alumni like Ralph Fiennes all over her office. In my heart, I knew I would never be on one of those cards. She was an absolute cock.

For the first year, I had to report in to her each day with a full economic forecast: what I'd spent, what I was spending. Later on, she also insisted on weighing me on a set of scales. Every. Single. Morning. Hard to believe, but apparently I was thin enough to make her suspect I was anorexic. I'm convinced it was to show me who was boss.

'The only person I'm thanking when I get my fucking BAFTA is myself,' I thought, whenever I trudged from her office.

In the first week we had an introductory talk from the school principal. I listened to very little because I was hypnotized by his hairdo – a cross between the Bride of Frankenstein and a feather duster. When he walked in I felt the urge to shout out, 'Stretch your neck up a bit, there's a cobweb that needs cleaning!'

'We're going to dismember you, pull you apart limb by limb, and then piece you back together again.' I kid you not. Those were his first words. Many of us were taken apart but never put back together again. Ask my therapist.

I was reminded of the dance teacher Lydia Grant in the intro of the 1980s cult classic *Fame*: 'You got big dreams? You want fame? Well, fame costs. And right here's where you start paying!' But that was fiction! This was real life! *My* life!

Before I went to RADA, I wasn't even aware of the smorgasbord of ways you could be told how utterly shit you were. Fatberg-in-a-fucking-sewer shit. God . . . I was so naive! By the end of the first week, my life-long dream was in tatters. There was something seriously wrong.

Part of the problem was that I could never take anything seriously. Lots of my contemporaries wanted to suffer for their art. I wanted to exert as little effort as was humanly possible – it was my survival mechanism kicking in . . .

We spent time at London Zoo. Yes, that's right, London fucking Zoo. On an acting course! We had to choose one animal, reptile or insect to study. The next time we got to class we would arrive in character.

Forty grand for this?

I don't know why, but I found myself instinctively drawn to the warthog enclosure. I read the information card:

The warthog spends the majority of its time grazing and wallowing in mud to relieve itself from the constant irritation of insects. Often birds will help it by sitting on its back and feeding off it.

Not only does a warthog get to sit on its arse all day, it doesn't even have to wash itself. I noted down a few eye movements, some wags of the tail. Occasionally, I'd have to swat something, but it was minimal.

When we got back to class it was toe-curling to see who was desperate to impress. I can't remember this budding starlet's name, so I'll call her Mimi. She reminded me of a unicorn on popping candy.

'I'm going to be a dragonfly!' she fizzed.

Surely, anyone with half a brain would have worked out that four hours of rapid wing movement could have you hospitalized?

Don't mind me, I'll just be on my arse. Maybe rolling around in some mud for a while, swatting the odd dragonfly . . .

Occasionally, Mimi would whizz past, panting uncontrollably . . .

'Wonderful, Mimi, you're fluttering with such *joie de vivre*,' the tutor called out.

'Tha— tha–nk . . . you.' As I had predicted, within half an hour Mimi was doubled over and heaving in a corner.

For the end-of-module test, the tutor chose a creature on our behalf. We had to go away, study it and then perform it.

'Daisy, I've been thinking. You'd make a perfect flamingo!'

'A fucking flamingo?' Nothing like drawing attention to my big nose! I would like to add that the same tutor also told me I had the body shape of a Dorito.

Cut to three hours of me standing on one leg and craning my neck up and down while a kangaroo hopped around me shouting *boing!* and a gecko lay motionless against a wall, bar a few blinks and the occasional head jerk.

I don't know about any other actors, but I have never since had to use *anything* I learned in animal class in any professional acting job. Ever.

Sometimes I wondered what the tutors actually got paid for. One beardy old thespian who turned up with his dinner still stuck to his jumper mainly said, 'Do it better.' Except I never remember him saying that to the boys:

'Oh Tom, daaaahling. That was wonderful. Wonderful! The way you brought Lysander to life was simply sensational . . .'

'And Daisy . . . Daisy, Daisy, Daisy. Your Hermia was wooden and rather frumpy. Do it better.'

He waved his hand dismissively, like he was batting away a fly.

The lessons on the Stanislavski method were appalling. Stanislavski was a Russian dude who taught actors to recall emotions from their own lives and channel them to make a role believable. The problem for me was that

# RADA

## STYLE/ COMEDY PROJECT – TERM 6

**PRODUCTION:** The Recruiting Officer     **DIRECTOR:** ▮▮▮▮▮▮▮

STUDENT: Daisy-May Cooper

1. Professionalism:
    Please comment on the student's professionalism relating to:
    - Attendance and punctuality
    - Preparation for rehearsals
    - Line learning
    - Relationship to other actors

**Directors Comments:** You lost three days of rehearsal for unavoidable reasons, but were generally punctual and ready to work. We discussed your learning lines as early as possible in the process, but you were still on the book at slightly too late a stage. You approached your work intelligently and took notes well. Your relationship with your fellow actors was open and engaged and you took a full and active part, bringing sound instincts and excellent suggestions into play.

2. Skill development:
    In relation to the requirement of the production, please comment on the actor's skill development
    - Vocal technique – audibility, transformation and listening skills
    - Movement technique – flexibility, spatial awareness and transformation
    - Textual skills relating to character as written and rhythm and pace of the whole text
    - Imaginative process in personal character development and ensemble work.

**Directors Comments:** You developed two distinct and coherent characters both of which you inhabited fully and showed yourself to be an actor with a strong and delightful flair for comedy (Costar Pearmain in particular was a joy to witness.) This deserves to be supported by greater vocal clarity and flexibilty and subtlety.  Your spatial awareness on stage was excellent and you were able to create a sense of place on a bare stage and you listened well and showed a good sense of rhythm and pace.  I felt you were fully engaged imaginatively in this project and only wish there had been more time to work with you on the particular demands of this text. You were a strong presence in the rehearsal room, were missed when absent, and were a valuable member of the ensemble

Signed by: ▮▮▮▮▮▮▮                                              Date:27.05.09

Year 2 Style/Comedy Summer 2009

Stanislavski was born in Moscow in 1863. He had a lot of bad shit to draw on – revolution, war, famine, death . . . nicely topped off by Stalin – a fucking dictator!

But at RADA they *loved* the Stanislavski method. One tyrannical tutor basked in the twisted cruelness of it all.

'Daisy . . . what's your worst childhood memory?'

'Erm . . . probably my Auntie Alison crashing her car when I was around six and my family having to switch her life support off?'

'Not good enough . . . Think of something worse . . .'

She pointed menacingly at the next person.

'And you . . . what's your's?'

'Erm . . .'

'Come on. There must be something.'

'The . . . the . . . the . . . abortion I had at fifteen . . .'

Silence.

'Great!' The teacher clapped her hands triumphantly.

'I want you right back in that place. Fifteen years old and in that clinic having that abortion! *Be* the character, don't *play* the character!'

I think some of the other students loved it but, honestly, it broke me. I could never pull myself back together after those classes. I felt as if all the stuffing had been ripped out of me. I'd never be whole again.

Maybe I'd always just wanted to make people laugh? At home, I was forever trying to cheer Mum up with silly jokes. At school, I'd been the class clown. The feeling of

# ROYAL ACADEMY of DRAMATIC ART.

Year 1 Speech and Verse. Summer 2008 (11 6 08)

DAISY MARY COOPER.

You started with your Reading. I am sure that you like to read , possibly you enjoy it more when you do not read aloud. For it took you a while to find the style of the writer vocally. In a way, you were holding the text inwardly. You were tense. You held your jaw tightly. You monitored your expression from the neck. You lost breath in a kind of tension release. Then , whilst this inner outer battle took place, you gave yourself very little room, mentally as well as physically.

"Even over The Flatland" came next. You seemed to lose the concentration on your subject. Your attention seemed to be taken up with speaking the poem rather than in giving the poem to your listeners. Imagery was not well suggested always. You almost spoke prose at times and ,at other times, a poetic tone floated over over your phrases .

Then you came to your scene from Henry VI part I. This seemed much more rehearsed. You seemed ready to speak for your character, and your diction was more imaginatively suited to your characterization. But your liking to take refuge into consideration led you to include an overlay of commentary.
Analysis, appreciation, commentary or consideration are suitable for armchair study. In performance, it is the RESULT of these that you play, that you bring to artistic life. At present you seem a bit stranded between the two.

bringing people together with laughter and navigating that fine line between tragedy and hysteria had always appealed to me.

At RADA, I couldn't even play Lady Macbeth without an audience sniggering. Unknowingly, my face would contort like Mr Bean's. Tutors called me Plasticine Face. Yet, in my head, I was a serious actress. I pictured myself sweeping up the stairs to receive my Oscar. I was Charlize Theron in *Monster* or Meryl Streep in *Sophie's Choice*: all the actresses whose performances I pored over, studying them word for word. But when it came to it, people just laughed.

I had trouble crying when I was acting too. It just didn't happen. Others could turn on the waterworks in a heartbeat. Literally, they just had to remember the time their mum refused them a Drumstick lolly aged six and their eyes moistened.

I tried everything. Every childhood indignity. Every school humiliation. Every crap boyfriend I'd ever shagged and who'd dumped me. Nada.

And that gremlin visited me again and again:

You don't know what the fuck you're doing, do you, Daisy May Cooper? What on earth is going on with your hands? Do you actually know what your next line is? Well . . . do you?

It got so bad that I started dabbing Olbas oil under my eyes. Then I started smearing it. Momentarily, my Lady

1 Monday
336-30

08 Dasy home weekend

09 — very down after Macbeth

10 Peformance.

worry weekend coming!

11 Finished Ballet Both Friday

12 for Manchester - I went

13 & there are no problems

14

TO DO                    Phone Shane

15 Laundry

Bathroom

16

17

December MTWTFSS MTWTFSS MTWTFSS MTWTFSS MTWTFSS
2008      1 2 3 4 5 6 7   8 9 10 11 12 13 14   15 16 17 18 19 20 21   22 23 24 25 26 27 28   29 30 31

12 DEC

Macbeth took a turn for the better. I cried. I wailed. I stumbled off to the side ravaged by guilt over the death of Duncan. The Olbas oil had found its way into my eyeball and it was stinging like buggery.

'Daisy! Outstanding! You're really starting to own the part!' the tutor trilled.

She was such an arsehole.

Then, not long into the course, we were asked to write and rehearse a monologue. Its strength and power had to come from within. We were to dig deep and draw on emotional trauma: love, betrayal, anger, joy, death.

For a whole week I put off writing mine. Every time I sat in front of my laptop I became paralysed by a grinding, stultifying writer's block.

'I can't do this, Dad.'

I rang home so many times to announce I was giving the whole thing up.

'Dais. Stick at it, love. You're amazing . . .'

Dad did that Lionel Dahmer thing again. He told me how much he regretted being made redundant from a job he didn't even like. How could I give up on the one thing I'd always wanted?

The day of the monologue drew closer. I still hadn't written a single word.

Every time I stumbled into the rehearsal room, Mimi was on her knees, sobbing, wringing her hands and grabbing at her chest: 'Why? Why? Oh God. Why?'

**2** Tuesday 337-29

Dee said that Daisy
was a great Lady
         Macbeth
so she few words
         better

mmmm?
Struggling with her
fight tor -
         very
         difficult

---

Royal Academy of Dramatic Art

## SHAKESPEARE PROJECT

### TERM 4 – AUTUMN TERM 2008

**PRODUCTION:** MACBETH          **DIRECTOR:**

**STUDENT NAME:** Daisy May Cooper

It is useful for the students to be given written feedback on this production from the director. We would therefore be grateful if you could complete the comment section over the page. The comments should incorporate both the rehearsal process and the performance process, and should contain constructive comments to move the student forward in their training.

**These comments will be photocopied, and a copy given to the student.**

1. **Professionalism:**
    Please comment on the student's professionalism relating to:
      • Attendance and punctuality, Preparation for rehearsals
      • Line learning, Relationship to other actors

**Directors Comments:**

Daisy was reliable, punctual and generally well prepared. Line learning was initially a challenge, however, but she met deadlines appropriately. She can work for detailed accuracy, however, for both her own benefit and her scene partners.

2. **Skill development:**
In relation to the requirement of the production, please comment on the actor's skill development
  • Vocal technique – audibility, transformation and listening skills
  • Movement technique – flexibility, spatial awareness and transformation
  • Textual skills relating to character as written and rhythm and pace of the whole text
  • Imaginative process in personal character development and ensemble work.

**Directors Comments:**

Daisy's strengths are her imagination and her emotional availability, but she can develop greater confidence in her relationship to language. She can generate great intensity, but if this is not rooted in her
3. **Any Other Comments:** central core then body and voice become strained. This led at times to either a screechy quality for Lady Macbeth or a dropping off of vocal energy. In rehearsal, Daisy was able to move to a place of greater strength and status but this slipped back a bit in performance.

Bit much, I thought. But the same question had crossed my mind.

I sat back at my screen. Still nothing.

I panicked. Then I logged on to the internet. There was so much to distract me! YouTube was brand new and loads of videos were 'going viral'. The one with the monkey doing black-belt karate was hilarious! And Charlie the unicorn on a quest to find candy mountain made me piss myself. Especially the part where he got a kidney stolen after being knocked out in a cave.

I returned to my monologue. Nothing.

I called up the new Leona Lewis video. If anyone could reach the depths of despair, it was Leona. I stood in front of my mirror belting out 'A Moment Like This' into my curling tongs. Nothing.

Fuck. Fuck. Fuck.

Every time I thought about the worst things that had happened in my life, I just couldn't go there. Maybe I could write a monologue about my Pez dispenser getting jammed that time? I doubted it was what my tutor was angling for. It *was* fucking infuriating, though!

Eventually, the day arrived. Other classmates left no stone unturned. There were tears, there was joy, there was laughter. They rode that emotional rollercoaster until the monorail ran out.

My monologue was short and sweet.

I took a deep breath and raised my eyes skyward. I

placed my hand on my heart. I held the room in the palm of my hand as I spoke about how I couldn't live a lie any longer. I had to face the truth. I clasped my chest when I spoke about a relationship that had ended. But instead of looking back to heartache, I treasured the memories.

It was so short, you could have confused it for a poem.

I lowered myself into my seat. I sensed a slight bewilderment on the faces of several students, but no one said a word. Solemnly, I bowed my head. I silently hoped to God that none of them owned Steps' second album, *Steptacular*, or could remember any of the lyrics to their 1999 hit single 'After the Love Has Gone'.

'Thank you, Daisy. A little short, but that was wonderful and moving.' It must have been the only time that tutor ever praised me.

What a fucking shitshow, I thought.

A lot of bollocks got bandied around at RADA. It would be far too depressing for me to share all the negative comments they made to me, but these are the highlights:

'I don't know why you're here. You have no talent.'

In second place: 'You're one of these actresses that's here by fluke, aren't you?'

And trailing a close third was the withering: 'Have you considered teaching, Daisy?'

I tried not to listen to it and took to doodling all over

my scripts. The amount of cock and balls I doodled over my feedback notes would have made the painter Hieronymus Bosch jealous.

As it turned out, Charlie was having an equally hard time. He'd got into Exeter uni and had gone off to study sports science. No one knew why. He absolutely hated sport. He got past two years of his degree and dropped out, having spent all his student loan on drinks at a dodgy nightclub. He'd been working shifts in Pizza Hut back in Cirencester.

'My life is just as crap right now, Charlie. Come to London,' I suggested.

Secretly, I was quite pleased that Charlie had turned out to be a failure, as it took the heat off me for a while.

'Can I?' Charlie sounded quite pathetic.

He didn't want to go home. Mum and Dad had been struggling to pay their mortgage. With hardly any money coming in, they were talking about selling the house.

'You can sleep on my floor . . .'

There were shower cubicles bigger than my room in halls.

'Oh, mate, that's amazing.'

Charlie didn't think it was so amazing when he was forced to loiter around the shared kitchen while I had sex with whichever random I brought home.

Charlie stayed on my floor for a whole year. When I invited him to my place, I just meant he could sleep on

AND GEOFF'S PLAY — LOOKING FORWARD
TO SEEING IT.

AGAIN — YOU WERE <u>WONDERFUL</u>,

WITH KINDEST REGARDS,

Vivian    (MUNN —
        RADA TEACHER,
        DIRECTOR).

---

30.4.2010

DEAR DAISY-MAY —

   I FELT COMPELLED TO WRITE
TO YOU TO CONGRATULATE YOU
AGAIN ON YOUR PERFORMANCE AS
FAYE IN 'IRON'. IT WAS SO TRUE
AND GREAT THEATRE WHICH HIT
YOU IN THE PIT OF THE STOMACH.

   NO-ONE CAN TAKE THAT AWAY
FROM YOU — WHAT YOU OFFERED WAS
VERY SPECIAL AND IN THE THEATRE
IT SHOULD BE STANDARD, BUT BELIEVE
ME IT IS VERY RARELY SEEN AND
YOU PRODUCED IT — I WAS INSPIRED
BY YOUR WORK AND ENCOURAGED.

   GOOD LUCK WITH THE AGENTS

King's College London

Daisy Cooper

having completed the approved programme of study and satisfied the
examiners has this day been admitted to the Kings College award
(validated for the Royal Academy of Dramatic Art) of

Bachelor of Arts

*in*

Acting

WITH HONOURS

1 August 2010

Chairman of Council

Richard H. Trainor

Principal

· *King's College London is a constituent college of the University of London* ·

April 29, 2010


Dear Daisy,

I came to see The Tree and thought your performance was
outstanding.

Please contact me on                    and we can arrange for you
to come into the office for a meeting if that suits you.


Signed
7th May
2010


Pat tweetered to
smear Daisy with
agents.

my floor for a weekend, maybe a week, tops, but honestly, without him I would have lost my mind. He is the only person who kept me sane throughout my whole time at RADA.

I'd finally made it through the degree I'd tried so hard to get a place on. Prestigious RADA had been calling out to me for years, and yet when I made it there it didn't seem to count for much at all. I expected my big break to come and, instead, precisely zero agents banged down my door after I graduated, although I did find one in the end. The Coen brothers never called. Charlie and I moved back to Cirencester, where Mum and Dad had moved into a rental property after having to sell their house. Charlie and I shared a room. Dad was unemployed. Again.

# CHAPTER 14
# THE WILDERNESS

Every day is the same. I wake up to the sun illuminating the curtain. The birds begin their dawn chorus and my heart sinks. Another day. Where the fuck are we going to get some money from?

I'd run out of baccy. I needed baccy. I could make a small pouch of Amber Leaf last a full two weeks.

I had a ramekin full of fag butts outside the back door; no filters, because they cost too much, just roach. I'd carefully unpeel the Rizlas and put the second-hand tobacco back into the pouch. It was usually damp from being left outside. Mum wouldn't let me keep it inside the house because it stank. My fingers stank bad enough, she said. I felt like Fagin from *Oliver Twist* – all I needed was the fingerless gloves.

I smoke my first rollie of the morning. It's disgusting, but it hits the spot.

The last of this recycled baccy would see me through the rest of the day, but then I'd be well and truly fucked. I'd have to tell Mum, Dad and Charlie that I needed to take money out of the food budget, and I knew they'd hit the roof, because there was no budget. There was nothing.

Then a thought comes to me: Auntie Jane got me that chain for my eighteenth birthday. I'd pawned the silver cross for seven quid a couple of weeks ago, but did I pawn the chain? I don't think I bothered. It was so thin and probably only weighed a few grams. It would have been humiliating taking that in, but the standards I had a week ago were different from the ones I had today: my dignity was slipping further away every day, like the sand in an hour-glass.

Meticulously, I go through the drawer, but all of the treasure that was once in there was taken long ago. It was like being a burglar in your own house – rifling through the drawers for spare change, robbing yourself over and over again. A quid? How had I overlooked that? Of course. It's a fucking euro, that's why. I shove it back in there, so I can find it again in another couple of weeks when I'm desperate and make the same mistake.

Charlie comes into the bedroom, fresh from the bath, and shakes a couple of cans of deodorant on the windowsill to see which one is less empty.

'What are you looking for?'

'Do you remember that silver chain I had with the cross?'

'No. Why? Do you think it's in there?'

He kneels down next to me to help me look. I can see

he's already spending the chain's worth on deodorant. I stop him.

'I've run out of baccy.'

'Give up, then.'

'I can't.'

'So, you're gonna pawn it for baccy?'

I say nothing, but I can feel his eyes boring into the back of my head.

'You know Dad needs bus money for his interview tomorrow.'

'I haven't even found it yet.'

But he's right, as soon as I find it I'm pawning it for baccy.

'You're so fucking selfish!'

He storms out of the room.

Yes, I am fucking selfish. I never used to be, but I am now. I feel like a heroin addict. How much do heroin addicts have to find every day to get their fix? Ten quid? At least my Amber Leaf only costs £3.19.

Yes! I find it, it was in here all along. But it's even thinner than I remembered.

It takes me twenty-five minutes to walk into town. On my way to the pawn shop I walk past the Costa coffee and see two women laughing over lattes. How civilized. I feel like the little matchgirl, peering in the window of the toy shop on Christmas Eve. What must it be like to have money in your purse and to walk into Costa to meet a mate for a coffee? It had been a long time since I'd met a mate here.

A really long time – the last time I met up with anyone must have been over six months ago.

I remember feeling sick with anxiety on my way to meet my mate that day. Praying that she wouldn't offer to buy me a coffee, because I wouldn't be able to buy the next round. It was always the same:

I'd walk in and she would've already found a table.

We'd hug.

Chat shit for a minute or so.

She'd head towards the queue.

'I'm getting a latte. What are you having?' she'd ask.

'Tap water.'

'You sure you don't want an Americano?'

No, I don't want an Americano. I want tap water, because tap water is free. And if you buy me an Americano, I won't be able to buy you one back. Because I have no money. I don't even carry a purse any more because the only thing in it is a Tesco Clubcard.

We'll finish our drinks, and I'll be in the middle of telling you a funny anecdote, but inside I'll be screaming because I can see you're staring at your empty cup and I know you are waiting for my stupid story to end so I can buy you another coffee. And I'll feel ashamed, because all I want to do is buy you one, of course I do, but I can't, and you think it's because I'm not picking up your social cues. But you're wrong, I'm picking them up like a fucking satellite dish, and I'm battling on with the anecdote in a bid to distract you from the fact I still haven't offered to buy you a fucking coffee.

You'll get impatient and you'll join the queue again and get another latte. You'll come back to the table and I'll feel that you're a little bit cooler towards me than you were. We chat trivial shit, but in your eyes I can see you think I'm a tight cunt. I know that later you'll phone our friends and say, 'She didn't even offer to buy me a fucking coffee,' and they'll say, 'She never does! She's a fucking user, that's why I don't hang around with her any more.'

That time six months ago, she comes back to the table with a glass bottle of mineral water. Fuck. *I asked for fucking tap water.*

I pour the water into a glass of ice, knowing that this will be the last time I see my mate for a while. She pours sugar into her latte and smiles. She proceeds to tell me about how the new guy she's dating's knob bends to the left. I laugh and savour this time with her because I know that I've only got the time it takes her to finish that drink for her to still want to be my friend.

That's why I stopped seeing my friends. Correction: that's why they stopped seeing me. You wouldn't think it, but having friends costs money.

*

The pawn-shop window is filled with the treasures of desperate people. Engagement rings pawned to top up the electric meter, an antique ruby ring passed down from a grandmother. Sentimental value means fuck all here; it's all about the weight.

My mum had pawned my granny's engagement ring not long ago, when the dog needed to go to the vet. I loved that ring. When Granny lost her battle to breast cancer, she gave the ring to Mum.

'She loved you so much, you know,' Mum would tell me.

She'd take the ring from her finger and let me try it on, saying, 'This will be yours one day.'

No it won't. It'll end up in the hands of that arsehole. It was priceless, but he valued it at two hundred and fifty quid.

The pawnbroker was an arsehole. I don't think he even owned the shop, he just worked there, but he acted like he fucking owned it. He had all the sensitivity of a bloodthirsty shark, and when the shop doorbell tinkled and I sulked in, he'd look up at me with a smile curling at the corner of his mouth. This wolf had been expecting Little Red Riding Hood.

I say he'd look up at me. One eye definitely did, but he was boss-eyed. I used to call him Moonshoe to Charlie, as he always had one eye looking up at the moon and the other at his shoe. Charlie didn't really get the joke as he never ventured into the shop. It was always me, taking a hit for the team.

'Hello again,' he says when I walk in with the chain.

Then he says nothing as I walk to the counter, eyeballing me with his one good eye and smirking.

The doorbell tinkles again and a middle-aged woman walks in. She starts looking in the glass cabinets. Moonshoe leaves me at the counter and walks over to her. I can wait, obviously, because I'm scum.

'Can I help you at all?' he asks her, in a nice, gentle tone at least two octaves higher than the one he speaks to me with.

'Just having a look, thank you.'

'Well, just let me know if you need any help.'

He gets back behind the counter.

'What've you got today?' He sighs, not really interested. He knows he's already got my best stuff. This is just the scraps now.

I pull out the pathetic chain. He grimaces, as if I've just taken a turd out of my top pocket. I want to punch him so hard in his face that his lazy eyeball will roll back straight.

He puffs out another sigh and drops the chain carelessly on his scales to weigh the last bit of my soul.

'Three pounds sixty-seven.' He smiles at me with what might be pity.

This has caught the attention of the middle-aged

woman, who is earwigging while pretending to look in a cabinet at an angle that gives her a good view of the shame on my face.

'Yup, that's fine,' I say. 'Just give me the money so I can get the fuck out of here.'

'The sixty-seven pence will have to be in coppers, I haven't got any silver.'

Fucking arsehole is loving this. He empties a bag of pennies and counts the sixty-seven pence, slowly sliding each coin to me across the counter. I don't have a purse so I put them in my pocket. I could just walk out when he gets to nineteen, as my baccy costs £3.19, but every penny counts and, my God, do we need every penny.

'Sixty-six . . . sixty-seven.'

I swipe the last two pennies up and charge out the shop.

'See you again *soon*,' he calls out after me. Arsehole.

He would see me again soon. I'd be back in a couple of weeks with a silver trophy of my grandfather's that I'd find hidden in the garage.

I walk to Tesco to get my baccy, all the while daydreaming about winning the lottery and buying that shitty pawnshop to play golf in. In my dream, I gleefully smash up the cabinets with my clubs, employing Moonshoe to hold the golf tee while I take a shot, and every day that he drags himself into work, I'll smile and say, 'Hello, *again*.'

I sit on a bench in the graveyard and roll a fag. I like it in here. You don't bump into people you know.

I used to sit on the bench outside the church, but I was a sitting duck for old schoolfriends of Mum's. All my old schoolfriends had moved to London to make successes of themselves, but their mums remained. They would come bounding over and ask me that question that would make me curl up and crumble like a vampire in the sunlight.

'Daisy! How's the acting going?'

It's not 'going'. It's truly stagnant – actually, no, it's not stagnant, it's actually going backwards. You see, I left RADA a year ago and not only have I failed to get a part in anything, I'm actually worse off than before I went to RADA.

No, no one to bump into in the graveyard. Just me, my rollies and some bloke called R. Jefferson who died in the 1800s from smallpox.

I walk to the library. We can't afford internet now, so I use the computers here every morning to see if my agent has emailed.

I open my inbox. One unread message:

*Save 50% on Viagra for up to 12 prescriptions a year*

It's still only half nine. My agent might just be getting into work. Maybe she'll email me at ten?

I auditioned three weeks ago for two lines in a BBC Three comedy called *Phone Shop*.

I thought I did OK. Usually, I'm appalling in auditions, but it's pretty hard to fuck up two lines. The director seemed to like me. I thought I felt him squeeze my hand as we shook goodbye. Maybe that was his way of saying I had got it, but surely I would have heard by now? Maybe they're considering me for a bigger part? Maybe they saw I had potential? Unlikely. Highly unlikely.

Fuck it, I'll chase my agent anyway.

Hi there,

Dais here. Sorry to be a pain in the arse. Just wondered if you'd heard anything back from Phone Shop?

I hit send.

I hear the sound of a flush behind me. Smiley walks out of the library toilet. He's had his morning dump. He's been homeless for as long as I've lived here, and wearing army combat clothing for longer than that. We call him Smiley because he has a pocket mirror, which he spends eight hours a day, usually outside the Memorial Hospital, just smiling into. Rumour has it that he was discharged from the army with a head injury.

Smiley throws his soiled backpack on to the floor and collapses into a plastic chair. Right on cue, he opens his pocket mirror and beams at himself. Most of his teeth are missing. I'd love to know what he is seeing. How nice must it be to escape into that mirror and not see how shit things really are.

I sit and wait for a reply from my agent. I'll give it half an hour. I spend the time stalking my old RADA classmates on Facebook. Selin has put a trailer up for an ITV drama she's in about the serial killers Fred and Rose West. A couple of seconds of her flash up: she's playing their daughter Heather.

It was filmed up the road in Gloucester. For fuck's sake. I should have been put up for that. She's from London and I have a West Country accent! This is so fucking unfair. Be happy for Selin, I tell myself, she deserves this. She really deserves this. Be happy for her.

I can't, though, I just can't. I wish that I could, but I can't.

Alex has commented:

So proud of you, hun xx

Of course you are, you're in a blockbuster, a film with Meryl Streep, playing a younger version of Margaret Thatcher. You have the success to be able to be proud of her. I don't. I have nothing. I have absolutely nothing.

I am proud of Selin. I'm proud of Alex. I'm so proud of them. I just hate myself. That's all.

I can feel self-loathing creep down my throat and tighten my lungs. It's like tar: thick and black and hot. I catch a reflection of myself in the screen and it's disgusting: I've put on weight, my teeth are brown from smoking rollies with no filters and the rings around my eyes are puffy and weirdly green. I'm physically repulsed by myself. I've been avoiding mirrors for such a long time I even brush my teeth with my eyes closed so I don't catch myself.

An email pops up: it's my agent's assistant!

Hi Daisy

Unfortunately, it didn't work out this time. They really liked you but have chosen to take a different path with the role.

Hope you're well!

Georgie x x x

*A different path with the role?* How deep does this character have to be for them to find a different path? She has two fucking lines?!

Three weeks I've been waiting, hoping, praying. I've thought of nothing else but the squeeze of that hand-shake and the opportunity it held. It was my one bit of hope and it's gone.

A Polish guy behind me is itching to get on to the computer. I log off.

'All yours, mate.'

I walk back up the dual carriageway to the house with the intention of taking a Nytol and sleeping all day.

*

Dad eventually managed to get a job at our old school, working in 'Inclusion' – essentially, a room where they dumped the naughty kids to stop them from disrupting the lessons. They were meant to be doing work, but Dad was too soft. He wanted them to like him. He would just let them sit around making fishing floats all day, as long as they promised to get their workbooks out, should my dad see the headmistress approaching.

Weirdly, they were all nuts about fishing. They couldn't concentrate in class at all, but after school they would sit and watch a float bob up and down on a lake for hours on end.

Dad took home £9k a year and Mum couldn't get a job for love nor money. Not even Tesco wanted her.

Rent was £1,000 a month. That was before anything else. So we were already short on rent even before basics like food, water, council tax, heating, and all the rest.

Understandably, our landlady wanted us out. Poor cow hadn't received any rent in, like, three months and we were on borrowed time.

We were going to be evicted and we had nowhere to go.

Mum went to the council to talk to a lady about emergency housing.

'I'm afraid the best we can do is put you up in bedsits, separately.'

Yup, that's right, separately, and not even anywhere near where we lived or each other.

'We have one for your daughter in Bristol and one for your husband in Weston-super-Mare.'

Fucking hell, was this really happening?

Mum declined.

'Something will come up,' she said, as she tried to make a curry for lunch from a tin of Value tomatoes and some out-of-date back-of-the-cupboard curry powder.

'I lit a candle and said a prayer in church today. I didn't have 20p to pay to light the candle. I hope God isn't shitty about that,' she said.

There was a knock at the door. Not bailiffs this time: the figures through the bubbled door glass were svelte. We all hid under the kitchen table anyway.

You could never be too sure.

Silence.

Had they gone?

We heard keys in the door. Can't be Dad; he doesn't finish work till half three. Mum came out from under the table.

Shit, had he got the sack for letting those kids fuck about?

'I'm here to show a possible tenant around,' a woman called out.

Mum froze. Fuck. It was the landlady.

'You did receive a letter from me telling you it was today?'

We probably did, but if anything looked like a bill, we'd shove it unopened into the boiler cupboard.

She stared in shock, past my mum. The house was in an absolute fucking state and stank of crap curry. She swallowed down her rage in one gulp as Charlie and I emerged from under the kitchen table, like two convicts handing themselves over to the police.

'Could you please leave?' she asked, obviously trying to remain calm in the presence of her possible future tenant.

I grabbed my baccy and jammed my feet into my trainers. I looked down at the floor as I made my way to the front door with Charlie and Mum in tow, not wanting to catch her glare.

'I'm so sorry about this,' the landlady said to the man who was with her.

'No problem,' he replied.

I knew that voice. No, it just couldn't be. If it was, then God had put more twists in my life than a comedy of errors. I looked up. I didn't want to. But I did.

*It's fucking Moonshoe!*

Of all the fucking people . . .

In all the fucking world . . .

It had to be fucking Moonshoe.

He had his good eye on me. The other was eyeing up my cat, who had decided to puke up a furball on the carpet.

He wasn't smirking this time. He was absolutely horri-fied.

The landlady stared at the cat. The rental contract we signed said strictly no pets.

We got out of the house, and the three of us ran to the phone box in the park. Mum was now completely hysterical. She made a collect call to the school and asked the receptionist to put her through to Dad. Charlie and I stood outside the phone box.

'So, God was shitty about Mum not paying for that candle,' Charlie joked.

'What?'

He scuffed some mud from the side of his shoe on to the concrete, embarrassed.

'Never mind.'

Dad answered the phone. Mum told him what had happened, but she exaggerated wildly.

'It was awful, Paul, the house was a complete mess. The way she looked at me, it was like I was scum. She told me to get out of the house! She was so bloody rude!'

Mum burst into tears.

Granted, the landlady had been cold, but we hadn't been paying her rent, we had got a cat, a dog and a budgie in the house, even though we weren't meant to. The house was an utter shithole and she was meant to be showing a future tenant around. So yeah, I think she had every right, really.

'Your father is coming to the house now to sort this out.'

Mum always referred to Dad as 'Your father' when things got serious.

We stood on the pavement outside the house waiting for Dad to arrive, which he did shortly afterwards. But he didn't come to greet us first. He was red with rage, fuelled by the tearful phone call from his wife, and he was storming towards the front door. Oh God, what was he going to do? We chased after him, shouting 'Dad!', but he already had his key in the door. The door opened and all I heard was him shouting at the top of his voice.

'How dare you be rude to my wife!'

We finally caught up with him.

'I beg your pardon?' she bit back.

'My wife said you were rude to her!'

'No, I wasn't!'

I now found myself standing next to Moonshoe. We both hung our heads to avoid confrontation. For once, we were united – he was just as embarrassed as I was.

'Yes, you were!'

My mum chimed in meekly.

'Sorry . . . I may have been a bit upset, when I was telling Paul on the phone . . . about you coming into our house.'

'*Your* house? It's *my* house!' the landlady shouted.

Moonshoe slipped past a gap between Charlie and my mum and out through the front door. The landlady followed him.

She turned and shouted, 'And I want you all out by the end of the week!' And slammed the door behind her.

There was silence for a minute as the four of us stood in the hallway before my dad finally piped up, 'So she wasn't rude?'

'I felt like she was being rude!' Mum cried.

It would have been funny if it had been a sketch in a sitcom but, at the time, we couldn't laugh. This was our lives: our landlady had given us four days to not only pack up all our shit and get out but find somewhere else to live.

Some years later, Charlie and I are doing a book signing in a small bookshop in Cirencester. There's a queue of over seven hundred people outside. There's a group of women in Swindon Town football tops approaching our stand. They are all singing a line from the show: 'He's dead, he's dead, he's dead!' We have a chat about Swindon Town Football Club while Charlie and I sign their books and I pose for a selfie. They wave goodbye and, as they do, a guy and his girlfriend are next in line. The man is holding a copy of our *This Country* book.

I look up. It isn't . . . No, it can't be. Yes, it fucking is! *It's fucking Moonshoe.*

'Hi, guys, love the show.'

He's holding his book out, but I'm not taking it, I'm just staring back in shock.

'Love the bit where Kerry's mum shouts, "Tomato, honestly!" Kerry's mum is our fave!'

He doesn't remember me. I don't believe it. He doesn't remember me at all.

'I know you. You used to work at the pawn shop.'

He stops. He's confused, but flattered that I know him.

'Yeah, yeah, I did! Did you used to go in there?'

'Yeah, I did.'

'No way! That's mental.'

He turns to his girlfriend.

'Did you hear that, Jackie? They used to come in the pawn shop!'

He beams at her, and I don't know why, but my heart completely melts. It's like all that old, painful rage dissolves in a single moment. He's so happy that I know him, and his lazy eye is rolling around in his head with excitement like a fucking pinball. He was an arsehole, but he sort of saved us in a weird way.

I take his book and sign it. God, I wish I had foreseen this. This is better than turning the pawn shop into my own personal golf course.

'Your show got me through a really hard time,' he says. 'So thank you for that.'

Fuck. That felt really good. Not in a vengeful way. That just felt really fucking good.

He takes a selfie with us. I shake hands with him and his girlfriend.

The next group of people in line are approaching the table, but I have just enough time to whisper to Charlie,

'You know who that was, don't you?'
  'Who?'
  'Fucking Moonshoe!'
  'Fuck off.'
  'Seriously!'
  'He didn't recognize you?'
  'No.'
  'Fuck. Me.'

# CHAPTER 15
# THE JOB CENTRE

I walk into the Job Centre and sit on a seat next to a greasy-haired youth in a long leather *Matrix*-style coat. He opens it and from inside removes a half-empty two-litre bottle of Dr Pepper. It is obviously flat because it makes no sound when he opens it. How the fuck does someone have an inside coat pocket large enough to hold a two-litre bottle of Dr Pepper? He smells of fags and BO. That said, I probably smell the same.

'All right?' he grunts.

Fuck, I must have been staring. I smile and nod.

I get a strong waft of cheap alcohol. He wipes the residue of drink from the whiskers he is trying to grow.

'They're all cunts that work in here.'

He says it just loud enough that a woman who looks like Deirdre Barlow glances up from her desk. Drunks just can't whisper, can they?

I smile noncommittally and stare at the ground.

He gets out his wallet and opens it towards me. It's filled with razor blades.

'Do you know why I carry these?' he burps.

Oh great, I'm going to get sliced by a drunken Dr Pepper lunatic carrying razor blades. I can see the headlines in the *Wilts and Glos Standard*.

### GIRL BLEEDS TO DEATH IN
### LOCAL JOB CENTRE

Local girl Daisy May Cooper
innocent victim in shocking incident

That'll be embarrassing. Not only will people know that I was at the fucking Job Centre but, somehow, I got murdered in one. Well, I suppose it's fame of a sort, I thought. In my mind I wandered through my own funeral, Bette Midler's 'Wind Beneath My Wings' playing as people file in, dressed in the deepest, darkest black, my grieving boyfriend and hysterical parents, my sobbing friends and the piles of flowers on my grave . . . Shit! Where am I going with this?

He takes out a razor blade, cuts his arm with it and proceeds to suck the blood from his arm as casually as someone would blow their nose into a tissue.

'People don't think vampires exist, but they do. Have you seen *Twilight*? It's shit. They got us all wrong. We don't fucking shimmer.'

*Christ*, I think. I only came here so I could get my £100 Job Seeker benefits. Now I'm in a conversation with a vampire who likes to wear a long leather jacket over an

Asda tracksuit. Poor bastard can only afford to give a hint of vampire when it comes to clothing. That probably explains why he's here.

'Mr Davidson?'

A young job adviser calls from his desk to the vampire.

The vampire takes another swig from his bottle and gets up. I can see fresh piss stains in his crotch. He catches me looking.

'Fucking cunt,' he says, under his rank, acrid breath. I don't know if that was aimed at the job adviser or me.

He walks over to the desk and falls into the chair opposite the young adviser. He leans back so the chair is only on two legs, like the school gobshite.

Brilliant, the job adviser can deal with the nutjob now. I take a leaflet from the wall about 'Working Tax Credits and You' and look at it. But I'm not reading it. I'm ear-wigging.

'Mr Davidson, I received a call from Stratton House Hotel, saying that you didn't turn up for your interview.'

The vampire suddenly becomes angrily animated.

'Listen. Right. I went to get the bus. I waited for, like, twenty minutes, and the bus didn't even bother showing up, like. So how is that even my fault? If I had walked, right . . . it would have taken me, like, two days from my house.'

Fucking hell, this was brilliant. He should have flown there – he is a vampire, after all. The 'two days' thing really tickles me, and I stifle a laugh. Vampires are so fucking dramatic.

'Well, you really should have called them to let them know.'

'I did! But no one picked up.'

'How many times did you try?'

'Like, eleven times!'

'Miss Cooper?'

'*Miss Cooper!*'

A middle-aged bloke behind a desk is shouting my name. I'd been so immersed in what was going on I hadn't heard anyone call. He beckons me over to his desk.

I get up. It's annoying, as I was quite enjoying the story. I walk over and take a seat. He types something on his computer.

'How are you?'

*How am I?* I want to fucking kill myself.

'Yeah, good thanks.'

'Let's have a look here . . .'

He clicks his mouse a few times and glides it across an 'Arsenal FC' mousepad while he rests his chin on his hand. He takes a sip of coffee from a mug that has a personalized picture of his son on it. It's badly pixellated and faded from the dishwasher. I bet he doesn't want to be here either. I bet he'd rather be sat with his son at the home end in the Emirates Stadium.

'You registered last week, is that right?'

Man, stating the fucking obvious, it's right there on your screen.

'Yes, that's right.' I nod politely.

I'm desperate for him to know that I'm not like the vampire lunatic. That I actually was someone once, before all this shit, that I have a degree and that I absolutely don't belong here.

'You have a BA with Honours? Which university?'

'No, drama school.'

'Right . . . an actor, then?'

'Yes.'

'I knew an actor once . . .'

Here we fucking go.

'Oh, really? How interesting.'

'You ever see a comedy called *The Brittas Empire*? It was about a leisure centre.'

'Not sure . . . maybe rings a bell.'

Even he knows an actor more successful than me.

Silence.

'Let me see what happens if I type "Arts" into the job search.'

Silence.

He types, clicks, raises an eyebrow.

'Don't suppose you want to be a Father Christmas in a grotto in a shopping centre in Swindon?'

I politely titter. Humiliating.

'They're looking for a DJ in a club in Cheltenham?'

For fuck's sake, just stop it.

'Yeah, sorry, not much in the way of acting jobs round here.'

'I'm just looking for something sort of part-time? Something that I can fit in around auditions? Maybe some evening work as well.'

Who am I kidding? I haven't been offered an audition in weeks. The only reason I want to work in the evening is so that no one will see me. Fuck doing a retail or café job during the day, when everyone and his nan can waltz in and see I've failed at everything. Yes, I definitely want something at night – I can successfully lead a double life then. I can skulk to work after sunset and be part of the weird night-time world, do my work unnoticed, anonymously, and return before the sun is up.

'OK, let's have a look . . .'

'Any cleaning jobs going? That would be perfect.'

'Not that I can see . . . they usually get snapped up pretty quickly. I'd be very surprised to see something still on here.'

Seriously? Are cleaning jobs now rarer to find than a good-looking single man who doesn't have some weird sexual fetish? Fucking hell, how long have I been out of the job game?

'Here's something. A kitchen porter in the Taj Indian restaurant. National minimum wage. Evening hours.'

'What's a kitchen porter?'

He leans into the screen and pushes his glasses towards the bridge of his nose as he recites the job description.

'To clean and wash up all kitchen and service items in an efficient manner.'

'Pot wash, then?'

'Yeah. Do you want me to give them a call?'

I shrug. At least I can listen to my iPod while I'm scraping tandoori chicken off a pan. On second thoughts, actually, I can't. I pawned the bastard thing. But I do have my old Discman, as long as I can find it. I know it's somewhere in the house, just a question of where Mum has put it. The evening hours and working in a kitchen mean that no one will see me. I nod in reply. He picks up the phone.

'Hello? Is that Mr Khan? It's Martin here from Cirencester Job Centre. I have a young lady here who is interested in the kitchen porter job . . . oh, right . . . OK, well . . . really? Oh well, that's good news. Well, thanks anyway.'

He hangs up the phone.

'It's gone, I'm afraid. They had forty-odd people apply for it.'

'Are you kidding?'

'Unfortunately not. Let's have another look.'

People say it's hard to make it as an actor, but it is starting to look like it might be easier for me to get a part in a blockbuster film than a pot-wash job in a curry house.

He takes another swig from his mug.

'Is that your son?'

'Hmmm?'

I point to the mug; he looks at it.

'No, I don't know who that is. This mug has been here for ever.'

He continues to click.

'*Fuck off, then!*'

Christ, Vampire is kicking off. He's being led out by a very short bald man with bottle-end glasses in a too-tight white shirt.

'*Get the fuck off me, Mole-Man!*'

I try not to laugh; he does look like a fat little mole. Like one of those crap *Wind in the Willows* animations that you had on a cheap VHS.

It's the most pathetic tussle I've ever seen. Vampire drunkenly kicks a desk, stumbling and only managing to move it a tiny bit. Mole-Man is trying to put him into some sort of citizen's arrest but only succeeds in exposing a horrible hairy crack as his trousers give up the fight with his belly and sink towards his knees.

Vampire is holding on to a rack of leaflets while Mole-Man is trying to push him out of the automatic doors like a battering ram. What's even more hilarious is that they are *both* shouting for someone to call the police.

Another job adviser – a thin, gangly bloke in his twenties – runs to the aid of Mole-Man while everyone looks on with open mouths. They both push the vampire out of the door, like they're pushing a piano on to a removal truck. Vampire falls through the open automatic doors and out into the street in a heap of leather jacket and Lonsdale trainers.

Mole-Man turns back to the room, wipes the sweat from his bright red bald head and adjusts his trousers. He's met with pathetic applause from Deirdre Barlow and another frizzy-haired woman who looks like an ageing *Gladiators* contestant. She is poking her head out of the hatch in the Job Centre kitchenette.

Gangly-job-adviser-man pats Mole-Man on the back, but Mole-Man ignores him. He's too busy looking around the room for more appreciation.

There's a knock at the window. Deirdre Barlow opens the plastic blinds to reveal Vampire, his middle finger pressed up against the glass. He smiles, revealing blackened teeth. His molars are missing. Doesn't look much like a vampire, I thought.

'Ignore him, Carol,' Mole-Man barks breathlessly.

Vampire now has both middle fingers up against the window. He mouths 'Fat cunt' at Mole-Man.

Mole-Man picks up the phone and feigns phoning the police. Vampire laughs and throws a pinecone hard at the window before stumbling off.

I turn to my job adviser.

'Does this happen often?'

'Not really, no,' he says.

*Jobseeker's*
**Allowance**

Your reference is
Please tell us this number
if you get in touch with us

**MISS D M COOPER**

Phone      0845 6088578
TEXTPHONE for the deaf/hard of
hearing ONLY 0845 6088551

Date 20 May 2011

Dear Miss Cooper

## YOUR CLAIM FOR JOBSEEKER'S ALLOWANCE

## A CHANGE IN YOUR JOBSEEKER'S ALLOWANCE

We have looked at your claim again following a recent change.

We cannot pay you an allowance from 19 April 2011. This is because:

you are working for 16 hours or more a week.

If you are not going to get any money at the end of your first week's work, you can apply for money from the Social Fund until you get your first earnings. Ask us if you want more information about this. We have sent you a sheet about other help you may get after you stop getting an allowance.

If you want a full explanation of why your Jobseeker's Allowance has changed, please get in touch with us. Our phone number and address are at the top of this letter.

## OTHER HELP YOU MAY BE ENTITLED TO

You may be entitled to other help. To find out more about this ask us for leaflet INF2 "Other help you may be entitled to".

## HOUSING BENEFIT AND COUNCIL TAX BENEFIT

You could get Housing Benefit or Council Tax Benefit. Get in touch with your local council as soon as possible. If you are already getting Housing Benefit or Council Tax Benefit you should show them this letter.

## IF YOU WANT TO KNOW MORE ABOUT THIS DECISION OR IF YOU THINK IT IS WRONG

Please contact us and we will give an explanation. Our address and phone number are at the top of this letter. You should contact us within one month of the date of this letter, or we may not be able to consider any dispute.

# CHAPTER 16
## *DOC MARTIN*

have been to endless auditions for soap operas and daytime dramas. Nothing. I have been emailing my less than enthusiastic agent for weeks. Nothing. I've lowered my expectations from a supporting role to playing a skeleton in a GP's surgery on *Doctors*. Honestly, I'd be a packet of pork scratchings behind the bar of the Old Vic if only someone would employ me.

I know that I am being edged out of existence by my agent. I'm a fart that's lingered around too long in a lift, silently choking its human cargo. The lift doors need to slide open so that this fart can drift away. If she's embarrassed by me, why doesn't she say? I'm a piece of dog shit stubbornly embedded in the grip of her Gucci trainers. If she was brave, she'd take a wire brush to me and scrub me out, but she hasn't got the balls, so I'm being politely ignored, she's not returning my calls.

Our landlady did kick us out, and she got a new tenant, so Mum, Dad, Charlie and I moved into a new rental place. It was tiny. Even smaller with all Mum's stuff bursting from every room. You needed to have done a fucking SAS course just to get up the stairs. But the new landlord didn't want to see any references – thank God, because our previous landlady wouldn't even have referred us to a rubbish tip. She threatened to come after us for lost rent. I couldn't walk near our old street just in case.

One night, I just had to get out of the house. Just close the door behind me and forget about it all. I had enough cash for a lime and soda in the local. I wanted to drink alone, but there was a guy at the bar – it was like Daffy Duck's face had formed an unlikely union with Bear Grylls' body and he had let himself go a bit. A lot, actually. Plus he had unsightly nose hair and a random moustache! A fucking moustache? What was I thinking? His only attractive quality was his melodic Welsh accent. Nick was 100 per cent fit-as-fuck if I shut my eyes and just listened.

'I'm a chef,' he said, and smiled and winked.

'What do you cook?' I honestly couldn't have cared less. Food was a sore point. Mum had taken to foraging in the reduced aisles again, and in the hedgerows for sloes and mushrooms. She called it being self-sufficient. I called it something else entirely. And Dad was out of work again.

'Well, mainly I heat up stuff.'

'Nice.'

'What's your favourite meal?'

'Dunno. Chinese?'

'I heat up a mean Chinese.'

His name was Nick. Turned out he worked as a chef in an old people's home and pinged a microwave for a living. He lived in a flat in town. 'Chef' was over-egging the pudding. Undercooked jacket potatoes and warm prawn mayo was his speciality. But he was offering me a drink . . .

I spotted an opportunity. If I shagged him, then I could get drunk and not have to walk or spend money getting home. Plus, I could get a free meal. My self-esteem was at an all-time low and I figured it was only polite to shag someone if they bought you wine. Seriously, that's how shit I felt. Even if the shag was crap, this seemed like a holy trinity of positives.

The shag was really terrible.

Not long after, my less than enthusiastic agent bothered to get in touch.

Hi Daisy, I've got this potentially brilliant gig for you. Auditions for Doc Martin. You know, the ITV drama? For the role of the receptionist?

Do I know it? Fuck yeah! It's one of the biggest success stories in television and it's got a surly and uptight Martin Clunes in it. It's a serious step up from any daytime soap. And this part wouldn't just be one episode. I'd get to answer the phone throughout the *whole series*. In a *West Country accent*, which I can *so* do. I could say things like:

## Fwd: Doc Martin; Daisy May Cooper

From:
Sent: 04 February 2011 15:38:18
To:
Cc:

1 attachment
Ep.2 26.01.11.pdf (149.0 KB) ,

Hello lovely lady

As discussed here are all the details for 'Doc Martin' next Tuesday.

Have a wonderful weekend

xox

Begin forwarded message:

**From:**
**Date:** 4 February 2011 11:59:44 GMT
**To:**
**Subject: Doc Martin; Daisy May Cooper**

Hey

As discussed please find attached Episode 2 of the new series of DOC MARTIN.

We'd love to get it to Daisy May to have a look at new regular character of Morwenna (she first appears in Ep.2 and then is right across the series). Basic character breakdown is below...

is directing, and                              is producing for Buffalo for ITV1.
Overall dates for the series are: 28 March - 29 July '11, filming in Port Isaac, Cornwall.

Hope she likes it. It would be great to meet her on Tuesday (8th February) at 11.00am at the Doc Martin Production Office, One Lyric Square, London, W6 0NB (entrance next to the Lyric Hammersmith Theatre)
She'll be meeting                              I will be there, and we'll just look at a couple of scenes, of her choice, to put on tape.

thanks & speak soon,

Silence.

32     **INT. CHEMIST'S - MORNING**                                       32

MRS TISHELL, in one of the aisles, is with a customer.

Behind the counter pricing items, MORWENNA NEWCROSS (22) ex-
Bevy leader. Bright, lacking propriety and with an abundance
of attitude. Harry ENTERS.

                    HARRY
          Hey. I need some cod liver oil,
          please? In the capsules.

                    MORWENNA
          Behind the line.

As they talk Morwenna gets a box of capsules, bags it, Harry
pays (Morwenna doesn't hand over the bag).

                    HARRY
          Huh?

                    MORWENNA
          The line for people with fish
          breath.

                    HARRY
          Sorry.

                    MORWENNA
               (indicates)
          Breath mints are in that aisle.

                    HARRY
          Did you hear what happened to me?
               (proudly)
          Passed a kidney stone.

He waits for the reaction. Morwenna waits.

                    HARRY (CONT'D)
               (indicates a couple of
               inches )
          This big, it was. Thought I was
          going to die.

Mrs Tishell comes to the till with purchases bags them up.

                    MORWENNA
          When are you going to invite me for
          a tour of the stiffs?

                    MRS TISHELL
          Morwenna, that is hardly seemly
          talk.

'There's a woman with an erectile dysfunction? . . . Let me see what's written down . . . I know it's a mistake, Doc, but it's not my job to write the prescriptions. I just answer the phone.'

I was all over that part! OK, it wasn't a huge role, but it was proper acting with the promise of being a recurring character. This equalled regular income. And if viewers got to know me, they would love me. Yes! Yes! Yes!

'Sure. Just send me the time and place,' I replied, coolly.

There was no way I was going to give my agent the satisfaction of hearing me get super-excited, only for me to be let down again. Besides, I was tempering my enthusiasm with a cautious optimism. I was seriously beginning to doubt myself. It's such hard work rehearsing lines for parts which never materialize and to listen to producers saying:

'Sorry, love, not this time.'

Or 'You were great, just not quite what we were looking for.'

Or, worst of all, 'We were looking for someone with more . . .' They can't even bring themselves to finish the sentence. Bastards.

Over the next few weeks, I scraped the cash together to get to the Holloway Road in London for the auditions. I borrowed money off Debs, Mum's old cleaner. At the time, she was a single mum, in a council house, with three kids. I felt terrible. And it's even more awful when you can read what people are thinking:

*Why doesn't she just get a job? This acting lark has clearly not worked out for her . . .*

Here's why: one, if I didn't act, I might as well kill myself. Two, there were very few jobs in Cirencester. And three, there were zero jobs I could waltz out of at a moment's notice to get a coach to London to attend an audition for a shitty part that I probably wouldn't get.

In total, there were four auditions for *Doc Martin*. Each time I auditioned I got through to the next round. I wished it wasn't so gruelling. Every time it felt like there was so much riding on it, and I was still so anxious after RADA. Also, there was the added stress of having to print audition scripts out at the library, which cost 20p a sheet. Once, my agent rang me:

'Daisy, I got a message from *Call the Midwife* and they said you were really unprepared for the part. It's not surprising you're not getting any work.' Her tone was so condescending.

'The script was sixty pages long and I couldn't print off the script because that's £12 I don't have,' I felt like saying. But I couldn't say that to her because she wouldn't have understood. Instead, sometimes I noted scripts down by hand off the computer screen so I didn't have to ask anyone for money.

On the last audition for *Doc Martin*, my sandals were

falling apart and I had to walk from Victoria Coach Station to the venue with duct tape holding them together.

After every round of auditions, my gloom started to lift. I was sure this was going to be *it*! Each time, I read and re-read the script and rehearsed my lines until I could recite them in my sleep.

In the end, it was whittled down to two of us: the choice was between me and the actress Jessica Ransom.

Mum and Dad were beside themselves, especially as the landlady from our old house had finally tracked them down. She was demanding her missing rent, and money for carpet cleaning. She said that after we left there was shit covering her house and it smelled like an elephant's crotch, what with Mum's menagerie.

'When Dais makes it big,' Dad kept saying, 'she'll take care of all of us. She's always had the talent. She just needs the chance. She'll buy us the house of our dreams.'

No pressure or anything.

'Let's just see what happens. We've been here before,' I'd say.

'We know, love. But we know you can do it.'

I didn't want to get anyone's hopes up, least of all my own, but I was due a break. I desperately needed something to look forward to, given the chaos of home and Nick, who I'd pretty much moved in with. In my head, I'd get the part on *Doc Martin* and flounce out of his life in a dramatic exit stage left.

'I'm too good for you, you weird sex freak,' I'd say. 'I've got the bright lights and the big city coming straight at me. Laters!'

No exaggeration, Nick was a sex freak. I found that out on an early date, after we had a conversation about Charlie's love of takeaways.

'He adores Chinese. Can't get enough of it,' I told Nick innocently.

'So, if you were to order any takeaway in the world, what would it be?'

It wasn't a proper question as, at the time, takeaways in Cirencester didn't get much more exciting than McDonald's. Now, it's gone all metropolitan. It's even got a street-food stall called Thai Me Up.

'Chilli beef, probably. And Charlie loves that too.'

'Chilli beef?' Nick attempted to look seductive. 'If you like chilli beef, then I wonder whether our sexual interests might be the same?' he purred.

'Erm . . . sorry?' It was hard to see the connection. 'What is it exactly you want to do with chilli beef?'

Suddenly, I had visions of Portuguese Polly back in Shepherd's Bush peeling raw bacon from the packet and dangling it in her mouth before chewing it. It was the least erotic vision I'd ever had.

'No, I just mean something more experimental than vanilla sex.'

Chowing down every night on his greasy chips, over-cooked chicken and burnt burgers before giving him a half-arsed blower was experimental for me. What more did he fucking want?

'What exactly did you have in mind?' I asked cautiously.

'It really arouses me to be . . . like an object . . .'

'Like an object? . . . like a sex object?'

Maybe he wanted me to catcall him? Or wolf-whistle at him in his pissy boxer shorts?

'No . . . like a proper object . . .'

'A proper object?'

'Like . . . a footstool . . .'

Of all the objects in the universe, I could not have predicted he was going to say a fucking footstool.

'Well, what do you say?' His eyebrows raised. He smiled and I watched the plaque glisten on his incisors.

I thought about it. Honestly, I would have preferred to put a fork under my big toenail and punt a fucking wall than get off on Nick being a footstool. But I would be escaping home soon and I had access to an unlimited supply of his booze. Plus, when he went to work in the morning I had peace and quiet *all day*. Why would I jeopardize all of that over a mere technicality? Fuck it, I'll do it.

'Well, we could try it . . .'

'That would be amazing.'

He was so grateful.

On the first night he wanted me to watch a film while he crouched naked on the carpet on all fours. I could rest my feet on his back for the whole one hour and forty-two minutes of *How to Train Your Dragon 2*. It felt a bit awkward, but a bottle of wine eased the pain.

'How is it for you?' I asked tentatively.

'Fucking a-mazing, Dais. Fucking brilliant.'

I shit you not, Nick managed to maintain a stonking boner all the way up until the credits rolled. He could usually barely get his wonky knob up during straight sex. And if he did, it didn't last for long.

Just treat it like any acting job, I kept telling myself. Dais, you can do this.

I was nervous, though. Fetishes often escalate, don't they? Was the footstool a gateway to more hardcore inanimate objects? Like the bidets you get in posh bathrooms? Or one of those kneeler chairs for chronic back pain old people use?

He started texting me if I was out:

Daisy, when you come in, I will be standing in the corner of the room. Do not talk to me. Take your coat off and hang it on my face and watch Homes Under the Hammer like I'm not even there. Remember. Do not talk to me. I AM A COAT STAND. Nick x

A fucking coat stand? I wanted to ask whether he might simply consider going down on me. It clearly hadn't crossed his mind that I wasn't getting as much pleasure out of this as he was. Not even a fanny flutter.

The minute I got in and placed my jacket over the top of his head, out of the corner of my eye, I saw his dick rising through his boxers like a parking barrier. He would've stood there for ever, until I told him otherwise.

It didn't stop there. He also loved being a human rug while I walked over him in heels. I remember my sweaty Primark stilettos making imprints in his milk-white, chubby back. If I went to the shops, he wanted to be left at home tied up with one of his dad's horrible paisley ties. I got my acting skills on . . .

'OK, slave,' I'd say, trying to find something to tie him to. I did try tying him to the heated towel rail once, but he burnt his wrists. So I ended up tying him to the curtain pole, which was a bit of a pain in the arse, as I had to balance on the bed to reach up to it and shut the curtains around his wonky bell end – which was now flashing the bakery across the road. He always insisted on being completely starkers and he had whiteheads on his arse. I imagine it was from wearing his chef trousers while working in a sweaty kitchen.

Just to remind you all, I was getting absolutely fuck all out of this other than booze: a three-quid bottle of

Chardonnay in his fridge and some warm Jägermeister – an unwanted Christmas gift – on his windowsill. Who the fuck gets off on being tied up while your dominant potters around Tesco? The problem was, I didn't have any cash to spend in Tesco and he would only get off if I was gone a long time, so I resorted to reading *Heat* magazine and having a gander at the reduced section. Sometimes I would do laps around the market place in the hope of wasting time. If I came back too soon, he would be disappointed and his boner would wilt like a piece of iceberg lettuce on an oven hob.

We never did anything nice together. Living out his object fantasies seemed to take up most of my time. And it was tiring being asked to act as his dominatrix all the time, like he was a toddler:

'Please, miss, can I use the toilet?'

'Not now, but in five minutes time you may.' That felt very cruel, because when I'm busting for a piss, I can never just hold it in, but it was what he wanted me to say.

But by far the cruellest thing was when he wanted to be a human ashtray.

'Just smoke while you're watching TV and flick the ash here,' he said.

Oh, for fuck's sake . . . really? My face fell as he opened his mouth and stuck out his tongue. It was fat and it had a carpet of white coating like he had thrush. I got a waft of his breath. It was like rotting garlic.

If I was watching TV, he begged for the footstool-ash-tray combo. He positioned himself on all fours with his tongue out while I put my feet up, drank wine, watched *Location Location Location* and flicked my ash his way. I tried to do it casually, but it occurred to me that I could get arrested for this. It was well dodge. He loved me stubbing my fag out on him. He winced with pleasure. I winced in pain.

After months of this, it's not that hard to see why the lure of *Doc Martin* consumed me. Daisy, you *have* to get this part. You *have* to.

I checked my emails at the library every morning and once again in the afternoon every single day after the final audition. Then, an email landed.

> The producers thought you were great, Daisy but, unfortunately, they've decided to give the part to Jessica Ransom. Sorry, but there is a bit of good news – they still want you to film on location with the team in Cornwall. You'll have four lines in an episode and play a young mum. It's £700. I'll send on the details – are you interested? Ness xx

Fuck. My heart plummeted. Four lines? Well done to Jessica, though. I mean, at that moment, I fucking hated her, but well done. She'd ace it. It was myself I hated more. Why wasn't I good enough? Why hadn't I knocked their socks off? But . . . four lines . . . and I'd get to film on location in Portwenn, or whatever it's called in real life. And that seven hundred quid would help pay off Mum and Dad's rent arrears. Plus, I'd get to be on TV.

I emailed back saying yes straight away. Then, panic set in. How was I going to get to Cornwall? I couldn't ask Debs for more money. Maybe Nick would lend me the fare? Maybe I could raise the stakes in return and suggest he be a vodka luge ice sculpture shaped like a naked man with a six-pack. I could suck him off and pretend real alcohol was flowing. It could be a farewell fetish before I dumped him.

Just as I was thinking about how I could scrounge money from him, he texted me asking to meet me outside the church in the town square. Which was unusual. Other than the weird sex, we mainly communicated in grunts. It was amazing to me how we could grunt in so many meaningful ways. I saw him waiting on the bench – a slob in his dirty chef's whites. Well, more grey, really. His greasy, lank hair hung around his face. Honest to God, I thought. Why am I with him?

'OK?' I muttered, trying not to sit too close.

'I want you to move out.'

I wasn't expecting that. It was meant to be me doing the breaking up, and I was pretty pissed off that he'd got in there first.

'What the fuck? What?'

'It's about the sex. You're too vanilla.'

This was priceless, coming from someone who thought a good shag was just something that lasted longer than ten minutes.

'Um . . . *vanilla*?' I sputtered.

'I love all the object stuff, but you're boring in bed and you've got fat. And when I saw your shoes at the bottom of the stairs the other day, my heart sank that you were still there.' I was incandescent with rage and I smacked him full on the cheek.

'You toad! You are a fucking moron!' I shouted as loud as I could. The old dears passing by stopped to listen to the unfolding drama. Now I had an audience I was in my element. I stood up and, in my best dramatic voice, I berated him for being the most unkind, uncouth, uncaring boyfriend *ever*. He'd never even made me come! One silver-hair shouted: 'You give it to him, girl! All men are bastards.'

I left with their applause ringing in my ears. I walked to the flat, collected my stuff and, on the way out, picked up the glass of coins that he kept on the windowsill and two unopened bottles of Chardonnay. *Doc Martin*, here I come!

The afternoon I was due to leave was a nightmare. It turned out I needn't have worried about the train fare, as the production company would pay for my ticket. I just had to pick it up from the machine at the station. Cue major wobble. I had to insert my debit card to get the ticket. I didn't know if I needed to claim it back on expenses or whether it had been prepaid. If it wasn't pre-paid, there wasn't going to be enough to cover it in my account. I inserted the card and shut my eyes. I waited for the beep telling me the machine had rejected it. It didn't come. The fare had been prepaid. Thank fuck.

I had instructions that a taxi would pick me up from Bodmin Parkway, the nearest station to the set, and take me to a hotel. I would stay overnight, do the shoot the next day, stay overnight again and then come home.

The minute I sat on the train I breathed a sigh of relief. I wasn't even pissed off any more about Jessica Ransom. I was thrilled I was going to be on the real set of a real production doing a real job. My first since RADA – three years ago.

The countryside rolled by. I was still pissed off about Nick. I was very fucking annoyed about my inability to cut him off when I had the chance, which should have been at around the time of the coat stand. Don't worry about it, I thought. What's done is done. Like I didn't know how it felt to have your pride hurt?

Then I felt my phone buzz. It was a text from Mum. She must have been at the library, sending it from one of those websites you can text from for free, because it was a message I couldn't reply to.

Daisy, can you get a payday loan out? The landlady's
coming round. She says she's taking us to court. Please.
Can you call me?

I waited for a bit before I rang Charlie.

'Is Mum back home?'

'Yup. Let me get her. She's in bits.'

'I know. Can you put her on? Quickly. I don't have
much credit on my phone and I'm on the train so I might
cut out if we go into a tunnel.'

Charlie handed the phone to Mum. She was crying.

'Is there any way you can do a payday loan?'

'Mum, I'm on the train. I don't have access to a computer.'

'I don't mean to do this to you. I know you have
your audition, but when you get there, can you get to a
computer?'

'Mum, I don't get there till late.'

'Please, Dais. I can't deal with this stress. She's coming
round. Please.'

'I can't . . . I'm on the train . . .'

'Please, Dais . . .'

'OK . . . I'll see what I can do, Mum.'

'Thanks. Sorry, Dais. You know I hate to do this. I'll
message later.'

I could hardly understand Mum through her sobbing. It was heartbreaking. My belly was grinding with worry that she and Dad had their hopes pinned on me to lift us out of our financial mess. The pressure was suffocating. And I had that wobbly feeling at the top of my legs and a churning like I was about to come on my period. Fuck. I'd forgotten it comes every month. No tampons or towels. This is all I fucking need. When I pulled my pants down in the toilet, it hadn't started. I rolled up some tissue paper and lined the crotch with it anyway, just in case.

I was so stressed out, and just as I was bending over, arse in the air, I sensed the expanse of the train carriage beyond me. The door was slowly gliding open and a teenager minding his touring bike was staring right up my chuff.

'So sorry!' I apologized, before hammering on the shut and lock sign. 'Shut, you fucker!' I muttered under my breath, but it took too long. I smiled politely when I eventually freed myself from the toilet.

'So sorry! Not every day you see what a girl's had for dinner,' I joked with the teenager. He shuffled awkwardly and looked at his feet.

Back in my seat, I tried to focus on the script that had been sent to me. And my four lines. The scene started with me sitting opposite Martin Clunes in his office, holding my baby son.

Martin Clunes: What's the problem, then?

Me: Well, he's been up all night with a temperature.

Martin Clunes: Has he been eating?

Me: Yes, he's eating fine, it's just his temperature.

*(Jessica Ransom runs in.)*

Receptionist: There's been an emergency. Some
   bloke's collapsed down at the harbour.

Martin Clunes: *(to me)* Make an appointment with the
   receptionist. That's her.

Receptionist: He's a cute one. What's his name?

Me: Boris.

Receptionist: No, seriously, what's his name?

Me: That is his name.

Receptionist: Oh.

Another text from Mum:

Have you got to a computer yet? I don't know what to do
Daisy. Please — can you get the payday loan?

By the time I arrived, Mum had called me at least three
times. And left more messages. I kept telling her I was
still on the train, but she was hysterical. When I got to
the hotel, I was close to using up all my credit. Now the
guy behind the desk was asking for a card.

'Could we take a bank card, please, Miss Cooper?

We need to charge £10 to it to pre-authorize any room service.'

'You need to take £10?' I didn't have £10 on my card. I didn't know how to tell him. There was a queue forming.

'Oh, I won't be ordering room service,' I said.

'I understand, Miss Cooper, but we still need to take it. We need to check the card is valid, but don't worry, we'll refund straight away if you don't order anything.'

'I won't order anything.'

'OK . . . but we do need a valid card.'

I could hear harumphing and tutting from a middle-aged man wearing a stupid fedora holiday hat behind me. He looked like Grampy Rabbit from *Peppa Pig* in need of a sugar rush.

I stood there in silence. Think quickly, Daisy. I leaned in and whispered, 'I'm an actress, and my production company are paying for the hotel. Can you please call them and take their details?' I realized I sounded like a complete dick, like Kim Kardashian asking for white doves, some assorted organic nuts and the temperature of my room to be exactly seventy-eight degrees.

Grampy Rabbit coughed loudly and looked at his watch.

That night I ordered no food. I didn't know whether the production company were covering that or not. And when I opened the minibar in the room, each small bottle of gin and vodka and Bacardi was secured with an anti-tamper device. I couldn't even drink the miniatures and fill them back up with tap water. I resorted to chewing slowly on the Lotus biscuits that came with the tea and coffee.

I lay on the bed and worried about Mum and how she would be going mental because I'd stopped replying to her messages.

By the morning, I'd hardly slept. I looked at my phone. Mum had left several more texts, but I couldn't call. I couldn't bear to hear her voice or feel the guilt of not getting to a computer. There was a taxi picking me up and I went through my lines again before I headed to the foyer.

'Here for the show?' The driver turned down Radio Two's *Breakfast Show* on his stereo and leaned out of the car window. 'Taxi for Cooper. Fern Cottage, yeah?'

I acted like a pro.

'Yeah,' I said casually. 'Filming today.' I felt way cooler than when I learned all the dance moves to Britney's 'Stronger' in around 2000. You got this, Daisy, I thought.

'Yeah, we get lots like you coming down,' he continued.

As we drove, I sensed he was fishing for more info, but Mum was blowing up my phone. I didn't know how long I could keep the Grace Kelly aloofness up. I wanted to burst into tears.

When we got there, the cabbie said, 'Here you go,

lovely,' then called out, 'Break a leg!' after me as I got out of the car.

'Thanks!' I shouted back, clutching my phone and tripping over my loose sandal strap.

Inside, there was a stressed-out woman with a clip-board.

'Daisy May Cooper?' I said, almost apologetically.

'Daisy . . . Daisy . . . Daisy . . .' She looked down her list, hitting the tip of her biro against her front teeth.

'Ah, yes, Daisy. Through to Make-up, please, and then someone will direct you from there.'

She spun round, talking loudly into her headset micro-phone. I froze. Fuck me. The room was busier than ants crawling over a dropped wedge of Victoria sponge at a church fete. Workers with leads and mics and cameras swirled around me. It felt overwhelming. And as I stood there, my phone kept buzzing in my pocket.

I had to ask several people which way to go to Make-up, but no one looked like they had the time to show me. Shit. Then I felt the churn in my belly again. I'd forgot-ten. My fucking period. I hadn't come on yet, but it was edging closer. Still no tampons or towels. Maybe one of the Make-up girls would sort me out.

As it turned out, I got shoved into a trailer, but no one spoke to me. No one even introduced themselves to me. It took until I made my own TV series six years later to understand what most of these people running around even did. You don't get taught that at RADA. It could all have been a bit friendlier.

I got into my costume – a fetching green striped T-shirt and green trousers – and after a while a young guy came to get me. 'OK, Daisy, you're up now,' he said, and guided me on to the set. I was plonked on a seat in the prefab doctor's office. I had no clue what was going on.

Then Martin Clunes walked in. Fuck me. His ears were even bigger in real life. No one introduced us. It was massively intimidating. This was the first famous person I'd ever met – unless you counted a bloke who looked a bit like Greg Wallace from *Masterchef* but just turned out to be a bald man with glasses. I can't explain why, but my body was shuddering – it was an adrenaline rush I couldn't control.

'Hi,' he said.

'Hi,' I stuttered.

Then someone rushed in and dusted me over with a powder brush and then a baby got shoved in my arms like a turkey into a hot oven. I'd never held a baby before. All I knew was that there was a way to support their heads so their necks don't break. But I had no idea what position that was. The baby hated me. I saw its face swell, and it screamed as if it was being murdered, so they swapped him with his twin. (They always use twins, but the twin hated me just as much.) Martin was telling me how to hold the baby. We finally stopped the baby from crying by shining a torch on the ceiling and distracting it, like it was a cat.

'Right, are we ready? Are we rolling?' I heard a voice shout.

Martin Clunes: What's the problem, then?
Me: Well, he's been up all night . . .

My mind had gone completely blank. 'Oh. I'm so sorry. Can we start again?' I said. I couldn't get any of the words out.

'Don't worry. Don't be nervous. It's going to be fine.' Martin Clunes smiled at me, like he was my dad.

'Thanks.' How embarrassing. Christ, come on, Daisy.

'And take two . . .'

Martin Clunes: What's the problem, then?
Me: Well, he's been up all night with a temperature.
Martin Clunes: Has he been eating?
Me: Yes, he's shitting fine, it's just his . . .

Oh fuck. Did I say 'shitting'? Fuck. Fuck. Fuck.

'I'm so, so sorry.' I could feel myself going redder than a baboon's arse.

'Don't panic. I know. First-time nerves. You can do it.' Martin was very encouraging.

'And take three . . .'

Martin Clunes: What's the problem, then?

Me: Well, the temperature's been . . .

Fuck. Every take was worse than the last. The blood was pounding in my ears. When I looked down at the random baby, its cheeks had gone bright red and puffy. Even the sound guy was judging me. Readers, if you want to see a clip on YouTube, feel free. I can't bear to watch it.

'Come on. You can do this.' Martin was beginning to sound quite irritated now. More like a headmaster.

But no, I couldn't. I looked around the room, searching for someone or something to help me. There was a coat stand in the corner. Not that. Please, not that. But it was too late. Nick and his stonking boner popped into my head. Once seen, it can never be unseen. Martin was eyeballing me like I was a naughty schoolgirl.

When I looked down again, the baby was screwing its face up. Please, please, don't take a dump, I prayed. Then I felt that trickle in my pants. You know the one you get when the period you've been waiting for for ever finally decides to put in a fucking appearance. On set. On your first TV part. Fuck. I shuffled around, hoping it wouldn't go through the material and stain the trousers. Or, even worse, the fucking chair. And why is it that, when it comes, it comes like a fucking tsunami? And these aren't even my fucking trousers, they're from the costume department!

'Let's make this one a winner,' Martin said, through gritted teeth.

'Sorry, so sorry,' I said. I took a huge breath and exhaled slowly.

'And . . . take seven . . .'

Martin Clunes: What's the problem, then?
Me: Well, he's been up all night with a temperature.
Martin Clunes: Has he been eating?
Me: Yes, he's eating fine, it's just his temperature.
*(Jessica Ransom runs in.)*
Receptionist: There's been an emergency. Some
    bloke's collapsed down at the harbour.
Martin Clunes: *(to me)* Make an appointment with the
    receptionist. That's her.
Receptionist: He's a cute one. What's his name?
Me: Boris.
Receptionist: No, seriously, what's his name?
Me: That is his name.
Receptionist: Oh.

Oh. Thank. Fuck. Someone swooped in and took the baby off me. Martin, frowning, said goodbye.

I headed straight to the bathroom and whipped off the trousers. There was period blood all over the crotch, so

```
                          CLIENT STATEMENT
                            21/06/2011
     Number:        Page: 1                        COOPER DAISY MAY




                                        Amount    Employer    Agency      PDSTG
     Description                         Received  Deductions  Deductions  Net Amount

     BUFFALO PICTURES        P/E 08/06/2011
     "DOC MARTIN: SERIES V"
     TOTAL GUARANTEED : 3OTH MAY 2011 @
             + HOLIDAY PAY @
     Commission
     VAT on Commission
     NHI
     Our Ref:


     STATEMENT TOTALS



                             PAYMENT METHOD

     Payee:                             By BACS    Our Ref:


     END OF STATEMENT                              Payment Total
```

*Doc Martin*, here I come!

I ran them under the tap and furiously scrubbed at them with soap, cursing Jessica fucking Ransom as I scrubbed harder and harder.

When I finally got back to the hotel, I rang Mum from reception to finally tell her I couldn't get to a computer to get the payday loan. I could hear she was very panicked.

'I gave the landlady the antique mirrors,' Mum said. Her voice was breaking with tears.

'The ones from Gran?'

'Yes. They're worth a bit, and I needed that woman to go.'

'OK, Mum. I'll be back tomorrow.'

A few months later, when the episode screened, all of my family gathered round to watch. Mum had also put a shout-out on Facebook – she was like Cirencester's answer to *The* fucking *Stage*.

People stopped me in the street beforehand. Worst of all was my old acting teacher, who clearly secretly thought I would never amount to anything. 'Oh, I hear you've got a small TV part,' she said.

'It's small this time, but they thought I was so good they asked me to come back with a bigger part,' I lied.

That lie is one I would repeat to Mum and Dad. Tragic.

What was even more tragic was that, in the end, most of my – four – lines had been cut. I was awful. I looked on in horror.

Receptionist: He's a cute one. What's his name?

Me: Boris.

Receptionist: No, seriously, what's his name?

Me: That is his name.

Receptionist: Oh.

I felt like a party balloon that was slowly deflating. Mum and Dad tried to lift my spirits, but I didn't feel like celebrating at all. It was a shame, because Charlie and I had taken a load of 2ps to the bank and bought in a few bottles of Chardonnay. We drank them and dreamed about ordering our favourite: chilli beef.

# CHAPTER 17
# *KERRY'S CAMERA*

Until Charlie and I shared a room at RADA, I had no idea he was creative.

Apart from the stop-motion animation films we made as kids, Charlie's strengths were maths and science at school. He was wound more tightly than a virgin on prom night. No one expected him to pursue a crazy, artistic career. He was going to be an accountant or a banker or something *very* straight.

All that changed when, one night, he invited a mate to sleep on my floor. As there was barely space for a fart in that room, I wondered how we were all going to fit in.

'You fucking selfish prick! How dare you bring a mate back?' I yelled. I was so close to completely losing my shit.

Charlie and I always bickered, but this time it felt different. I watched as he stumbled down the corridor. Later, I found him crouched in a ball on the stairs. Tears streamed down his face. He blubbered in waves and did this weird flicking thing with his hair. He looked like a lonesome, wet Elvis.

'I hate myself. I don't know who I am. I don't know who I'm supposed to be!' he sobbed.

Fuck!

I had no idea Charlie was even capable of having an identity crisis. Apparently, while he'd been at Exeter uni he'd taught himself to play the guitar and I'd noticed he'd had his ear pierced. Charlie was a rebel without a cause. All these years, he'd been pushing down his creativity.

'Maybe it's time you came out of the closet, Charlie?' I put my arm around him.

Sympathy had never been my strong point, but I tried my best.

'You can be whoever you want to be. Who wants to be a banker anyway? They're all cunts.'

This wasn't entirely true. This was before the financial crisis, when people still thought the credit crunch was a fucking breakfast cereal. Besides, we actually could have done with a banker in our house . . .

From that moment onwards, he and I imagined stories together. Whenever I got back from classes we made up skits and stupid songs about people we knew from Cirencester. Mum sent us the local newspaper regularly and we thumbed through it. Although we took the piss out of everyone and everything, I guess it was our way of admitting that we missed home. And we really did miss home.

One of our early efforts was a song about a man raising money for a disabled teenager. It was a worthy cause, but this guy turned out to be the biggest fucking narcissist on the planet. Other people held jumble sales or ran a half-marathon, but he lived out his pathetic superstar fantasy by recording an album under the guise of saving a kid's life. I mean, who does that?

> He spent all the money on a photo shoot,
> He spent all the money on the CD covers,
> He spent all the money on the studio,
> So there's no money left for the life-support
>     machine . . .

As I say, it was early work. But I hope you can appreciate the raw talent.

Another song we put together was about a red-meat-loving racist butcher whose son announced he was turning vegetarian. Its natural comic potential seemed obvious to me and Charlie. And, for one of our stupidest songs to date, we drew on the old music-hall tradition and created 'Rang Up the Dong', which was about nothing in particular.

And when Charlie and I eventually made it back to Cirencester and we were sharing a room, like the crusty old grandparents in *Charlie and the Chocolate Factory*, making shit up became our only escape. We had so little money and so little hope. We camped out in the garage and recorded classics such as 'I Live in Cirencester'.

I live in Cirencester,
Stratton ain't much better . . .

Friday night, twelve o'clock,
Let's all go to The Rock.
Six quid to get in!?
Five quid for a gin!?
The Rock can suck my cock,
Go up to 17 Black,
There's no room to swing a cat.
I end up in the Abbey,
With Kenny Cook drinking shandy . . .

I live in Cirencester,
Stratton ain't much better . . .

Walking into town,
Woolworths has been shut down.
All there is is
Bloody Burtons, New Look, Fat Face and Dorothy
    Perkins.
If I want to get some decent clothes,
I'll have to go to Cheltenham.
Five quid for the bloody bus!
You gotta be bloody joking!

Kenny Cook was the local drunk who could always be found in the park with a can of Special Brew. Locally, the video went viral and it can still be found on YouTube. Christ, like I needed any encouragement . . .

But something Jessica Ransom said to me after the *Doc Martin* shoot had stuck in my mind. I'd told her about my post-RADA nightmare and how I'd found it impossible to get work. And how my audition nerves were worse than coming down off a weekend Bacardi Breezer binge. She mentioned that she had started writing her own material.

'Maybe you could do the same?' she suggested. I'd never thought about it before. I was so caught up with trying to make it as an actress in other people's shows and being reliant on other people's scripts.

Maybe I could? I thought.

I started writing. Just to make Charlie laugh, I created a character called Kerry. She was like so many girls from around where we lived. Kerry ended up being based on one of the school bullies from when I was at Deer Park Secondary. She was oafish and selfish, but underneath it all she had a big heart.

And I created Kerry's mum – the character whose voice I also act on *This Country* but who you never see. Then we started filming two-minute sketches. The videos got absolutely zero views on YouTube, but Charlie and I pissed ourselves. It was like being back in our old house filming Matchmakers landing on our neighbour's tits.

Unfortunately, every now and again reality kicked in.

After doing an assortment of shit jobs and signing on, Charlie and I got a cleaning job. Of all the jobs we'd done, this one was scraping the bottom of the fucking barrel. It was £100 a month for three hours a night, in an office block in Cirencester. Charlie and I got the three-hour shift down to twenty minutes.

The head honcho at the cleaning company was a guy called Terry. He had a nervous tic and an unrivalled enthusiasm for industrial cleaning products. I couldn't fathom how anyone could get off on the mere mention of a squeegee, but he could.

Terry was never satisfied with our work and left passive-aggressive notes on desktops and in the bathrooms.

During yesterday's visit, I cleaned the sink area with a stainless-steel cleaner. I also used it on the urinals to take all the scum off. It came up well. Strike is the best chemical to use on the floors. I'll be coming on site next week to see you guys on Tuesday evening . . .

If you're so fucking good at cleaning, why aren't you doing it? I thought.

Admittedly, Charlie and I were substandard. Hoovering was a lot of effort. Instead, I cast my eye across the

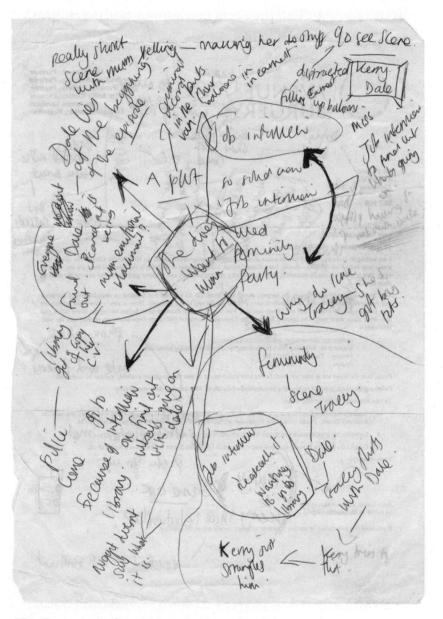

*This Country* started as a shit-storm in my head.

floor and picked up the most offending particles by hand. Henry Hoover rarely got a look-in. If we were feeling energetic, we emptied the bins.

In my defence, a lot of time got taken up wrestling Toblerone-length turds from the Ladies. Without fail, one was there winking at me every fucking night. It took a bog brush and a fair amount of oomph to cut it in half. I liked to imagine the turds were curled out by the office hottie – size six with pert tits and stilettos – the sort men throw themselves in front of to open a door.

Like Cirencester's answer to Dalziel and Pascoe, we created criminal profiles of the people who worked there, based on the state of their desks – a half-drunk cup of coffee; kids' pictures in a frame; a cute kitten mouse mat; a chewed pencil end. That was a highly strung insomniac who used his family as a smokescreen for an international cat-smuggling ring.

After a while the staff began waging a war with us. They left out presents for us, like they were leaving tidbits out for the mice that no one ever sees but everyone knows visit. Crumbs on the carpets; pencil shavings on desks. It was a message: if you won't clean our shit, we'll make sure we give you something to clean . . .

One night, around the time of my audition for the small part on *Call the Midwife*, which I obviously didn't get, I was greeted with a very fucking unwelcome present in the Men's.

Often, I'd take my lines in and rehearse them as I 'cleaned'. I'd position them on the mirror ledge, glancing at them and reciting the words in my head as I gave the sinks a cursory wipe.

'Cursory' may be an exaggeration.

An empty packet of Quavers had been left on the radiator. I was saving it until last. Strange place to leave a crisp packet, but anyway . . .

I wasn't feeling confident about the audition. Actually, I felt awful about it. There's a point when you've been through so much disappointment that you predict failure before it's even happened. It didn't help that the script was sixty pages long and I'd only had time to copy part of it out at the local library.

'Come on, Dais, you can do this!' Dad again. Always in my head, but even his encouragement had begun falling on deaf ears.

It was time to tackle the Quavers. The packet looked slightly bloated and it was slumped like an old drunk outside a pub. I brought the bin over and grabbed it. Liquid exploded from it and drenched down the front of my T-shirt.

For fuck's sake. Who would do that? Just leave an old Quavers packet half filled with water on a radiator? Fucking animals!

I looked in the mirror. My white T-shirt had a strange tinge of yellow about it. I scrunched up the wet patch and held it to my nose. The smell was strong, like ammonia. Fuck. It wasn't water. It was piss.

When I looked at myself in the mirror, there were bags under my eyes and my skin was pallid. Why would anyone give me an acting role? Tears rolled down my face as the smell of piss wafted up to meet my nostrils. It felt like the last straw . . .

The next day, Terry surpassed himself:

> I passed by early this morning. Can I suggest that when you see pencil shavings on a desk you wipe the whole desk down thoroughly? I've found that if I move things to one side and give the cloth a good rinse out before each sweep it leaves very little residue and the desktop comes up sparkling.

Who was this guy? Mrs fucking Doubtfire?!

Actually, mate, I spent most of last night scrubbing piss off the men's bathroom floor, then myself, and then sobbing into the mirror, all right?

But for someone who fantasized about sanitation solutions, Terry was very fucking squeamish when it came to mess – especially women's mess. He visibly recoiled at any mention of periods. I took my pleasure wherever I could. I loved it when he dropped in to check on us.

'Terry. I need stronger cleaning fluid. A crimson wave has deluged the Ladies.'

'Terry, the desks didn't get cleaned because a sanitary towel with more wings than a KFC chicken bargain bucket is jammed down the S-bend.'

'Terry, the disposal unit is *overflowing*. It's like Dolmio day on the second floor . . .'

Terry's eyes darted around, looking everywhere else but at me. It was obvious he despised me.

At home, our *Kerry* videos got slowly better. So much so that Dad suggested we write a proper scripted comedy based around the character. Charlie and I cleaned by night and wrote by day.

At first, we put together four pages of script. To be clear, we didn't actually know what a proper script was or how to present it. It didn't matter. It was more important that we got our ideas down.

Alongside Kerry and her mum, Charlie and I developed a character called Dale, who was later to become Kurtan in *This Country*. We kept on writing . . .

The complaints at work escalated, going from passive aggressive to just fucking aggressive.

The manager on the second floor asked yesterday whether the cleaners were on holiday. Banana skins rotting in the waste-paper bins; filth all round the photocopier and scum on the splashbacks in the urinals. I distinctly remember telling you exactly how these should be cleaned . . .

Kerry films Selin.

Kerry
what's your name?

Selin.
Selin

Kerry.
who your best mate.

Selin
you

Kerry
how long have you known you've been a Gay.

Selin.
fuck off.

Kerry (laughs)
Selin
no seriously Kerry, fuck off, I aint gonna do it if
your gonna be a knob.

---

Selin has Camera.
~~Kerry~~
Selin
whats your name

Kerry
Kerry.

Selin
whats your second name

Kerry
muttlow.

Selin
who's your best mate?

Kerry
you.

LONG silence

Kerry
ask me another Question then.
Selin
I cant think of any.
Kerry
~~Just~~ Come on!
Selin
alright... fucksake.
who is your ..... worst enemy.
Kerry
well siân at the moment
Selin
why
Kerry
coz she basically wrote on
damens wall on facebook ~~that~~ not
to trust me coz I'm a shit stirrer.
Selin
Thats ~~trag out of order~~ did she really?

kerry.
ok, 3 2 1 go.

___

~~Selin~~
kerry.
if you see a red like flashy thing at the top right
that means its recording.

selin
ok.

kerry.
can you see it.

selin
Yeah... ok 3 2 1 ....    kerry. got it?   selin  Yeah.

selin ~~to~~
what do I do now...

kerry
press it twice to stop recording.

___

kerry.
just leave it there.  ~~right look through and see it~~

selin
Yea but theres no one to press it.

kerry.
yes, but I'll press it now. and then we run over here,
do it. Its recording now. Go.... Quickly.

selin.
done?

kerry.
Yeah.

selin
can we watch it back.

kerry.
Yeah.

selin               kerry. hang on a sec
lets see then.

Well why don't you put that sombrero on her
head · · · · · · · · · ·

LONG PAUSE.

Is that funnier? · · · · · · ·

NO.
Why don't you do that impression of Liz next door & for
you've been framed ... thats funny.
NO.
Why not?
Coz no one knows who Liz is.
I do .... she lives next door.

Kerry - Aright

Selin - mum says I cant see you anymore.

Kerry - what? Why?

Selin - whats that?

Kerry - Camera

Selin - did you nick it?

Kerry - no, my stepdad tony ~~got it for me~~ bought it me.

Selin - why?          whats your mum getting wory for?

Kerry - I dunno? ~~whats your mum tut wona see me then~~?

Selin - Coz you was on the front page of the standard.

Kerry - honest mate. I would never play football at chosterton
cemetary honest. That was pugsley. I'd never ~~do~~
~~that~~ disregpect you or your nans grave.

Selins mum shouts: whos that?

~~Selin~~ - kerry.

~~Kerry~~
Selins mum - well she~~s~~ aint comingin.

~~~Scene cuts~~~

Kerry - park then?

Selins mum - what?

Selin - Im going to the park.

Selin mum - no your not.

Selin shuts the door.

Scene cuts.

Kerry on dokey Ride — cuts.
Selin ~~cuts~~ on ride —
Both on ride.

We continued writing until we had ten pages of script. The series of sketches we created was called *Kerry's Camera*. Our first script was called 'Kerry Gets a New Camera', which Charlie filmed. It was a skit where Kerry and Dale play Scrabble and want to know if 'Dave' is a proper word. I sent the script to my more-than-useless agent. She didn't reply. I rang her.

'Hi, it's Daisy . . . Daisy Cooper? Just wondering whether you . . .'

'Daisy who?'

Oh, great. My fucking agent can't even remember who I am. Humiliating.

'Daisy Cooper? I'm on your books. The *Doc Martin* job?'

'Oh, Daisy. Yes, Daisy. So sorry. I've been so busy sticking my tongue up Kate Winslet's arse I've found it difficult to remember anyone else . . .'

She didn't actually say that last bit, but she might as well have done.

'I sent you a script I've been working on . . . I was just . . . erm . . . wondering if you'd had a chance to . . . ?'

'No.'

As far as I know, my agent never did read our script. If I'd waited for her, I would still be jabbing at Toblerone turds in an office toilet.

I got impatient and went to the library and researched production companies. Then, I sent out emails to *hundreds* of them with the videos we made of Kerry attached. It felt as hopeless as catapulting satellites into outer space. Just me and Charlie and our ideas and all the blood, sweat and tears it took to get our work together hurtling out there into the cosmos. But at least I was doing *something* . . .

We waited weeks. Nobody replied.

I checked my email. Again.

Dear Daisy,

Many thanks for your email. The clips you recorded are fun, though I worry that they share a similar territory to the Gilbert character in The Morgana Show. But I'd be happy to read the script, so please email it to me.

*The Morgana Show* had been created by comedian Morgana Robinson and had appeared on Channel 4 a few years before. The only real similarity between Kerry and Morgana was the home-video feel.

I read on. Fucking hell! I had to do a double-take at the email signature.

The message was from a woman called Anna who worked at Avalon. *What? Avalon? The* Avalon? Avalon — one of the most amazing production companies in the UK. The company that produces Harry Hill and Lee Mack and discovers loads of new comic talent. Yes! *Yes!* YES!

Oh. My. God. In that moment, all the shitty jobs I'd ever done paled into insignificance. This was *it*! Somebody, somewhere, in a big, fancy office in London, actually thought we were funny.

I dashed off a reply.

Please find attached a script. As I said before, I really believe this is something very exciting and I've already had a lot of interest from the head of the comedy department at the BBC.

The bit about the BBC was utter bollocks but if I didn't blow my own trumpet, who was going to?

The email I received back was a request that Charlie and I come in for a chat.

A chat? A fucking *chat*?

I wanted to chat more than a twelve-year-old with ADHD (which could be me, by the way).

'Yes!' I replied emphatically.

I ran to tell Charlie. Charlie always gives the impression that he doesn't give a shit, but it's just for show. Underneath, Charlie cares. He really, really cares. And this was a massive boost to our self-confidence.

For weeks we strutted around our home town like two horny cocks. I was willing people to come up and ask me the same, tired question:

'What are you doing now? I hear the acting stuff didn't work out . . .'

I'd already rehearsed my answer:

'Actually, we've got a meeting with a proper production company. Yeah. Me and Charlie. We'll have our own comedy series soon.'

'Really? Gosh, we thought you were joking about all that stuff . . .'

'Joke's on you, motherfuckers!'

As we counted down the days to our meeting, our cleaning went further downhill. Mrs Doubtfire was close to igniting.

> I have received more complaints from staff. It leads me to question whether you are turning up to work at all. Except that I know you are because a rather unsavoury outline of male genitalia was discovered in the dust accumulated on the marketing manager's desk. I will be coming this evening to discuss this with you personally. Could you please update me with any cleaning solutions you need me to order . . . I noticed you were out of sponge scourers . . .

Ever since the invitation from Anna at Avalon I'd been itching to write to Terry and tell him to stick his cleaning job right up his Gary Glitter. But I couldn't. That job was all we had. We just needed it to tide us over until we'd be getting paid *gazillions*.

*

The day of the 'chat' with Avalon arrived. Charlie and I were so anxious we booked the 5.30 a.m. National Express coach from Cirencester. You could never be too careful. What if a lorry shed its load on the M4? Or the coach driver suffered a heart attack and we got stranded at Membury Welcome Break, unable to reach Anna, who'd be chewing her ballpoint pen in a meeting that Charlie and I never made it to? What a fucking comic twist that would turn out to be. All these years in the wilderness, only to be stuck in Harry Ramsden's sharing a full-fat Coke while the time of our big meeting came and went.

We arrived in Victoria Coach Station four hours early.

There were only so many Costa coffees we could stretch to, so we pounded the pavement near Avalon's offices around trendy Ladbroke Grove for an absolute age. We were shitting ourselves. Around fifteen minutes before our slot we edged open the glass doors. It felt like we were entering the set of a movie.

The building was a renovated warehouse and when we went in the receptionist swivelled coolly in her seat. In the foyer, a massive cut-out of Harry Hill smiled down at us. One of Simon Bird beamed at us. I swore Simon gave me and Charlie the big thumbs-up as we signed the visitors' book.

'Anna will see you in the meeting room. Would you like a tea or a coffee?' the receptionist chirped melodically.

Would a monster glass of Chardonnay be out of the question? I stopped myself from asking, but Christ, I needed something to calm my nerves.

Anna was waiting in the meeting room with our script laid out in front of her.

'Charlie. Daisy. Thank you for coming.'

'That's OK.' We shuffled around uneasily.

'Gosh! Relax! You both look like deers in the head-lights!' Anna helpfully pointed out.

Deers in the headlights were exactly who we were. Why did she have to point that out? We were two twenty-somethings from the middle of fucking nowhere attending one of the biggest meetings of our lives – wouldn't you be crapping yourself just a tad?

Anna was intimidating purely because we thought she was important. And we blindly accepted that she knew more about how our ideas could be successful than we ever could.

'We've read the script. We feel it's got potential, but it needs . . . it needs to be more like Lee Mack's *Not Going Out*.'

'Lee Mack's *Not Going Out*?'

As much as Charlie and I loved Lee Mack's *Not Going Out*, the material we'd written was as far from Lee Mack's *Not Going Out* as you could get. Wasn't that obvious?

I glanced over at Charlie. He looked utterly confused.

Anna reeled off a load of words we did not have a

fucking clue about. She talked about treatments and log-lines and biographies and stuff we'd never heard of, and that they never teach you at fucking RADA.

When we asked some questions, Anna launched into several 'hilarious' anecdotes about her time on *Big Brother* – also not helpful – the pinnacle of hilarity being when she had to chat to Jade Goody's mum Jackiey in the Green Room. This took up three quarters of the meeting.

By the time the glass door opened and we were vomited out into the corridor, I was none the wiser. Was that it? We'd come all this way to London to be entertained with stories from Anna's own career? So . . . is Avalon interested or not? What is it that they actually want us to do?

The whole thing was utterly bewildering. We made our way down in the lift in silence.

As the doors pinged open I looked up at the card-board cut-out of Harry Hill. Harry wasn't smiling any more. His lip was now curled up in a sneer. And Simon Bird's thumbs had taken a downward turn.

Shit.

What upset us the most was Anna's tone. It was so condescending. Granted, she would have had no idea that we'd got on a bus four hours too early, or that we could barely afford the bus in the first place. But we had expected her to be . . . well . . . a bit more encouraging? . . . Maybe a bit more nurturing of new talent? Maybe?

In our hearts, Charlie and I both knew the meeting had nosedived.

'What shall we do?' we asked as we shared a cup of coffee in Leicester Square before heading back to Victoria.

'Maybe we could write to Ricky Gervais? Or Peter Kay? They've got their own TV series and they must have been in the same predicament once? Ricky Gervais will definitely know what to do . . . definitely,' Charlie said.

It was a long shot. And how could we even reach them?

When we got back to Cirencester I dropped a note to my agent. I told her about the meeting and how Avalon said they were interested but we weren't exactly sure what they wanted. I asked if she could help mediate so it could be made clearer exactly what it was we needed to produce.

We weren't being dicks. We were being exactly the opposite. This meant *absolutely everything* to us. We just wanted to get it right.

We waited a month for another meeting with Avalon. Again, Charlie and I travelled down to London . . . on a slightly later bus this time.

We made the same trip to Ladbroke Grove. Harry Hill's expression wasn't any more upbeat, but I had a

379

better feeling about what the chat might bring. I hoped Anna would lay out exactly what it was Avalon needed, maybe provide us with some advice or examples so we knew we were on the right track.

Anna met us in the same room. She didn't smile like she'd done when we first met her. In fact, she looked pretty pissed off. A drink was not on offer.

'I don't want any more emails from your agent saying we are not doing enough for you!' she hissed.

'Pardon?'

Fucking hell! Was this woman for real?

'What did you not get about our last meeting? What exactly was it you did not understand? If you don't grow up, you're never going to make it in this industry,' she snapped.

Grow up? We were barely out of college and this was the first script we'd ever sent to anyone. We explained all of this in our first meeting. What was it *she* didn't understand?

Christ, Anna banged on and on. I smiled feebly and tried not to cry. I could feel Charlie's foot gyrating wildly under the desk. He was holding back the tears, too. We'd waited a whole month – for *this*?

It was also clear that she didn't want me to play the character of Kerry. But the whole point about writing my own material was that I'd written a character I could play.

How far does this woman's imagination go? I wondered. Answer: fucking nowhere!

Charlie and I sat there like two naughty schoolchildren and took one of the most unholy and unjustified of bollockings. It washed over us, wave after wave. But, weirdly, we took it. Not once did we interrupt and defend ourselves. It makes me cringe now to think of how we kowtowed to an absolute cunt because we were so in awe of her being a hot-shot London producer.

As far as I knew, our agent had just passed on our confusion and asked for some clarity. But Anna had been an absolute arsehole. We didn't know it then, but she was to be the first of many arseholes we would meet on the road to making *This Country*.

On the bus home, I thought about the letter I had been composing in my head to send to Terry. The one about us getting our own comedy series and how last night's Toblerone turd was the last I'd ever be evacuating. And how he'd have to deal with all that messy menstruation stuff himself.

I didn't write the letter.

Charlie and I needed that job. I hated so, so much that we needed that job, but we did need it. Badly.

# CHAPTER 18
## *THIS COUNTRY*

harlie and I didn't want to work with Avalon. This was gutting. We'd poured everything into our meeting, but it was clear from the outset that they didn't get where we were coming from.

We wanted an amazing production company behind us, but we didn't want to compromise our material. That said, we were eager for advice and someone to help us shape it into something that worked.

I wish we'd stuck to our guns on the 'no compromise' rule, because the next few years were an utter shit-show.

Charlie and I continued cleaning. Even the Toblerone turds started mocking us.

Then, another production company called Lucky Giant got in touch. It was the UK comedy arm of NBC Universal, an American company. One producer there had got round to viewing the material I'd sent, only it was so long ago I'd forgotten I'd ever sent it to them. He was called David Simpson and he called my agent. By now, the fact that I was still alive had escaped her notice altogether. Embarrassing.

Eventually, she teamed us up with a literary agent. I breathed a sigh of relief. I'm sure she did too. How many ways can your *own fucking* agent tell you she holds out no hope for you?

But we still had hope, even though we were pretty anxious that our first meeting with the new agent was just going to be a repeat of Avalon.

The meeting was near Oxford Street in London and, again, Charlie and I made our way there by coach. Everything about it was massively intimidating. The foyer was covered in plush carpet and lots of people were running around trying to pretend they were important.

Then, we met Laura. And around twelve dogs. Yup. Weird and unnecessary. The offices were awash with dribbling, salivating, farting dogs. Apparently, the agency collected destitute pups like it collected clients.

'So, I've had a look at your script and I can set up the meeting with Lucky Giant for you,' Laura said, as she nuzzled a chihuahua.

'Oh, brilliant,' I replied, batting a Labrador puppy away from my crotch. It could obviously sniff that I'd just come on my period.

Meanwhile, Charlie was being eyeballed by an arrogant Jack Russell who he came to despise.

'Lucky Giant. Yes . . . I can set up a meeting with . . .'

'Set up a meeting with . . . ?'

Laura had a strange habit of never finishing a sentence.

Instead, she just tailed off and stared intently while breathing menacingly like Darth Vader. It was hard to tell if we just bored the shit out of her, or she was mesmerized by the size of my nose, or she was actually dead.

Fast-forward seven years and Laura became the inspiration for *This Country*'s Big Mandy, who falls asleep with her eyes open. Funny how you remember things . . .

Laura was quite proactive, though, and she did set up the meeting. I loved the sound of Lucky Giant. It felt lucky. A second chance. And they were giants. So they must be giants of the TV industry, right? Dais, we're on to a winner . . .

When we met with the producer, David, he liked our script. But he did want us to develop another with him that would be a sure-fire success. That's OK – we needed top industry advice. At least he didn't suggest our script should be more like Lee Mack's *Not Going Out*.

Me and Charlie warmed to David because he was a junior in the company. Immediately, we related to him. He looked like the fat guy with glasses from *Jurassic Park* who gets eaten by the dilophosaurus in the torrential rain.

Charlie and I made many of our early business decisions based on whether we felt sorry for whoever it was or if they looked vaguely suicidal. David ticked both of those boxes.

Should we trust Lucky Giant? Well, what choice did we have? Neither ITV nor the BBC had written back to us . . .

We'd love to work with them, we said.

This feeling didn't last.

We were so far down the list of priorities at Lucky Giant that the vending machine was developing its own script ahead of us.

A new script took a year. A *whole fucking year*! One more year of us cleaning in a shitty office block; one more year of Terry's passive-aggressive notes and one more year of me travelling to auditions that flopped like a shit soufflé.

Quickly, we learned that David had all the creative genius of a fucking PowerPoint presentation. He had no idea how to write a script. He had no idea about comedy. He was a guy who loved templates and formulas.

'Here's an episode of *The Simpsons*. Write something that matches it,' he said. In Lucky Giant's hands, comedy writing was more clinical than a GP with an index finger shoved up your arsehole. Some scriptwriters might suit that, but not me and Charlie.

'Do you have a bad feeling about this?' Charlie asked me early on.

'Yup. But it's the only chance we've got . . .'

We felt trapped, but we agreed to stick with it.

David promised to introduce us to a top director. I've

forgotten the guy's name so I'll just call him Mike. Our first proper pilot? Yes! *Yes!* YES! We were all over that. For the first time, we'd see the seeds of a show . . . *our* show. And this guy was a *top* director.

Even better, Mike wanted to meet us in Cirencester – our home turf. He wanted to get a sense of our ideas and our characters in the flesh.

Mum got over-excited and cooked loads of food in the tiny kitchen of our rented house. And Charlie and I mapped out a tour of the area so we could show Mike around all the places featured in our script.

His visit was a massive fucking disappointment.

'Fucking train. Middle of nowhere. Takes ages. You can't even get a train direct to Cirencester!' I shit you not. Those were Mike's first words when we picked him up from Kemble station – one whole hour from London.

We'd waited months for this dynamo to visit. Anyway, wasn't that the whole point of *This Country*? It wasn't fucking London!

We took Mike into town and around the marketplace . . .

'So, Mike, this is the pub . . . you know, the one in our script? Where all the funny stuff happens?'

'Sorry, hang on a minute. I have to get this . . .' Mike's mobile was forever ringing. He spoke to his colleagues. He spoke to a mate. He spoke to his wife. I'm sure his fucking dead hamster called. He spoke to everyone. They were all so much more important than talking to us about our script and our pilot.

In the end, we made a single-scene pilot with Mike. It was awful. It was so far removed from my and Charlie's vision that when we watched it back we wanted to die. The scene was of Kerry in the living room, but it was utterly static. None of the improvisation Charlie and I were good at featured in it. It was flatter than Kendall Jenner's chest if it had been run over by a steamroller in a world of very dense gravity.

We've waited all this time for *this*?

The last time we met Mike was in a Zizzi restaurant in central London. He behaved like a lunatic. Who orders pork belly in an Italian restaurant and then demolishes the waitress for not bringing English mustard?

'Why have fucking pork on the menu if you don't have any English mustard to go with it?' he said a bit aggressively.

'I'm sorry, sir . . .' The waitress looked like she was about to faint.

Charlie stepped in. He couldn't bear it any longer.

'It's an Italian restaurant, Mike. That's probably why they don't serve English mustard . . .'

We didn't ever want to see Mike again.

'Hey, dudes. Fancy meeting up? Fleshing out some more ideas?'

Mike left many messages on our voicemail.

*No, Mike. We don't want to meet up. We'd rather be stripped naked and have our private parts smeared with English mustard before being spit-roasted over hot coals than have you anywhere near our ideas.*

And we didn't want to be embarrassed by him like that in a restaurant ever again. We'd rather just pay the bill and never return.

'Please, please, can we film our own taster tape?' we pleaded with David.

So, were we beggars now? That was how Lucky Giant made us feel. But funnily, instead of breaking us, it had the opposite effect. As the time dragged on, we got *way* braver about our ideas, even though we couldn't bring ourselves to break from Lucky Giant.

Every crap script David had wanted and the crap teaser tape we'd made with Mike only made it clearer to us exactly what we *didn't* want. We'd spent so many hours writing the bare bones of *This Country*. Our humour was so specific and so unique to us that every disappointment only told us that it couldn't be anything else.

And if this taster failed, we wanted it to be on our heads. We didn't want it to be because someone who was comically inept wanted us to wear silly hats or bang on about drinking in Wetherspoons or do shit jokes about eating kebabs.

Yup. David wanted us to do this *all of the time*. His humour began and ended with jokes about big tits and lager louts, like clicking on some awful edition of LAD-bible.

The teaser tape we made by ourselves was exactly what we wanted. We improvised just like we do on *This Country*. There was no static camera, no set-up scene. It was me on the hoof, interacting with people around Cirencester. It was everything we had wanted to do *two years ago*, but no one had listened.

We watched it back. Yes! *Yes!* YES! This is *our* show, *our* vision. Fuck yeah! *At last!*

Wherever our new tape would take us, we were proud of it. It was all that mattered.

The tape got re-sent to BBC and ITV. We waited.

Both made contact soon after and wanted to set up meetings. Are you fucking kidding? Charlie and I were beside ourselves. Fucking hell!

With a don't-care-a-monkey's-fuck recklessness, I started to recompose my letter to Terry. Not only could we not clean his shitty office block any longer because we were making our own comedy series, but this comedy series would be on mainstream TV! He could shove his microfibre mop so far up his arse it tickled his tonsils.

But . . . then a strange thing happened. Almost overnight we got reshuffled at Lucky Giant. We got elevated from being the wart on the heel of someone's foot to at least armpit height, even if that armpit smelled like a Fray Bentos pie.

What happened next will make you fucking weep. Why Charlie and I still didn't tell Lucky Giant where to get off, we don't know. Naivety? Low self-esteem? A fucking momentary frontal lobotomy? Take your pick . . .

The armpit was called Mario Styliandes, Lucky Giant's chief executive. The same chief executive who had taken *absolutely no interest* in Charlie and me for the whole *two years* we had been developing our script. I'm not saying we hated Mario, but if he'd dropped down dead during our time with him, we would have had a massive party that would've lasted for days.

Mario was immaculately groomed – a cross between a younger Antonio Banderas but with a nose like Gérard Depardieu's. His temper knew no bounds. And maybe that was it? When it came down to it, we were just fucking scared of him.

The irony was that in the same week we got introduced to Mario we also had a meeting set up with Shane Allen – head of comedy at the BBC. Shane had emailed to say he was interested and he laid out the kind of money that might be on the table should a series be commissioned. It was lower than the fee on any commercial channel, but we didn't care. We just needed someone who understood us.

We were counting down the days until we were meeting Shane, but in a bizarre twist we got a message from his assistant the day before.

Shane is so sorry and he sends his apologies. He will not be able to attend tomorrow's meeting. Shane was at a birthday party yesterday and has had an unfortunate incident involving some random children and a bouncy castle for which he needed urgent medical attention . . .

I loved this guy already, even if he had just cancelled on us. A bouncy castle? Children? Fucking priceless!

But this is where it went completely tits up. Because had Shane met us that day, we would have avoided the next episode in our lives. We would have avoided the bit where Mario took complete control of our script and oversaw all the rewrites on it. And the bit when we met with the BBC (but not Shane), but then how the BBC got cut out of *any* future deal, on Mario's instructions. And the bit where we started creating a pilot for ITV with *none* of our original material, purely because there was more money on the table. And of course the bit where all the lifeblood got sucked out of everything we'd ever dreamed of.

Six months on: cut to the next teaser tape, complete with a brand-new script (100 million drafts later). According to Mario, *this* was the tape that ITV would not be able to say no to. This would be the tape that would knock their fucking socks off.

I want you to suspend disbelief for one moment:

Kerry is not Kerry any more. She does not steal stuff from the local shop. She is not the spoilt, selfish, flawed yet loveable character we created. She is bland and washed out and . . . what's the word they keep using? Oh yes . . . 'likeable'. How I fucking hate the word 'likeable'.

Suddenly Kerry is saving dogs and being nice to old people and raising money for the local hospice.

And the worst bit? Dale, played by Charlie, and who *was* Kerry's cousin in our original script, is now transformed into Kerry's *love interest*.

Yes, Kerry is hopelessly in love with Kurtan. She buys a new bra and experiments with make-up to try to woo him. She spends whole episodes trying to impress him in the most base, crap and unsubtle of ways.

*But this is not Kerry!* Kerry is more asexual than a fucking amoeba – it's how I wrote her!

Was that the only thing these inept men could do with a female character? I thought. Just make her more feminine and hopelessly lovestruck? It showed all the imagination of a shadow moving through the fucking Dark Ages.

And did I mention what they wanted to do with Kerry's mum? They told us that having Kerry's mum being off-screen was never going to work. Viewers would find this too complicated. We'd have to cut her out completely or make her into a visible character.

If any of this sounds ridiculous, by far the most ridiculous thing about all of this was that Charlie and I *went along with all of it*. I acted out Kerry in exactly the way Lucky Giant wanted me to, even though every sinew in my body was screaming: *This is so wrong!*

During the filming of the new teaser tape, I remember looking over at Charlie, who was standing behind the monitor. He looked as lost as I was. And my audition gremlin returned with a vengeance. Only this time it wasn't a gremlin. It was a Toblerone turd with eyes and a mouth. It was poking up from the ladies' loo and grinning wildly . . .

'You don't know what the fuck you're doing, do you, Daisy May Cooper? What on earth is going on with your hands? Do you actually know what your next line is? Well . . . do you?'

The pilot was called *Carnival Day*. This is a taster. It is fucking horrendous:

Exterior: Cirencester town centre

KERRY and DALE (aka Kurtan) are walking through
     the town centre. There is a buzz around town as
     people prepare for the Cirencester Carnival,
     putting up bunting and posters. We see on Kerry's
     face that something is on her mind.
Dale: Oh yeah. Guess what, Gary Bumworth was
     helping me set up for the carnival last night and

one of the falcons escaped from the falconry
display and snatched a hotdog from the burger
van and started eating it on top of WHSmith's,
so Bumworth shot him with a crossbow and
the bird sanctuary reckons he owes them
£2,000.

Kerry: Dale, I've got something I need to tell you . . .

Dale: Oh, and batty old Anna is doing the tombola
this year so we can cheat.

Kerry: Yeah, but Dale, listen . . .

Dale: But yeah, apparently, they ain't doing Soak the
Parish Councillor this year, as Lee Tanner ruined it
last year by pissing in the sponge bucket.

Kerry: But you know the King and Queen
competition?

Dale: I can't wait for the King and Queen
competition!

Kerry (excited): Really, Dale? Because I've entered
us . . .

*(Kerry looks lovingly into Dale's eyes . . . )*

No! *No!* NO! STOP! *Stop!* STOP! Christ . . . it is pure
cringe.

ITV saw the new pilot. ITV hated the new pilot. It
wasn't anywhere close to our teaser tape, the one that
had been sent to the channel and which it had based a
potential commission on. Nothing like it. By now we'd

racked up a £350,000 debt with Lucky Giant and created something that *we absolutely hated*.

But Lucky Giant owned our scripts, our material, our characters – everything. We didn't know this until Charlie spoke to Laura, who was still our agent.

The only piece of scaffolding still holding us up was Terry and our fucking cleaning job. Oh, no . . . wait . . .

An email from Terry dropped into my inbox:

Daisy/Charlie,

After years of giving you the benefit of the doubt, of defending your less than professional standards to managers, we have come to the end of the road. The cloths that I specifically earmarked for the toilet areas have been found on desks, and the desks are still not satisfactorily clean.

I cannot defend such a disgusting use of microfibre, nor do I want to imagine the transfer of bacteria from one location to another. Please do not come to work tomorrow. I wish you all success in the future, but I trust you will not be cleaning for a living. Please do not ask for references. These will not be forthcoming.

Fuck. All these years I'd been crafting the perfect email to Terry in my head, I'd been imagining the day I'd tell him where to shove his stupid job. I was fucking pissed off Terry got there first. I thought of all the replies

I could send, but there was nothing. I was nothing. We were nothing.

I am lying on the broken mattress Charlie and I share at Mum and Dad's house. He is on the phone to our producer and I am trying to read his face.

'Hmmm, yeah . . . yeah . . . OK, well, thank you for letting us know. Bye.'

He hung up the landline.

'ITV are dropping the pilot.'

Silence.

'Well, fuck it, we'll just take it to another channel. What about the BBC?' I tried to reassure him, even though I felt like someone had dropped a bowling ball into the pit of my stomach.

His eyes become glassy.

'The production company are dropping us too.'

'Well . . . we'll start again. We'll go to another production company.'

'I've already spoken to Laura. She says we can't take it anywhere, the production company own all the rights. The only way we could would be to buy the rights back from them, at a cost of over £300,000.'

He didn't cry, but he looked like he was on the verge of it. We didn't have a pot to piss in and if we were to get back the ideas and characters we'd created, we'd have to pay the cost of a house to save them. *Our own ideas* would cost us money?! We didn't even own our own house; we were barely affording the £600 a month in rent.

'That's that. We had our chance and now it's gone,' he said, staring at a stain of dog piss on the carpet.

I felt like I was bleeding out on to the broken mattress. Three years of creating, three years of hopes and dreams just bled out and I was empty.

Charlie stormed out of the room.

'Where are you going?' I called out after him.

'I have to get out!' he shouted back at me. I heard the front door slam. He was going somewhere to cry, or possibly kill himself.

But Charlie didn't kill himself. He actually couldn't cry either.

When Mum and I found him he was at the side of a country lane kicking a gatepost in that weird, repressed way men do when they're fucking livid. His face had gone bright purple. No tears, just pure rage.

Mum and I remained on suicide watch for several days.

Weirdly, I felt the opposite. I can't deal with the small stuff. But this was big shit. *Really* big shit. Although we'd spent three years working at it, we had no TV series and we had no job either.

But I'd never felt so strong and powerful in my entire life. I became She-Ra having just ditched the fucking Masters of the Universe; Lara Croft leaping athletically over the debris of a ruined city; Wonder Woman with slightly less perky tits.

I emailed Shane Allen at the BBC. The title of the email read: 'Look what the cat dragged in'. We were drowning in the quicksand of a fucking swamp – may as well be funny, I thought.

I poured my heart out. I told Shane everything that had happened. How fucking awful Lucky Giant had been and how fucking awful the pilot was . . .

I had never met Shane.

Please, please. I just want to meet you and get your advice. I'll dress as the Karate Kid and stand outside your office until you talk to me. You can be my Mr Myagi. I just need your advice on what to do. Please, you are my only hope.
Daisy xx

Looking back, it was desperate, like Joan of Arc writing a letter to God.

With the last of my money I bought a karate outfit from a charity shop (what are the chances of finding one?) and booked my National Express ticket. I was prepared to camp outside the BBC for as long as it took.

But I didn't ever have to. The god of karma shone down on us like a blinding sunbeam. Shane emailed back. He said he thought about Kerry often and that he had never laughed so much as he did when he saw the teaser we'd created or the ten pages of our original script.

The bouncy castle incident remained a deep regret.

'Why stand outside the office looking like a complete twat when you can just come in and have a meeting?' he wrote.

He signed off the email with: 'Every little ting's gonna be all right.'

In a weird, utterly fucked-up way, we'd come full circle. Three years of utter hell to make us understand what *This Country* was. Three years of utter hell to make us understand who we were, to make us understand *exactly* what we wanted.

I cried. By now Charlie was a lighter shade of purple, but he was still very angry. And disbelieving . . .

He needn't have been.

Within weeks, Shane had negotiated our ideas and characters back from Lucky Giant and commissioned the first series of *This Country*, which finally aired in 2017. A massive fucking risk, but Shane took it.

And the rest, as they say, is TV history . . .

# SCRIPTS

Kerry

'Kerry' is a a comedy based around the life of Kerry Mutlow, A local chav who lives in a Beautiful Market town in the cotswolds. It is all filmed on a hand held cam (In the style of films such as Blair witch and Paranormal activity) documenting what life is like for an Unemployed Chav , with an array of colourful characters.

                    (*Knock at the door*)


                         KERRY

                        Alright?


                      KERRY'MUM

                     Who's that?

                         KERRY

                         Dale!

                     KERRY'S MUM

                        Who!?

                         KERRY

                        DALE!

                     KERRY'S MUM

Dale...not that Welsh streak of piss. Well tell him he's not coming
in until he takes off his shoes. He left mud all up the stairs last
                         time.


                         DALE

                  (*Nod's at camera*)

                    What's that?


                         KERRY

                        Camera.

DALE

Did you nick it?


KERRY

No.... my step dad Tony bought it me.


KERRY'S MUM

Wouldn't do that in his own house would he?


KERRY

How did it go?


DALE

Alright...just got back


KERRY'S MUM

Dale!


DALE

Yeah


KERRY'S MUM

Dale!?


DALE

Yeah

                    KERRY'S MUM

              What was he like then?


                       DALE

                    A prick


                    KERRY'S MUM

                    A dick?


                       DALE

                   No a prick


                    KERRY'S MUM

                     Why?


                       DALE

            (*He starts ranting and raving*)


  You're a disgrace, you gotta get off the drink and off the drugs and
             get a job, so I knocked him out


                    KERRY'S MUM

               You knocked him out?!

                       DALE

      Yeah, no one talks about my nana that way.


                    KERRY'S MUM

                     What?

                              KERRY

                    Jeremy slagged off his Nan


                            KERRY'S MUM

                So the little'uns yours or not then?


                              DALE

                Mercedes is but Sambuca's not.
                            KERRY'S MUM

                I always thought you two looked alike.


                              DALE

          Funny you should say that. Turns out she's my niece.


                            KERRY'S MUM

        I tell you what Dale you always come up smelling of roses, you.


                              DALE

                              Yeah..


                            KERRY'S MUM

                Your brother must be pleased then.


                              DALE

          He hasn't heard yet. He went down last week.


                            KERRY'S MUM

            Bloody 'ell, what did he do this time?
                              DALE

(*To camera*)

Hello, ladies my names Dale, pussy magnet of the south west... and
here's Kerry, the lezza.


KERRY

Fuck off Dale. Why don't you tell them your second name you fucking
gay?


DALE

Whatever


KERRY

Tell 'em then.


DALE

Nah... It doesn't matter.


KERRY

Tell 'em.


DALE

Nah


KERRY

His name is Dale.. Dale Winton. After the gay from pets win prizes.


DALE

Fuck off Kerry, ~~your surname is Oakey...~~ Kerry Oakey and you can't
~~sing for shite.~~

You ~~my~~ fanny fiddler.

KERRY

Give me my camera


DALE

Are you in a stress?


KERRY

Just give me my camera


DALE

Are you in a pissy with me?


KERRY

Just give me fucking Camera Dale.


DALE

What you so upset for.


KERRY

Just give me the fucking camera.


DALE

Fucking hell Kerry, I was only joking..


KERRY

~~I can't sing... Very funny..~~

I don't fiddle fannys dale... Ped

(Kerry walks away)

Dale

not even your own

KERRY NO!!

DALE (laughs)

~~You can!~~ ...— OK


KERRY

~~Why do you always take the piss out of me for it then?~~
SERIOUSLY DALE, say that one more time and we aint
gonna be mates


DALE

~~Like when?~~
~~I promise~~... Its only banter... I know your not a fanny
fiddler... Your a cock sucker.


KERRY

Like the time I sang for Nana's 80th at the Wheatsheaf.. And you said
I sounded like the reincarnation of Vikki pollard....


DALE

Yeah...


KERRY

I 'aint finished... that I sounded like the reincarnation of Vikki
pollard

If she came back as a cat with its tail caught in a food processor.


DALE

....you have to admit that was a good one.


KERRY

Fuck off.


(Car pulls up)

NUGGET

Alright dick heads

                              DALE

                    Alright Nugget you twat?




                             NUGGET

                    What's wrong with her?


                              DALE

                She's got her knickers in a twist.


                             NUGGET

                       About Tracey?


                             KERRY

                          What?


                             NUGGET

                      Tracey Chambers


                             KERRY

                     What about her?


                             NUGGET

                   You 'aint heard then?


                             KERRY

                       Heard what?

NUGGET

What Tracey been saying 'bout you?


KERRY

No? What she said?

NUGGET

That you're a full blown lezzer.


KERRY

What?!


NUGGET

That you are always looking at her tits. That's why Carly didn't
invite you to her hen party at the outdoor pool coz they didn't want
you perving at them in their bikini's. They've even made up
a song about you and posted it on face book.


KERRY

I'm not a LEZZER!

Nugget - A say lezzer.
She didn't say lezzer.
She said being a fiddler

Looks at Dale... everyone is silent


DALE

You do wear boxer shorts Kerry.


KERRY

Because their more comfortable!


DALE

And you're the best darts player at the Kings arms....

                    KERRY

              I'm NOT A LEZZER.




                    KERRY

You tell Tracey Chambers to meet me at the amphitheatre at 3 o'clock
         and we'll deal with this man to man.


                (They laugh)

                   NUGGET

           What you gonna do to her?


                    BONE

                 Rape her?


                (They all laugh)

                  CRUSTY

      How would that work?... rub fannies?


                    DALE

     With a dildo, crusty you fucking dip shit.


                   CRUSTY

               Up the fanny?


                   NUGGET

               Or the asse..?

                         KERRY

            Up neither... I'm not raping anyone...




                         NUGGET

            You can get ones that go up both


                          DALE

            Just tell her to be there.


                     *(They drive off)*


                          DALE

                     You alright?


                         KERRY

                     I'm fine.


                          DALE

  You know, if you ever swung that way, I would still be your mate.


                         KERRY
                         Fucking
            I'm not a lezzer Dale.


                          DALE

I know... Just saying, that's all.... Plus my auntie sue is still
doin' them Ann summers parties so If you wanted any of those rubber
cocks, she can get them on the cheap.

                    KERRY

I don't want any Rubber cocks... for fucks sake dale I like blokes
o.k.


                    DALE

             Really?

                    KERRY

             YES!


                    DALE

       So what you gonna do to her then?


                    KERRY

             I don't know yet.


                    DALE

You know what we would do to her back in Wales don't you?


                    KERRY

             What...?


                    DALE

             Egg the cow


                    KERRY

       Is that slang for punch

DALE

No... just throw eggs at her.


KERRY

fanny fiddler.

I can't believe people think I'm a ~~Lez~~. ~~thats really~~

~~fucked me off~~ ~~I was really fucking buzzin~~ No


DALE

Well, maybe if you wore a dress once in a while...


KERRY

I did... For my nan's funeral and you said I looked like rose west.


DALE

Fred west. I told you you shouldn't curl your hair when you have
such a scowly face... ~~I could have said something worse~~


KERRY

~~Worse than Fred fucking West?~~ cheers.


DALE

~~I could have said Ted Bundy.~~

I dunno. it but spoke it was weird.

I different uped to ~~drting up~~. It was like

~~KERRY~~ mike Tyson in a dress

Why's Ted Bundy worse?


DALE

I dunno... ~~He killed more people?~~

                              KERRY

                              Cheers



                              DALE

You know I'm only messin... I reckon you could scrub up quite nice
                        if you wanted to.



                              KERRY

                           You reckon?



                              DALE

                 Yeah I do.... If you had a shave.



                      She hits him hard.

                              DALE

                    You little fucker...


*(Kerry runs off and Dale puts the camera to one side chases her and*
           *gets her in a headlock. They play fight)*

                              DALE

          Can you smell what the Rock is cooking?



                          *(He farts)*

       *(They are interrupted by a police office)*



                              PC

                    You can't do that

DALE

What?


PC

That, (*he points at them*) you can't do that.


DALE

What this?


(*Kerry is still on the ground. |Dale farts on her head*)


PC

No... I mean no fighting.


DALE

But I can still do this?


(*Dale farts again. Dale and Kerry laugh*)


P.C

Seriously... I'm gonna have to ask you to move...


DALE

Good... Coz it stinks round here.


KERRY

How's it goin' P.C... I heard that you're still training to be a
special CUNT-stable

DALE

Did he really used to piss himself?


KERRY

All the time... and he breast fed till he was five.


P.C

No I never


KERRY

That's not what Gary Bumford said. Your mum told his mum.


P.C

You really are the scum of the earth Kerry ~~Dales~~ mother


KERRY

And you're a mat pissin tit sucker.

(Kerry & Dale both laugh)

P.C

I ~~hand~~ saw something quite funny ~~today~~ today...
~~I'm going to have to arrest you~~


KERRY

what, ~~telling the truth?~~
a dipshit in a police outfit / what are ya looking in
the mirror.


DALES PHONE RINGS


P.C

~~No I don't, i remember that no Kerry~~
Ha ha ... my god you are nutty ~~arty~~ Kerry ....
no — it was online... It was a song someone
wrote ... something about you — a prawn ring and
a Grannys farms.

Kerry ....
that was
a good
1